The Bible and African Culture

Zapf Chancery Tertiary Level Publications

A Guide to Academic Writing by C. B. Peter (1994)
Africa in the 21st Century by Eric M. Aseka (1996)
Women in Development by Egara Kabaji (1997)
Introducing Social Science: A Guidebook by J. H. van Doorne (2000)
Elementary Statistics by J. H. van Doorne (2001)
Iteso Survival Rites on the Birth of Twins by Festus B. Omusolo (2001)
The Church in the New Millennium: Three Studies in the Acts of the Apostles by
     John Stott (2002)
Introduction to Philosophy in an African Perspective by Cletus N.Chukwu
     (2002)
Participatory Monitoring and Evaluation by Francis W. Mulwa and Simon
     N. Nguluu (2003)
Applied Ethics and HIV/AIDS in Africa by Cletus N. Chukwu (2003)
For God and Humanity: 100 Years of St. Paul's United Theological College
     Edited by Emily Onyango (2003)
Establishing and Managing School Libraries and Resource Centres by
     Margaret Makenzi and Raymond Ongus (2003)
Introduction to the Study of Religion by Nehemiah Nyaundi (2003)
A Guest in God's World: Memories of Madagascar by Patricia McGregor
     (2004)
Introduction to Critical Thinking by J. Kahiga Kiruki (2004)
Theological Education in Contemporary Africa edited by GrantLeMarquand
     and Joseph D. Galgalo (2004)
Looking Religion in the Eye edited by Kennedy Onkware (2004)
Computer Programming: Theory and Practice by Gerald Injendi (2005)
Demystifying Participatory Development by Francis W. Mulwa (2005)
Music Education in Kenya: A Historical Perspective by Hellen A. Odwar (2005)
Into the Sunshine: Integrating HIV/AIDS into Ethics Curriculum Edited by
     Charles Klagba and C. B. Peter (2005)
Integrating HIV/AIDS into Ethics Curriculum: Suggested Modules Edited by
     Charles Klagba (2005)
Dying Voice (An Anthropological Novel) by Andrew K. Tanui (2006)
Participatory Learning and Action (PLA): A Guide to Best Practice by Enoch
     Harun Opuka (2006)
*Science and Human Values: Essays in Science, Religion, and Modern Ethical
Issues* edited by Nehemiah Nyaundi and Kennedy Onkware (2006)
Understanding Adolescent Behaviour by Daniel Kasomo (2006)
     Students' Handbook for Guidance and Counselling by Daniel Kasomo
     (2007)
Business Organization and Management: Questions and Answers by Musa O.
     Nyakora (2007)

(Continued on page 224)

The Bible and African Culture
Mapping Transactional Inroads

The Rev. Dr. Humphrey Waweru, (PhD)
Lecturer, Department of Philosophy and Religious Studies, Kenyatta University, Nairobi, Kenya

Zapf Chancery
Eldoret, Kenya

First Published 2011
©Humphrey M. Waweru
All rights reserved.

Cover Concept and Design
C. B. Peter

Associate Designer and Typesetter
Nancy Njeri

Copyediting
Dr. Phyll Chesworth

Editor and Publishing Consultant
C. B. Peter

Printed by
Kijabe Printing Press,
P. O. Box 40,
Kijabe.

Published by

Zapf Chancery Publishers Africa,
C/o St. Paul's University
P. O. Box Private Bag - 00217
Limuru, Kenya.
Email: zapfchancerykenya@yahoo.co.uk
Mobile: 0721-222 311

ISBN 978-9966-1506-3-9

Acknowledgements

I am glad that tradition provides this forum for publicly thanking those special people who helped this book become a reality. For me, writing is a paradox: a mixture of loving it and hating it, of intense solitude and grateful community; and of personal beliefs freely expressed and needing the objective and loving scrutiny of trusted others.

So it is to those trusted others, who invested so much time and careful attention to reviewing my manuscript, that I am deeply grateful to the editor of Swedish Missiological Themes for having published some of the chapters of this book as articles in a series of Swedish Missiological Themes' Journals.

I am also deeply grateful to my daughters Caroline Wambui Mwangi currently undertaking her Computer Science (Programming) course in Middlesex University London, Grace Wanjiru Mwangi currently undertaking Environmental Studies Community Development in Kenyatta University and Mary Waithera Mwangi who is currently at home waiting for her 'O' Level results for their time and support during the writing of this book and even typing the draft manuscripts. They are definitely the power behind the success of this book.

But most of all, I am deeply grateful to my editor and publisher C. B. Peter. I have always loved and valued Peter's deeply as my mentor who always tells young scholars 'to publish or perish'. Working together on this project gave me an opportunity to develop a deep respect and appreciation for him as a consummate professional. He is the finest editor I have ever worked with-intuitively knowing when to push, support change, or accept, always with the goal of creating the finest book possible. He has been a joy to work with in this project.

And finally, thanks to my wife Catherine Muthoni Mwangi, a nurse by profession for her cheers from the sidelines and the much-needed reminders to smell the roses along the way. Catherine made it her duty to remind me that a scholar is not a scholar unless one has published. I dedicate this book to her.

Preface

There is good news in Africa! That is a paradigm shift in biblical studies in Africa. This is important information for those whose steady diet of western biblical scholarship and research has begun to make them believe that the vast majority of Africans are not concerned with African culture in relation to biblical studies. It is true our African societies require a paradigm shift in biblical scholarship. What is not true is that most of our ordinary readers are not keen in contextual Bible study. They are the source to contextual Bible reading in our times, particularly the oral texts which are then compared to the written ones.

In my opinion, it is time to engage in the dialogue that has silently been going on between the Bible and the African culture. We have to be involved in this conversation between the Bible and the African culture.

The purpose of this book is to provide a platform for such a conversation in order to allow the African culture to interact with the Biblical culture. This paradigm shift is what the members of the African community and they alone share. However it is good to note that the invention of other new theories regularly, and appropriately, evokes the same response of resistance from some of the specialists on whose special competence they impinge. Western biblical scholarship has dominated the field for so long, where the African culture has only been discarded as unviable to be compared with the biblical culture. This book brings in a new theory of contrapuntal which in turn implies a change in the rules governing the prior practice of normal science.

This therefore means that the proposal for a paradigm shift, from comparative, inculturation and indigenization to contextual and contrapuntal may not be received enthusiastically by the proponents of pure biblical scholarship as one might have thought. It does not mean the whole idea is wrong or will never pick up in African biblical scholarship. Rather, 'new theories regularly provoke resistance from some of the specialists on whose area of special competence we impinge. But as time goes by, our logicality will be given attention. Nevertheless, a shift introduced by this book does not necessarily mean a complete break from the previous paradigms. For paradigm shifts do not have to change radically. Rather some elements of the previous paradigm still remain in the new as they guarantee harmony in the particular society that is adopting the new theories.

This book is therefore written for those people with an interest in the way the African culture interacts with the biblical culture with similarities and differences to compliment each other. It is for people who do not know how to remain faithful to their culture as they engage with the new faith of Christianity. Hence this book handles subjects of interest such as age grading, marriage, dowry as well as reading the Bible through our own eyes.

Contents

Introduction

It has always been my desire to reflect on the debate that has been going on, in Africa concerning the relationship between the African culture and the Bible. Why are African Christians becoming increasingly superficial? This debate has not been entertained even though it is right at our door step. Engaging in such a debate is a challenging task. This issue has been ignored and we seem most of the time unaware of it. Recently, I have been lecturing African theology, Biblical studies, Philosophy and Political science in a number of institutions around Nairobi, Kenya. Some of my students have been insisting that African Christians must have a complete transformation from their culture into the Christian Culture (Biblical). On the contrary, others insist that we ought to have a complete transformation from Christianity to our African culture. First, I thought it was naïve for University students to hold that opinion. It is impossible to abandon one's culture for another culture. However, it is possible to incorporate new cultures, thereby making our culture dynamic.

As a result of a heated debate in the lecture halls, I decided to write this book as an attempt to engage in this debate in a more scholarly manner. I have expounded on African culture and philosophy and shown how it relates to Christianity. I have also discussed the future of biblical hermeneutics and theology in Africa. The setting for this reflection is providential, for it comes at a time when African biblical scholarship is in need of a paradigm shift. It is providential because we have the advantage of relating the African culture to specific teachings in the Bible. It is my hope that the insights shared here will project the discipline of Christian theology, especially hermeneutics and exegesis, beyond the parameters to which many of us are accustomed.

This *Introduction* summarises all major arguments in the book in order to bring out the real issues of contention. Here an introduction of the main theme of the book is spelt out. The main task of this *Introduction* is to inform the reader of what to expect and set the tone for the arguments.

Chapter 1 reflects on the African culture and the Bible. It defines what we mean by culture, both from African and biblical perspectives. It reflects on culture as a tool of civilization and also demonstrates the possibilities and limitations of dialogue between the African culture and the Bible.

The main purpose of this chapter is to demonstrate that the encounter between the Bible and Africa is not a one-way affair: from Bible to Africa. Both of them could alternate their roles from subject to object, because none of them has remained static. The culture[1] of a people is dynamic. There are no people without cultural heritage. One interesting thing within the African culture is that it is similar in almost all areas, hence an outline of the three common areas for intercultural dialogue.

Due to the diversity of the cultures of the African people, Chapter 2 outlines the culture of the Kikuyu people as an example of African culture. It explains who the Kikuyu people are, their location, religion as well as their way of life. It is impossible to deal with African culture without being specific due to diversity of life in Africa. This is because though African culture is rich, it is not uniform. It has similarities, but there are also differences from one place to another and from one community to another.

Then chapter three deals with the mapping of the transaction between the African culture and the Bible. This is juxtaposing the two. It argues that, Africa will no longer be acted upon, but is herself

---

[1]This word may specifically refer to the African way of life in terms of acting, behaving, and knowledge of the people manifested in art, music, dance, drama, housing, clothing, spiritual as well as governance.

an actor. Also, the Bible is no longer the agent, but is the object of the actions of both ordinary and academic readers.[2] It outlines the development of the transaction in order to demonstrate that the dialogue has been going on for quite a long time. Here, an historical overview of this development is outlined to demonstrate that Christianity was planted on the African soil and watered by African rivers and that without these two it would definitely dry up.

Hence chapter four outlines an interesting theme concerning the methodologies for a transaction between the African culture and the Bible. In this chapter a paradigm shift has been introduced. A new way of thinking has been brought forward and a new methodology of contrapuntal introduced. It is not possible to do theology without a method, so here methods are explained and the preferred method is demonstrated.

This methodology allows a smooth juxtaposition so as to assess the encounter between Africa and the Bible as a 'dialogue' or a 'transaction'. Both these two words are used here with their economic and legal connotations to avoid controversy. While missionaries brought the Bible as 'a package deal', they did not always have their own ways. Africans were also able to negotiate and survive the scourge by relativising, resisting and even modifying the Bible with uncanny creativity (West 2001: 83). Africans in their own ways were able to negotiate and transact with the text for their own good.

This is followed by chapter five which discusses the fundamental issue of inter-religious dialogue between African culture and the Bible. Here, we have engaged in dialogue with certain texts to show what we mean by the word dialogue. It is not only erroneous but also unfortunate that for ideological reasons, biblical studies in Africa

---

[2]A large number of African readers of the Bible are not educated in the academic ways of dealing with the Bible, and they are commonly referred to as ordinary readers, while the educated are usually referred to as professional readers (for more information see Gerald West 1993). However both of these readers uses culture to dialogue with the sacred text.

have been done in isolation of African culture. It has been assumed that our people could abandon their cultures completely in order to become Christians. Here we have demonstrated that African culture can dialogue with the Bible without compromising the biblical message. We have used the contrapuntal method in reading biblical texts through our own lenses.

Then chapter six reflects on the issue of African worship as a means of transaction and scholarship. The purpose of this chapter is to demonstrate that we can do mission work through transacting with African culture and the Bible. More people could understand the Biblical message if it was preached through culture as a means of mission to our people.

Humankind is a matter of gender balance hence chapter seven is a reflection of the role of women in this transaction both in the African setting and in the Gospel of John. This is followed by our chapter eight which discusses dowry as a major issue in the African culture. Here dowry is explained as one of the key issues that demonstrate a real transaction between the African culture and the Bible.

Last and not the least is chapter nine which offers the summary of the book and demonstrates that conversation, dialogue, listening or debating between the African culture and the Biblical culture is a key transaction if Christianity is to remain relevant in the African setting. The only way to make Africans become real rather than superficial Christians is to engage in the inter-religious dialogue between the African culture and the Bible. This book demonstrates that Africans have tools (oral text) for transacting business with the sacred text.

CHAPTER ONE

African Culture and the Bible

When the Bible arrived in Africa, it found a fertile ground to germinate on. Africans were so receptive to Chistianity that, it took a very short time for the missionaries to convert them to new ways of life. This meant abandoning their African culture.[1] This means that the African Church was born as an independent identiy rather than a suplement appended to the Jewish synagogue or a European church. African Christians are therefore not Jewish proselytes. They are not second-class Jews who have come in as late comers.

This was the early temptation for the Church, which was by the mercy of God overcome at the council of Jerusalem (Acts 15). The African Christians are the people associated and identified with Christ Jesus. A defining moment of realisation that this was happening occurred during the council of Jerusalem. The apostles who presided over that council recognised that God was taking out of the Gentiles a people for himself within their own culture (Acts 15:14). Peter who may have learnt the hard way through the encounter in Cornellius' house (Acts 10:34), was able to use that experience to

---

[1]Every society has its own culture and the word culture means patterns of behaviour, which are customary in any society. These are sets of customs, which may be economical, political, judicial, religious and technological. Such distinguish that culture and the society to which it belongs. Cultural patterns are passed on from one generation (*riika*) to another through time by means of education (education here refers to both informal and formal ways of learning).

argue convincingly that God has no favourites. 1 Peter 2:9-10 also demonstrates this perception:

> But you are the chosen race, the King's priests, the holy nation, God's own people, chosen to proclaim the wonderful acts of God, who called you out of darkness into his own marvellous light. But one time you were not God's people, but now you are his people; at one time you did not know God's mercy but now you have received his mercy.

Therefore we need to understand that the Bible and culture engagement is a process of coming together, the meeting of life with life, hence such a process of engagement is rarely completed within a particular generation. Several generations of believers are needed to firm up and reap the fruits of that engagement. We are not going to find once and for all the biblical answer to a particular cultural problem. It does not work like that the Bible and culture engagement is not about answers to issues. It is about how a community and people of God come to see themselves as called into the people of God and how they come to participate in that community within their own culture.

What is Culture?

The word culture comes from the Latin word *cultura* derived from *colere*, which means 'to cultivate'. It generally refers to the way of life of a particular people.[2] That includes their socio-political and economic activities and practices. It is passed down from one generation (*riika*) to another. Specifically, culture refers to the arts, systems of beliefs, societal institutions, behaviour, dress, language, rituals and norms (law and morality) of a people. The common patterns of culture are language, ritual, art-forms, design and

---

[2]Mugambi (2001:17) argues that culture is the revelation of a people's self-understanding and self-expression, in their own context.

architecture as well as structures of time. Such patterns do help people to understand themselves in relation to their environment[3].

There are various definitions of culture. For example, Tylor (1874) defines culture as:

That complex whole which includes knowledge, belief, art, morals, law, custom, and any other capabilities and habits acquired by man as a member of society.

For JNK Mugambi culture is the total manifestation of a people's self-understanding and self- expression, through politics, economics, ethics, aesthetics as well as kinship and religion.[4]

Kroeber A and Kluckhohn C (1952) argue that culture is not more than a set of cultural objects. Such objects are defined by anthropologist White L (1949) as 'the symbolate' that which is created by the act of symbolisation as objects of their own kind of symbolization.

Cultural anthropologists usually use the term 'culture' to refer to the universal human capacity and activities to classify, codify and communicate their experiences materially and symbolically. The view of scholars (Waweru 2007:177) has long been that it is the enhanced capacity that defines feature of humans. However, some primatologists have identified aspects of culture such as learned tool making and use among humankind's earliest generations in the humankingdom.

Other scholars like Williams (1976: 87) concluded that contemporary definitions of culture should be classified into three possibilities or a blending of the following three factors:
1. A general process of intellectual, spiritual, and aesthetic development
2. A particular way of life, whether of a people, period, or a group
3. The works and practices of intellectual and especially artistic activity.

---

[3]John Macquarrie in his book 'Principles of Christian Theology', London (1966:12), argues that no one can escape sharing in the mentality and intellectual climate of his own culture.

These definitions reflect differing theories used in understanding human activities and the criteria for evaluating them. The combination of these possibilities gives birth to a worldview of the people of a given society. With such an understanding, African peoples had their own culture which not only influenced their way of interpreting the Bible but has also had a great impact in their lives.

The Concept of African Culture

When discussing 'African culture' scholars prefer to use the word in the plural form, that is, 'cultures' because there is no 'one' African culture. Just like in other societies, African culture is manifested in the peoples (Africans) activities and practices. These include artifacts such as music, oral literature, lifestyle, food, painting, sculpture, theater and drama.[5] So, African culture is manifested in economic and social activities. As stated above, culture includes art, science, as well as moral systems. The African people had distinctive spiritual, material, intellectual and emotional beliefs – which together characterized their religion. Religious beliefs emphasized ways of living together, value systems and traditions.

Therefore to the Africans, culture is that which they apply to that which describes a wider variety of societies. In the early 1930s, sub-cultures or groups with distinctive characteristics within a larger culture began to be the subject of study by anthropologists (cf. Louis Leakey (1933); Kenyatta (1938)).

Sociologists followed suit and from 1950s started reflecting on culture as symbols. They viewed culture in terms of symbols as

---

[4]J.N.K. Mugambi, 'Religion in the Social Transformation of Africa', in Laurenti Magesa and Zablon Nthamburi, democracy and reconciliation: A challenge for African Christianity (Nairobi: Acton, 1999), 73-97.

[5]To the African people it is the past, ancient that seemed to live again in day-to-day life. It is the past that spoke to their generations telling of deeds long forgotten, of deeds that are no longer known to revive the memory. This is the real culture of the people, whereby we go by the past rather than the future.

demonstrated in the legacy of Clifford Geertz (1973) and Victor Turner (1967), who argued that symbols[6] are both the practices of social actors and the context that gives such practices meaning. Therefore, symbols not only make culture possible, but also reproducible and readable. Hence symbols are the 'webs of significance' which offer regularity, unity and order to the common life of a group.

Because of the closeness of the African communities, there are many similarities in their cultures. More specifically, neighbouring communities tend to influence culture of each other. This makes the concept of African culture not easily definable. However it should be taken as the way people think, behave as a group which gives them identity in relation to others.

Influence of Christianity

African cultures were greatly undermined more than any other cultures in the world when Europeans imposed colonial rule in the 19th century and led missions to convert Africans to Christianity. Draper (2002: 16) argues that the peoples of the Mojority world[7] only came to recognize their specific position in culture at the end of a long history of colonial domination as well as their cultural dispossession and economic exploitation.

When European missionaries arrived in Africa, they did not in any way try to understand or appreciate the African culture. They were taken aback by practices like traditional circumcision, praying facing Mount Kenya, mode of dressing and pouring libation. To the missionaries, who had just witnessed developments in Europe

---

[6]See Anthony P. Cohen (1985) who argues that, symbols give the limits of cultured thought whereby people of the same culture rely on such symbols to frame their thoughts and expressions in intelligible terms.

[7]Although this term is not used by Draper in this specific reference, It is commonly used by postcolonial thinkers to refer to the Two-Thirds World (meaning Asia, Latin America and Africa- see Waweru (2005: 15).

especially in the 18th and 19th centuries, the way of life of Africans seemed backward. They therefore thought that Africans were uncivilised.

They equated 'culture' to 'civilization' and embarked on a mission to 'civilise' Africans. This resulted in the imposition of western discourse to Africans. This process of 'civilising' Africans was not only unpleasant but also brought to fore the inequalities between European societies and African societies.

This way of thinking led to the classification of Europeans as more civilized than Africans.[8] They also described the European culture as superior to that of the African. It is this kind of thinking that made some European scholars to add the concept of popular culture into the definition of culture. So, scholars like Matthew Arnold (1822-1888) regarded culture as simply the result of 'the best that has been thought and said in the world.'

Therefore, to the Europeans culture referred to elite activities such as European art and classical music. Similarly, the word cultured was used to describe people who participated in these activities. This came to be known as 'high culture', which was the culture of the ruling class seen to be different from the popular culture of the ordinary peoples. This interpretation may have added to the classification of people as 'rich' or 'poor' in the capitalistic world. Thus, the interaction of African culture with Christianity has had a great impact on the ways of life of Africans. They have adopted aspects of European culture while at the same time retaining some traditional practices.

---

[8]See Kibicho (2006:66), who argues that the missionaries were greatly inhibited in their perception and evaluation of African humanity and religion by what was there described as "a two-pronged prejudgment which the Europeans, including the missionaries, held regarding non-European peoples".

Culture as Dynamic

With globalisation, cultures, especially those of the African became and remained dynamic. There are no fixed boundaries between different cultures. They are constantly in flux, interacting and competing with one another. There are several cultures, religions, theologies and Christianities co-existing in Africa. Therefore, one is at a loss on how to describe any of them due to their diversity. However, given the diversity of the African people, all these terms make sense.

We can therefore argue that Africans have developed a more inclusive notion of culture as 'worldview'.[9] In this diversity of thought, a distinct and incommensurable worldview characterizes culture in terms of each ethnic group's way of life. They respect other people's culture without labeling it as 'civilized' or 'primitive'. They appreciate that differences in culture are dictated by environmental circumstances naturalisation; and that, because culture is dynamic, it changes over time.

Apart from the influence of Christianity and colonisation, African cultures have changed due to external influences and adjusting to the changing environments. Some of the main causes are inter-cultural marriages and interactions like through trade, migration or conquest.

Approaches to Religion

Because of the emergence of many religions, Race (1984) argues that there is a widely accepted approach to understanding religious pluralism. This approach advances three types of reactions: exclusivism, inclusivism or pluralism. The typology was developed within Christian theology for examining various Christian attitudes

---

[9]In my PhD thesis (2005:165-166), I have defined a worldview as a picture of the way things appear in sheer actuality, people's concept of nature, of self and society, where the most comprehensive ideas of order of life are expressed.

to African culture. In supporting this postulate, Heim S M (1995: 4), argues that it can also be used as a logical typology to analyse other religions' and cultures' attitudes towards religious pluralism. Below is a discussion on the three models.

Exclusivism
According to Knitter (1995: 4), the basis of exclusivism model is that there is only one religion and by extension one culture and all others are simply false. This model fosters a one way of thinking. Rather than a dialogue, it completely disregards other people's culture. This is the missionary principle perfected through evangelisation, which is inclined on conversion of others into one's own religion or culture.[10]

In this context, the Bible and African culture are viewed as falling along bi-polar dimensions with both cultures as two polar opposites. Each answers the question of truth consistently in one direction. If one agrees with one religion or culture then one would disagree with the other. This is the ideology the missionaries applied to imply that it was either Bible culture or African culture but not the two together because they cannot be both correct.

Post-colonial critics hold that this model absolutises one culture. For example, Kibicho (2006: 57) argues that this kind of exclusivism means undesirable connotations for many people. It denotes narrow-mindedness, arrogance, insensitivity to others, self-righteousness and bigotry. Such thinking made missionaries to evaluate humanity of the African from a negative context. They basically relied on their wrong view, perspective and standards. The result was dividing people into 'us' and 'them', 'insiders' and 'outsiders' and 'saved' and 'not saved' with negative consequences.

Further it meant that cooperation between the Africans and the Europeans was difficult, hence colonisation. This model even goes

---

[10]For Dube (2001:147) such is a colonial cultural bomb that "shatters and alienates the colonial subjects from themselves, their lands and their cultures."

further to suggest that the zeal to eliminate African culture and propagate the Biblical culture (cf. Western culture) was right. As we shall see below, the inclusive attitude is a better alternative to exclusivism.

Inclusivism

The inclusivism model views both the Bible and the African culture as holding elements of truth that are unique to the different traditions. Mbiti (2003) seems to capture this attitude aptly when he argues that whatever truth or presence of the spirit is found in other faiths is in someway anonymously Christian. This view mitigates the intolerance of exclusivism. It pours scorn on the resulting scenarios in the relationship from which missionaries evaluated African humanity and culture (Kibicho 2006: 57). In the context of colonialism, these relations were mainly those of master-slave or superior-inferior.

The inclusivism view condescends towards acceptance of other religions and cultures. Although it does not articulate support for or persecution of other faiths, it seems to advocate tolerance and respect for each other. It implies that there is no value in dialogue except to persuade the other party. There is nothing to learn if our culture is partially available elsewhere.

So, although the inclusive model tries to tone down the antagonistic relationship that exists between the Bible and African cultures, it seems to advocate subordination of one culture to the other. This has resulted in a stand-off between Christianity and the African elites. To make their stand very clear, some Africans later resorted to token measures like abandoning the western names.[11] This was because the missionaries behaved as though the Bible culture was more authoritative and therefore important and superior.

---

[11]By 1978 Ngugi was saying ' I have always thought of Christianity itself, as part and parcel of cultural imperialism. Christianity, in the past, has been used to rationalize imperialist domination and exploitation of peasants and workers' (1978:10).

It appears therefore that inclusivism does not go beyond mere tolerance, which was a mere white wash. Those who seek to go beyond tolerance appeal to pluralism, which is only possible through a dialogue between two cultures interplaying one another contrapuntally.

Pluralism

Netland (1991: 213) proposes a common model called pluralism, which genuinely accepts other cultures, as opposed to exclusivism and inclusivism. The central affirmation of this model is that we ought to be open to diverse ways of being human and recognise that there are diverse possibilities for our own lives. It therefore encourages us to tolerate both the Bible culture as well as the African culture. We should try and see the world from both points of view, because we can never totally abandon our own cultural practices.

Pluralism affirms that both the Bible culture and the African culture are equally legitimate ways of life. So it goes beyond tolerance as advocated in inclusivism to demand dialogue that may be mutually enriching. This is why Knitter (1995: 29-30), for example, argues that people should be encouraged towards a deeper experience within their own tradition and at the same time be open to dialogue with other traditions. The gist of pluralism is that until great faiths not merely tolerate but find positive values in the diversity of the human condition, we will have conflicts and ethnic tensions all the time (Sacks 2003: 200).

However there is also a major problem with pluralism because it is not easy to come up with a genuinely pluralistic model that is coherent and does not privilege any particular cultural practice. Some may think that an African philosophy and way of life (humanness) assesses the faith of the other in a way that transcends absolutism and relativism.

So are there any possibilities and limitations in the dialogue between the African culture and the Bible? How do these two interact with each other and to what extent does our culture affect the Bible or vice versa? To understand this phenomenon, we shall discuss the

the central models and philosophies in the dialogue between the African culture and the Bible.

We shall explore the African cultural aspect of *umundu* with reference to the Kikuyu people of Kenya to create a platform for peace within different ethnic groups and different strategies for an inter-cultural transaction. The aim is to applying *umundu* views on other African cultures and religions. However, a thorough understanding of the philosophy of *umundu* is necessary before applying it.

Humanism

Definition
The word *undu* stands for human. The term *umundu*[12] (humanism) is derived from *undu* and is used in general to describe African humanism. Most scholars associate *umundu* with Bantu languages commonly spoken in the entire East, Central and Southern Africa. There are over three hundred linguistic groups in Africa that use the term *undu/untu* or its variation. These people are believed to have a common ancestry.

In Kenya, *umundu* is associated mainly with the Bantu speaking people that inhabit central and western Kenya. In their various dialects, these people use the *undu* or its variations where referring to a person. Therefore, this group of related languages is referred to as Bantu and the speakers are called Bantu peoples. They include the Kikuyu, Luhya, and Swahili.

---

[12]The word *umundu* is one general term, which means humanism (*untu* in Swahili) and is used to describe the African humanism. In a general way most scholars associate this term with a loose Bantu speaking family of languages: the entire group of languages, spoken within East Africa where the word *undu or untu* stands for humanism.

The Concept of Umundu

What are the ideas at the core of *umundu?* To answer this question, we have to make a distinction between the implications of *undu* in cosmological and social-legal contexts.

In the cosmological context, *undu* is primarily used to define humans, that is, people or persons.[13] Human beings are distinguished from visible non-human things like animals, plants or minerals. They are also seen as distinct from invisible supernatural world of spirits, ancestors, gods or even God. Thus, scholars associate *umundu* with humanness.

In the socio-legal context, the term *undu* is used as the opposite of the inhuman. The inhuman refers to a person who transgresses the scope of humanity, that is, personhood or *umundu*. All societies have accepted norms on what constitutes human behaviour. Therefore, to be inhuman – the opposite of *umundu* – is to behave contrary to societal expectations.

People who are thought as inhuman in society include witches, sorcerers, murderers, rapists, thieves among others. In addition, those who generally transgress accepted code of conduct that regulates behaviour among people. The same applies to behaviour expected towards each other – based on age, gender, status or position in society.

Some spirits and gods are also thought to be inhuman. In most African societies, misfortunes such as death, diseases, drought or crop failure are blamed on evil spirits that are thought to be inhuman and bring afflictions. Most of the time, it is thought that the suffering occurs when our ancestors or spirits are offended.

---

[13]However in this cosmological domain little emphasis would be placed particularly in Islam and Christianity as major religions on difference between *undu* (person) and other ontological categories, but instead the essential continuity between these categories would be acknowledged.

Such calamities can only be avoided through the cooperation of family and community. They all come together to perform rituals that appease the spirits.

Umundu also refers to the attention that a person gives to another. It includes virtues like kindness, courtesy, compassion, consideration and friendliness. It is determined by even the attitude one displays to others and life in general. Therefore, *umundu* is more than just humanness. Being a human being does not necessarily mean that one has the qualities of *umundu*.

In summary, *umundu*, just like most fundamental concepts lacks a single definition or characterization. There is no one meaning agreed upon by all scholars. However, the above analysis clearly shows that the essence of *umundu* is humanness and communalism. In addition, *umundu* means a display of accepted value systems like respect of kinship and relationships, sharing, hospitality, compassion, empathy, humility and cooperation. It means what is morally good and brings dignity, respect, contentment and prosperity to others, self and the community at large. This is captured in the cardinal belief of *umundu* that a person is a person through others.

Application in Kikuyu Culture

Is there a relationship between *umundu* and pluralism propounded in intercultural dialogue among the Kikuyu? The concept of *umundu* can readily be identifiable among the Kikuyu. The Kikuyu community has attributes and traits that can easily be described as *umundu*. These include a sense of kinship and belonging, integration of strangers, solidarity, sympathy, compassion, patience, conformity, kindness and cooperation.

There are three basic concepts at the very core of humanism (*umundu*) that can be applied in the Kikuyu philosophy. These are interpreted from the three major humanistic statements as follows:

(a) *Kamuingi koyaga ndiri* - meaning 'a crowd is able to lift a mortar.' This is popularly used in the larger Murang'a County.

(b)   *Urutagwo mwiruti* – meaning 'we help one who is able to help oneself.' This is popularly used in the larger Kiambu County.

(c)   *Mugi ni mutare* – meaning 'the wise is advised.' This is popularly used in the larger Nyeri area including parts of Nyandarua.

The above three examples are applied in understanding the relevance of *umundu* for inter-cultural dialogue as follows:

(a) Kamuingi Koyaga Ndiri

This is a Kikuyu proverb literary translated as a 'crowd is able to lift a mortar.' A mortar is gadget commonly used by the Kikuyu to prepare porridge. It was believed to be one of the heaviest object in the community. It belonged to the whole clan, and so was used communally by individual families. No one single individual could carry it alone from one homestead to another. This called help from family members and even neighbours. Therefore, this proverb was used to show that we need each other all the time. In this context, we can argue that, similarly, no one culture is self-sufficient. Thus, a dialogue between our cultures, including that of the Bible culture is absolutely essential.

(b) Urutagwo Mwiruti

This Kikuyu proverb can be literary translated as 'we help one who is able to help oneself.' It means one must be able to help himself/ herself in a small way before being helped in a big way. It also means that one has to help others by participating in social activities before expecting them to help his/hers. In other words, individuals have to contribute what they can and society will do the same.

(c) Mugi ni Mutare

Mugi ni mutare, a Kikuyu proverb can be literary translated as 'the wise is advised'. This arises from the understanding that no one individual has the monopoly of knowledge and can claim to be wise on his or her own. Everyone has to accept advise from others so as to know. In simple terms we have to interact culturally with each other for us to be wise.

Therefore these three common and popular proverbs are the pillars of unity and in them *umundu* is fully realized and expressed. An African is never regarded as a loose entity to be dealt with strictly individually. His being and destiny is intertwined with that of others in the community. There are always others with whom he is associated with so as to safeguard the welfare of the community (Mbiti 1975: 177).

In this discourse, the ancestors are not left out. For example, when one is named after an ancestor, he or she is expected to emulate his or her character. Ancestors are considered part of the extended family. Therefore, in a way, *umundu* implies a deep respect and regard for African religious beliefs and practices.

Interaction Between the African Culture and Christianity
Terrorism in the world today has become a serious threat to peace and co-existence. The causes of terrorism include civilisations clash, ethnic conflicts and, cultural and religious differences. Africa has not been spared these conflicts as witnessed in the 1998 bombings of the US embassies in Kenya and Tanzania and the post-election violence in Kenya in 2007/2009. Can a consensus among African religions and cultures be a source of peace rather than conflict? There is an indication that intercultural researches can lead to understanding and identification of common aspects that could help bring about peace. This can bring about tolerance.[14] Cultural exchange is the key important thing that is required here.

---

[14]Postcolonial thinking is made up of mind-sets that have developed in reference to the end of colonilsation in the Majority World. Such mind-sets are still diverse and no clear definition on what they may mean exists. But the term is used in this book to imply the critic offered by a number of thinkers after colonialism faded (see Waweru 2007:23).

African communities have different attitudes (stereotypes) towards each other's religion.[15] Application of pluralistic religious models can help us set criteria for assessing the possibilities and limitations of *umundu* for intercultural religious dialogue. The concept of *umundu* needs to be transformed into a truly intercultural and religious philosophy. There is an Afrocentrism embedded in the grand narrative of *umundu* expressed into its core claims.

Umundu as a Point of Theological Transaction

One of the central debates taking place in Kenya today is about the role *umundu* can play in addressing multicultural and religious concerns. The main argument has been that *umundu* has strong multicultural and religious tendencies. The post-colonial thinkers argue that a decolonised assessment of the religious order based on interrelations, dialogue or mutual exposure is possible through the conduct which *umundu* prescribes.

Umundu inspires people to interact with others, to experience the difference of their humanness so as to inform and enrich their own. Mbiti (1969) and Kibicho (2006) have set their discussion in the framework of the philosophies of intercultural and religious dialogue. Setting the discussion in this context and in the light of the core ideas of *umundu* makes us realize that it can be ambivalent if not paradoxical. *Umundu* can be ambiguous because it accommodates various positions – exclusive, inclusive and pluralist. Therefore, *umundu* is potentially pluralist and inclusive.

As such to be *mundu* (humanness) is to affirm one's humanity by recognising the humanity of others in its variety of content and form. The core meaning of this contention is that *umundu* defines an individual in terms of the relationship with others. The assumption is that a vital force, a universal force unites the Gikuyu, for example,

---

[15]See Barbour 1998 who offers five types of attitude, absolutism, approximation of truth, identity of essence, cultural relativism and pluralistic dialogue.

with the other and this gives the impetus for the potential inclusive and pluralist orientation of *umundu*.

This, however, implies a desire for collectivist or communalist conceptions of individuality. As such *umundu* tends to bend towards accommodating cultures in which communality takes precedence over the individual. This is where the core for the uniqueness of *umundu* lies. It brings out the essence of *umundu* in socialism and its implications are unity and solidarity. The dictum is, we can only be people through other people; hence the African mantra 'I am because you are and because you are therefore I am' (Mbiti 1969). There lies the question about its real pluralistic nature. However it would only work from the point that ancestors are the founders of *umundu* and without them there is no *umundu*. For without them we are not and without us they are not.

However, contrary to such an assumption, a combined affirmation and critique of *umundu* shows that the philosophy of *umundu* is not always positive. It can be a powerful river for separating Africans from others if personality is emphasised. *Umundu* is not as pluralistic as it has been claimed to be. This has been clearly demonstrated in the detailed characterization of the philosophy

Conclusion

It is our conclusion here that for that anticipated impact to occur, the role of mother tongue (or vernacular) scripture is crucial. Mother tongue Scripture has a fundamental place in the engagement of Bible and culture. If people will recognize that *Ngai*, the God that have been known from time immemorial, is their saviour, and that the coming of the Bible (gospel) is what they have looked forward to, what they need, then God has ensured and continues to ensure that they will hear him each in their own language so they can marvel at his majesty and his love for them. So with this kind of understanding one is required to know the historical overview of the intercultural transaction. We then need to narrow down to a particular African culture, that is, that of the Kikuyu and use it in this engagement.

A Transaction between the African Culture and the Bible

CHAPTER TWO

The Kikuyu People

Origins

Kikuyu Country

The native homeland of the Kikuyu people is around Mt. Kenya, which is the only snow-capped Mountain along the equator. This Mountain is found in the Central Region of Kenya. This country of the Kikuyu people can be divided into three zones, high, middle and low land according to the altitude. High and middle country has an exceptionally temperate and health climate, as the altitude ranges from 4500 to 7000 feet above sea level, which keeps it cool all the year around. The low country has an altitude of 3000 ft above sea level. It has boggy areas, which are good for rice growing, but renders the area very unhealthy since it is infested with mosquitoes (Ambler 1988: 5).

The Kikuyu traditionally identify their land as beaconed by four mountains or ranges namely: Mt. Kenya (Kirinyaga- the holy shining mountain), Ol Donyo Sabuk, the Ngong Hills and the Aberdare (*Nyandarua*) Ranges. It is correct to state that there is no valley, which is not watered by a river or a stream in Kikuyu land. The sources of these rivers and reservoirs are the above mountains, which like an enormous sponge keep the moisture through the whole year. The vegetation is most luxuriant and often gigantic, of a standard only found within the equator. It is a common practice to find many

Kikuyus[1] in every part of the country including Uganda and Tanzania, where some have even risen to national leadership. The Kikuyu were in Murang'a by 1500 CE, Kabete by around 1750 CE.

.

Creation Myth

Like the Jews Kikuyu people have their own creation story (cf. Genesis 1-3). They traditionally believe that a man called Gikuyu was the founder of the tribe. This man had a wife named Mumbi, who gave birth to nine full daughters (meaning ten). The daughters married men provided by *Ngai* and lived in their father's land making their own families, which allowed them to retain their names as clans resulting to women domineering in Kikuyu society for a number of generations.

This explains the current division of the Kikuyu people into nine full clans as family groupings. According to the legend or the myth, women ruled the men for sometimes and seriously mistreated by them until they rebelled. The story explains a change in history from matriarchal to patriarchal organization.

Migration History

The Ancestors of the Kikuyu came to Kenya during the Bantu migrations of 1200-1600 CE. The Kikuyu were in search of good land that involved several continuous waves of migration and remigration along the large rivers like Tana. The Kikuyu became a distinct group by around 1600, and include some other families like the Meru, Aembu and Mbere people all surrounding Mt. Kenya.

One genetic line known to the Kikuyu is the **Thagicu**, thought to be the earliest Bantu settlers in the area, perhaps around 1200 CE. This seems to be the original group that also comprises the

---

[1]In ordinary East African English usage, one finds the plural for individuals occurring as both *Kikuyu* and *Kikuyu*s However the real name for this group of people is Gikuyu, which has now been reserved for the founder of the tribe, while adopting the term Kikuyu for the people who are the descendants of Gikuyu and Mumbi.

Kamba who today makes and incorporate some of those people in the Thaicu of today, related to the **Dhaiso** (*Segeju*) of northern coastal Tanzania. It was in Mukurue wa Nyagathanga in Murang'a County where an identifiable beginning for the modern Kikuyu people is defined. Later some moved to Nyeri in Mukurwe Division and finally spread to the whole area.

The Kikuyu found a small group of people called **Gumba** occupying the Mount Kirinyaga area with which they had a military conflict with and defeated them. The Gumba were allied with the **Athi** and the **Maasai** in the early 1800's. The Kikuyu people did not believe in killing one that is weaker than you but believed in assimilation, hence they assimilated both the Gumba and Athi and a large settlement of the Maasai through marriage. A small group of the remains of these smaller tribes called Dorobos are currently found in Kihara-Gachie area of Kiambu County and are the founders of St. James Anglican Church Gachie, which was consecrated on 19th January 2011 by the Rt. Rev. Timothy Ranji, Bishop of Mt. Kenya South.

Interaction

The Kikuyus' had no contact with the outside world apart from their cousins the Kamba who were trading in Mombasa until the arrival of the missionaries and settlers. The name for the mountain around which they are settled, Mt. Kenya, is actually a Kamba word because it was a Kamba guide who led the first white missionary or explorer, who when asked the name of the mountain, he gave him the Kamba name, *kere-nyaa*. That which has snow, and Kikuyu people used to call it *kirima kia Mwene Nyaga* (the mountain of the owner of ostriches). It is from this Kamba name that our country got its name – Kenya.

Reaction to Colonisation

The Kikuyu responded strongly to missionary and western education, perhaps more than any other tribe. Their proximity to the British colonial government in Nairobi and the settlers who desired the comfortable Central Highlands simultaneously gave them a great advantage and imposed on them the greatest burden of peoples under colonialism. This made them suffer more than any other group during liberation movement for Kenya's independence.

On a positive note the Kikuyu, however got the best chance to access education and opportunities for involvement in the new money economy and political changes in their country (hence the slogan 'Kikuyu love money'). They also experienced more than any other community the greatest cultural change due to both the opportunities and the oppression of their colonial masters. They developed a greater adaptability and used the British colonial system to overcome the system. These people almost completely abandoned their traditional customs, copying the missionaries and the colonialists.

When Kenya gained its independence and the modernisation entered its new era, many Kikuyu saw opportunities in business moved into cities and new areas to work. They had a desire for education and many Kikuyu have become scholars and university professors in many countries of the world. The Kikuyu people are capitalistic in almost everything they do. Many own or drive *matatus* (mini-van taxis). It is common for a Kikuyu to have many small or large enterprises simultaneously. They have a reputation for astute management of money and hard work.

The Bible was translated in Kikuyu over 100 years ago (1903), one of first in East Africa.

Education
The Kikuyu people are naturally educationist and they love it. Originally they had an informal system of education, which since has been replaced by a formal system of education[2]. This formal

---

[2]It would be rather unfortunate for Kikuyu people to retreat back to informal systems of education after having abandoned it for over a 100years. Quite a number of people are now insisting that we need to go back to our traditions such as sacrificing animals, but it is difficult for the Kikuyu community to retrogress.

education is now given priority for most Kikuyu families, even in the rural areas. Both boys and girls are now provided with education equally, making it possible to find both men and women in virtually every area of business and professional life. Rural families are closer to the traditional pattern of life.

However Kikuyu made an error by ignoring the informal system of education completely, they should have embraced both of them for instructions of their children. However they cannot afford the cost of going back to it. They have now to stick to the formal system and seriously work it out for the benefit of the whole community. But must continue with what is good in their culture like stories and songs as a way of enhancing community socialization.

Identity [Culture/Language]
The Kikuyu speak a Bantu language, making them culturally related to other Bantu-speaking peoples of East Africa. The Kikuyu are identified with other Highland Bantu peoples, primarily the Kamba, the Meru, the Embu, and the Chuka. These tribes of Central and Eastern Kenya can hear each other, even though they might not speak the other's language fluently. Kikuyu are traditionally an aggressive industrious agricultural people, who still live on small family plots, but large numbers of them are involved in all kinds of businesses, no matter what.

The stature of the Kikuyu depends on varied origins and the incorporation of many different refugees or migrant groups; hence they exhibit a wide range of height, physical build, and skin tone and facial features. The Kikuyu language and naming system are strong identification factors.

Language
The Kikuyu speak a Bantu language in the Northeastern Highland Bantu family. It has lexical similarities with Kamba, Embu and Meru. It exhibits three inherently intelligible dialects with local variations. Embu is very close and these two languages are intelligible with some dialects of Kamba. The Kikuyu language, often referred

to technically in its Kikuyu spelling *Gikuyu*, is written in a modified Roman alphabet developed by the missionaries. The language name is spelled *Gikuyu* due to a pattern of phonetic change in the Kikuyu grammar. This spelling is sometimes seen in English references.

The Gikuyu is the primary language, which is spoken by the older members of the family. The Kikuyu are very fond of their language and most multilingual Kikuyu prefer to speak Kikuyu with anyone who knows the language. Most of their Church services are mostly in Kikuyu, even in towns, with an English service mostly for the youth or services are bilingual. Kikuyu is a common language that you hear in many market places because of the strong influence of Kikuyu in the country.

The Kikuyu language is spoken by many people of other tribes and is commonly heard in Nairobi along with Swahili. In many schools, education is begun in the home language, but universally Swahili is taught, then used as a medium in upper elementary, when English is introduced. English is the language of secondary and advanced education. In urban areas, English is introduced in lower grades, and some children go to English-medium schools from the beginning. The educated Kikuyu will prefer the little children to communicate in English, while the learned will insist the use of Gikuyu language at home.

Kikuyu commonly speak Swahili, and English is quite common. Those who are reared in the cities do not speak it as fluently and often as those in the outlying areas. In recent years, urban families have come to use English and Swahili in the home and many Kikuyu children in Nairobi cannot easily talk directly to their grandparents in their mother tongue. This has irritated the elderly members of the family and an upsurge in the use of Gikuyu language is on the rise.

Socio-Political and Economic Organisation

Story, Song and Proverbs
The story, song and proverbs provide us with a rich source of African wisdom. These are all religious. They contain religious beliefs, ideas,

morals and warnings. They speak about God, the world, people and the nature of things and so on. They are set within the cultural and social environment of the people who have produced them and use them. The youth are still often taught through stories, songs, proverbs and other traditional teaching methods[3]. Like most cultures of the world, oral "literature" is a treasure, with its own oral history, legends and traditional stories. Like many other African peoples, the Kikuyu value proverbs and riddles. Rhetoric and verbal games are both entertainment and skill development. Such cultural treasure of the Kikuyu needs to be encouraged, particularly among the youth[4] for the purposes of socialization[5].

It is clear that music and dance are some of the pillars of the Kikuyu culture[6]. Today the country enjoys a vigorous Kikuyu recording industry, for both popular and gospel music sung in all manners whether in pentatonic scale and western music styles. Proverbs are also common within African culture. A proverb is a

---

[3] A *proverb* is a brief saying that presents a truth or some bit of useful wisdom. In a proverb the literal words say something but there is a different meaning behind them. It is the hidden meaning, which is important. A proverb thus requires interpretation. It is in this respect the users of Kikuyu proverbs are cautioned to make sure that whenever they use proverbs, they should be able to give its interpretation.

[4] Mr. Githiri Gathigi aged 95 years, commented that the Kikuyu had a very elaborate sung riddle game; a duet called the enigma poem or *gicandi* a set text poem of riddles. It is mostly sung in a duet and the players are in a competition. The duet is strikingly different than the normal singing of the Kikuyu performed by a soloist and a chorus. The poem is learned by heart. A decorated gourd rattle accompanies the singing. One *gicandi* may be as long as 127 stanzas. (An interview on 6th-1-2010),

[5] This word socialization refers to how people learn or acquire norms, traditions and values in a specific society. Through socialization process individuals are assisted to understand what is expected of them.

[6] Culture refers to behaviour learned as a result of living in groups, which tend to be patterned, and this is transmitted from generation to generation, through music and dance.

brief saying that presents a truth or some bit of useful wisdom. In a proverb the literal words say something but there is a different meaning behind them. It is the hidden meaning, which is important and must be decoded. The proverbs have a broader goal of cultivating in the members of the community the ability to appreciate and conform to the social values, norms and beliefs of that community.

Cultural Beliefs

The Kikuyu are incurably superstitious and they quite often hold some practices handed over from one generation to another. For instance, some Kikuyu still honour some traditional superstitions such as a taboo against whistling particularly at night. They believed that such would awaken the malicious spirits, which would finally disturb the peace of the society. However many people are less interested today with such practices and actual belief of such may miss the point.

The Kikuyu believed that children should not be counted at all, so even though their legend says Gikuyu had 10 daughters, they always say nine. So that When counting they will say 'full nine' instead of the word for ten. Nowadays this term is still used sometimes by old people or in a joking manner. The real word is still retained, *ikumi* (ten).

Courtship

In the Kikuyu society marriage occupy a special position of importance. It is the desire of every member of the society to build up his own family in order to extend and prolong his father's *Mbari* (clan). This results in strengthening the community as a whole. In the Kikuyu community boys and girls are left free to choose their mates for courtship, without interference on the part of the parents on either side. However advice on the choice of a good lady was always availed. From as early as age ten there is social intercourse between boys and girls, which provides them with an opportunity of becoming acquainted with one another for a considerable time before courtship begins making it almost impossible to choose a husband or wife hastily. The first stage in courtship is for the man to approach a lady in a very indirect manner. Once the lady accepts the love from the man she then proceeds to inform her parents about such an approach. This brings the courtship to a second stage.

In this second stage parents from the Man's side arrange to visit the lady's home with some gifts. No discussions about marriage are entertained at this level but information of interest between the man and the lady is given and the gifts left behind becomes a sign (*ithigi*) that someone has created a friendship in that home. No any other man will be allowed to engage the lady unless this first engagement is broken. So the parents of the man now goes home knowing that their son is in courtship with the lady. This makes the relationship to move into a third stage.

In this third stage the parents of the man start earnestly to collect goats and sheep, or cattle (today money is used for marriage) for the first instalment of the dowry (*ruracio*). Once parents of the man has given quite substantial amount of money or goats, sheep and cattle they move to the fourth stage. (See dowry in Chapter Eight).

Marriage
Here a final day is fixed on which all family members are gathered in order to sign the marriage contract. On the day in question all representatives of the two families and friends are invited. Plenty of food and drinks are served. The ceremony of marriage is conducted *(ngurario* or *gutinia kiande)*. This is followed by a big dance of *mugithi* (a train like song). Women are then invited to present a song called *gitiiro* which is special to women only and which marks the end of the marriage ceremony. Then the parents of the girl will arrange for a visit to the man's homestead, taking with them presents for the man's relatives. Such a visit will depend with the clan, some will do it sooner than others. It is commonly known as *Itara* (seeing the firewood place). From this time forward the lady is regarded as having been blessed and given away to the man's clan. The marriage is then considered to have taken place with the entire agreements concluded with dowry (to be discussed later in details).

Birth

The Kikuyu considered bad luck if one spoke openly about the coming birth of a child, because it was thought evil spirits might take the child. Even now they are sometimes troubled by the European practice of baby showers and mention of the expected date of birth, and especially the idea of choosing or mentioning the expected baby's name before birth. The Kikuyu believed that *mwana ndatumagirwo ngoi ate muciare* (before a child is born nobody should attempt to make the baby basket). These are some of the superstitions that Christians have been able to overcome. So if any one suggests that we go back to traditional beliefs there will be a direct clash with our Christian faith today.

Naming System

This community equally considered bad luck if one spoke openly about the naming of a child, because it was thought evil spirits might take the child. Even now they are sometimes troubled by the European practice of naming unborn children and especially the idea of choosing or mentioning the expected baby's name before birth. The Kikuyu people however have retained their naming system up to date. It is their cultural practice to balance the relationship between the family of the girl and of the boy through naming.

Although many things have changed in a positive note, naming of children in Kikuyu society has remained unchanged, therefore more than any other custom naming is a unique ritual pattern still surviving in Kikuyu land. The family identity is carried on in each generation by naming children in the following pattern: the first boy is named after the father's father, the second boy after the mother's father. The first girl is named after the father's mother, the second after the mother's mother.

Subsequent children are named similarly after the brothers and sisters of the father and mother; from eldest to youngest, alternating from father's to mother's family. As refugees are accepted into a clan the naming pattern will incorporate new lineages and integrate them into Kikuyu society and history. A Kikuyu marrying a non-

Kikuyu will follow this naming pattern, as part of enculturation[7] of members of the community.

Because of the rapid changes in the social and material culture, this naming pattern is an extremely strong and important factor of Kikuyu identity. This practice also has the positive value of ceremonially and literally incorporating a non-Kikuyu into the tribal lineage.

Thus the names of the parents in the other ethnic group will be added to the next generation of Kikuyu descendants. This mechanism incorporates the "mixed" children into one of the existing Kikuyu lineages, while allowing the Kikuyu social structure to grow and incorporate new lineages. This facilitates the introduction of whole new family lines while maintaining the same core structure and organization of Kikuyu identity. However unlike many African peoples Kikuyu names have no meanings (*ritwa ni mbuukio*), so Kikuyu names are not religious but traditional. You do not expect in this respect to have a name that has a religious significance within the society unless it is a nickname to a person depending on daily practice farming or business. However such persons have other names, which are traditional and meaningless, e.g. Wanjiku, Wambui, Kamau and Njoroge. These names simply refer to a clan as an age group without any religious connotations.

---

[7]Enculturation refers to the process of learning the culture of one's group, through different settings such as places where conflicts are being resolved, dowry being negotiated and in initiation ceremonies being conducted such as age grading systems. Most of the Kikuyu religious practices are all geared towards enculturation of individuals to their culture as part their worldview.

Religious Beliefs

Traditionally the Kikuyu held a worldview that has been referred to as ancestor worship[8]. They believed spirits of dead could be pleased or displeased like a living individual. The ancestors were honoured as intercessors with God and spiritual powers, hence the many tributes you hear in funerals today. They were honoured in the naming system, and people often explain the traditional belief that the actual spirit of the grandparent and other ancestors comes into the new child named after them. This has now changed due to acceptance of a more scientific worldview, Christian faith and longer life spans. (The grandparents are often still alive when the grandchildren are born; hence no ancestral spirits are required). Only through an ancestor does a Kikuyu name become religious. This shows the influence of religion in the life of the people. It also demonstrates that people with such names are in effect religious carriers.

The Kikuyu traditionally worship one God whom they call *Ngai*. This is the Maasai name *(Enkai)* for the One Creator God and was borrowed by both the Kikuyu and the Kamba. They believe *Ngai* is the creator and giver of all things. They thought *Ngai* lived in the sky. Yet they also thought of Ngai as living on Mt. Kenya. When the cloud was on the mountain, *Ngai* was said to live there. This name of God is used in the Kikuyu Bible and Christian worship and confessions. A common blessing is "Ngai *akurathime*" *May God bless you*.

As with peoples all over the world, high places were holy places. For their neighbors the Maasai, similarly the mountain (hill) of *Ol Doinyo Sapuk* (the Black Hill) and the hills of Ngong were holy places, as well as the peaks of the Mau Escarpment in the Rift Valley.

---

[8]World view denotes a theological concept rather than an attempt to provide a description of a type of religious phenomenon: it is used here to explain the picture of the way things in sheer actuality are, in relation to their world of religion (cf. Geertz 1968:302), so that their primal world view is their way of understanding life and the world which they live.

Their traditional religion is monotheistic and has many stories that can be related to Biblical stories. Their traditional religion involved sacrifices when things were not going well, which were offered under a *Mugumo* tree, generally on a high place. Even today, the *Mugumo* tree holds this place of honour as a sign of the sacred. In times of trouble, or in an annual special service, a family or village leader would take his family to the "high place" and pray for this family, ask forgiveness of sins and request help in drought or other needs. People who did these prayers were age graded through goat sacrifices. One cannot offer a sacrifice on behalf of his family or society before one is graded into a particular age grade. So initiation was an important aspect to the Kikuyu people.

Age-Set System
The most important stage of initiation to the Kikuyu people was a circumcision ceremony for both boys and girls by age grades of about five-year periods. All men within a circumcision group would take an age-grade name. This later helped even to know times in Kikuyu history, and peoples' ages could be gauged by age-grade names.

This system of age grading may have been copied from the early Thagicu, one of the ancestral groups of the Kikuyu, from Cushitic and Nilotic peoples. It was also a common practice among the Nguni people of Southern Africa, such as the Zulu. Other Kikuyu neighbors like the Maasai still had this age-grade system, organizing newly adult men into a warrior class and the graduating warriors into junior elders.

The practice of circumcision for boys is one of the strongest customs of the Kikuyu people still being followed, but only as a family matter and is done in hospital nowadays. Some of the old men still prefer to be called by their age-grade name, although as rapid cultural change has taken place, the age-grade system has basically died out. For the girls circumcision which caused early divisions in Christianity has lost some of its emphasis among Evangelical Christians. It is still practiced secretly among those with traditional beliefs. Most churches and civil societies still officially discourage it. Younger generations and more urban families have abandoned the practice. Traditionally, boys and girls were raised in a different manner. Girls were raised to work in the *shamba* (farm), while boys were expected to care for animals. Much has changed as Kikuyu sought education for both boys and girls and there is quite a liberal sharing of various tasks between the genders, especially in urban areas.

This is very important because while the family and the clan unite several groups of kinsfolk in the tribe and have a territorial unit, which acts independently, that is unity in diversity, the age grading system unite the whole tribe regardless of kinsfolk or boundaries. According to Kenyatta (1938) an important factor in unifying the Kikuyu society is the system of age grading (*riika*). As we have seen the *mbari* and the *muhiriga* systems help to form several groups of kinsfolk within the tribe acting independently, but the system of the age-system grading unites and solidifies the whole tribe in all its activities. They act as one body in all societal matters and have a strong bond of brotherhood and sisterhood among themselves. The age set system normally starts after circumcision. It is after the circumcision that an individual becomes mature person and therefore he or she is given responsibility in the community[9].

However leadership does not start with circumcision. The pre-circumcision period serves as a preparation and training for leadership. It will be unfair to neglect this pre-circumcision period. We shall now evaluate the role of leaders in three stages that make up the grading system of the Kikuyu community namely:

---

[9]After an initiation one becomes a full member of the society and responsibilities may now be given depending on one's age. An elder starts to be developed after circumcision, since this is the first stage of age grading. Baptism is the equivalent of this stage in the church tradition.

pre-circumcision period; after circumcision (warriors); and elders[10]. (To be discussed later into details).

Economic Organisation [Roles]

Many rural Kikuyu are very poor and everyone works for the benefit of the farm and the improvement of conditions for the next generation. However a few are among the richest in the country today within urban setting.

Girls

Girls are responsible for taking care of a baby brother or sister and also for helping the mother with the household chores. This still tends to be the case even in urban families who cannot afford to hire a maid.

Political Organisation

To the Kikuyu people charity begins at home. A Kikuyu family is an administrative unit whereby it has its own government and leadership. Every family had its own way of doing things *"Ndiakagwo ta ya wakinii"*(no man will govern his house like that of his fellow neighbour), or *'o rungu na muguwiire wa ruo'* (every creeper has its own lying style) so by nature Kikuyus are capitalistic. As the family gets children it extends to become a wider community. As people age in that family many more spring up and when grow up to the seventh and eight-generation new sub clans are formed. Such small clans are normally called in Kikuyu Mbari. So Mbari is a sub clan composed of a number of families who could trace their origin from a common ancestor[11].

---

[10]See a research by David Kamau conducted at Ikinu in 1989, concerning this age grading system, entitled: *The role of leaders in small Christian Communities: A case study of Ikinu Parish,* Nairobi Archdiocese (a thesis submitted in partial fulfillment of the requirements for the master of Theology 1990).

[11]See J. Middleton & G. Kershaw, (1965:25) for a detailed classification of the Kikuyu family and clans. These two scholars have attempted to write the history of the Kikuyu people.

One may leave his clan (*Mbari*) and settle somewhere else, particularly on buying a new piece of land at a distance. After some generations one may form his *mbari*. It is after the death of this man that his people will name the *mbari* after his name, in such a sub clan people know each other, they share several things a stream, village, land and market. In this understanding a family will occupy a *mucii* (home) signifying fire (*Mwaki*) while *mbari* will occupy *Ituura* (Village). When *mbari* grows up it becomes a *muhiriiga* (a full clan), which may occupy a whole range. People in this full clan usually call each other '*Nyumba*' literary people of the same house. The boundaries in Kikuyu land are rivers and ridges. If one was not able to buy land or clear a forest they could join another clan to do so jointly (J Middleton, & G. Kershaw 1965:25).

Today this buying of land by *mbari* has evolved as land buying companies, such as *Nyakinyua, Mboi Kamiti, Mwitumberia, Mwana Mwireri* and many others, which are common in Kikuyu Land. This may also be the origin of the word Harambee coined from the proverb *Kamuingi koya ndiri* (a group of people lifts the mortar), which implies that people must pull together for the common good, so as much Kikuyu are capitalistic they are also socialistic in away. The Kikuyu balanced between capitalism and socialism striking a balance on family and individual. This is a principal factor in Kikuyu tribal organization namely family and clan. The man assisted by his wife is usually regarded as the principle leader in each setting. In this tribal organization one of the most important issues is Age grading system in reference to the role of leaders.

Age Grading System

A common Kikuyu custom is that of circumcision and it is a very important rite of passage among the Kikuyu. It is during circumcision that an (individual passes from childhood to adulthood). People who are circumcised together are like brothers and sisters. It is the time they get a common name of age group (riika).

They are proud of being together. They organize themselves with their own leaders. Normally the boys who had shown some qualities of leadership before circumcision become the leaders of the newly circumcised men. As soon as the wound heals the newly circumcised men join the junior warriors. During this period of junior warriors, they are not allowed to take any active part in war until the senior warriors initiate them. So it is a period of initiation. It is during this period of initiation into warriors that the training takes place. The training takes the form of advice. They are given the following instructions:

1. It is their duty to defend the tribe from outside attack and once the council of warriors makes a decision they should never retreat. Today teenagers are taught by the church to defend their Christina faith.

2. The warriors should be ready to die for the community and for this reason; they take an oath never to retreat in war (this is how Kikuyu fought for independence from the British rule). The Church today trains the young converts before confirmation how to hold firm to their faith. They should never retreat in trials and temptations.

Therefore the role of leaders in both junior and senior warriors was, to know how to make proper judgment and be able to keep the discipline and instructions they give. The whole tribe must be in their heart and not self-seeking, always ready to listen to everybody. Their role as leaders was not so much not to command but to serve and guide the people. These are some of the qualities that the leaders must have and they are chosen on merits. According to Kenyatta (1938:25), every *riika* (age set) has its leader who was responsible for activities of his age set. His main duty was to keep harmony and discipline in the group. The role of a leader in this group was to settle minor disputes and quarrels between the members of his regiment. He also acted as a spokesman of the group in general matters. He was the chief composer and organizer of songs and dances of his *riika* and sometimes arranged competitions between his group and other group.

3. The role of leaders in the institution of elders. After the senior warriors, the next age set is the institution of elders, whose role is the government of the tribe. Some of the conditions to join the elders' institution are that a male person must have been retired from the senior warriors. The person must have been married and settled with his family. The logic behind the condition of marriage is that one who cannot manage or lead his family cannot be a leader of the tribe and nobody would listen to him. Again J. Kenyatta says: The government should be in the hands of council of elders. The position of elders should be determined by a system of age. No man should be allowed to hold a responsible position other than a warrior or become a member of council of elders unless he was married (1938:20) and had established his own homestead.

The institution of elders is as important as that of warriors if not more. Before a person becomes a full elder he had to go through various stages. These are stages of training for leadership, so that the community can recognize one. One had to give several goats (*Mburi cia kiama*) from one stage to the other.

Council of Boys (Ngutu)
The boys organize themselves. They have their own councils. The boys' organizations start in the family. On family level, they organise some games like throwing stones or dancing.[12] From the family, they move to *ituura* (village) organize how they are going to work as a team especially on the land. They move from one family to the other. When they go to pasture the goats, they put them together. They allocate positions from which to watch the goats. In their free time they organize dances. The name for their dance is called *nguchu*. As Cagnol (1933:75) puts it, "Another game

---

[12]See J. Kenyatta (1938:2), who is the Kikuyu to document the story of the Kikuyu people in a very detailed manner.

is the *giuthi*." Six holes are made in the ground and each player has six little balls which he has to get into the 22 holes according to a certain combination of numbers"(this is comparable to golf).

Normally in all these activities the council of boys, called *Ngutu,* is responsible for the organization. Within the council of boys there are some boys who show a sense of leadership, boys who are gifted in leading others. Such boys call for a meeting. They formulate regulations and rules to discipline the boys who might misbehave. As the boys approach circumcision, they have many dance competitions. The competitions are between different villages (*matuura or miaki*). It is during these competitions that boys show their talents in leadership. From these competitions a leader was identified. The winning village would mean that their organization was good and that discipline was kept. For C. Cagnolo it is perhaps in this direction that the Kikuyu boy has the best chance to display his individual talents[13]. The mothers listen with pride to find traces of special cleverness in these extempore productions. The community kept the boy child alert all his life through these challenges.

In short boys had their own activities and the role of leaders was to keep the discipline and give wise decisions and suggestions. It was under their responsibility to lead other boys in dances and games. This period for boys was very important because future leaders began to emerge at this stage. The Meru say "a *Mugambi* is - born *a Mugambi*" and the Kikuyu "a *Muthamaki* appoints himself in childhood". Both expressions convey the essential idea that leadership is inherent and does not depend on the payment of an entrance fee. None the less, a leader comes out quickly".[14]

Today we are able to deal with these boys during initiations organized by the Church. However the Church follow-ups are so limited that the boys are left on their own for the rest of their lives. This is

---

[13]C. Cagnolo, (1983:76) has explained the games of the Kikuyu people within their customs, traditions and folklore.

[14]H.E. Lambert (1957:101) gives a detailed way of how leaders were identified within Kikuyu Social and Political Institutions.

dangerous because many other groups have taken advantage of the boys and have started training them in other things. If we have left the tradition of training boys traditionally, the church must now come up clearly on how to move with the boys into other developmental stages. Otherwise the initiation does not end but starts with circumcision. Traditionally the next stage was the institution of warriors commonly known as the council of commons (*Kamatimu*).

The Council of Commons (*Kamatimu*)

This is a stage commonly known as a one goat elder. Once a senior warrior gets married he retires from military service. His father then arranges for him to be introduced into the council of commons. The father is required to pay a fee of one goat.[15] This is the beginning of the process of initiation. The individual person is now not a warrior but between a warrior and half an elder (commoner). He is a commoner because he is allowed to carry arms like a warrior with a spear, sword and arrows in case of an emergency, hence the name *kamatimu,*[16] the lowest level is the council of common.[17] According to Muriuki (1974:188-189) this lowest council was made up of junior elders, a group that consisted of all those men who had married and hence ceased to be active in military service. For anybody joining this council of common elders one had to give a goat and a calabash of beer. However today one may give sodas instead of bear? Recently

---

[15]See David Kamau 1990:41, where he argues that this goat is usually given by parents but not by individual. However if one is of age and parents are not willing one could give it on his behalf.

[16]The *Kamatimu* act as messengers to the *kiama,* and help in ordinary jobs like skinning animals, lighting fires, fetching firewood, roasting meat as well as carrying ceremonial articles, so these are not yet elders but learners (see J. Kenyatta 1938:107).

[17]Jomo Kenyatta, 1938>1984, states that when a man is married with his own home, he was supposed to join *kiama* (council) by paying one male goat or sheep and then he is initiated into a first grade of eldership (*kamatimu*)

the Roman Catholic priests in Ruku Parish gave sodas instead of beer in a ceremony at ndongoro, a popular site for initiation in Kabete location, Kikuyu District. Even then they were not regarded as full members of the Kiama and had more in common with the warriors.[18] So they had to give extra goats for their status to be up lifted.

The role of this council of commons is to act as messengers for the council of peace (council of senior elders). The members of the council of commons are not fully recognized elders and may not take part in the council of peace discussions and deliberations. However during the council of peace meetings the members of the council of commons are invited. But their role is to listen to how the meetings are conducted and how the issues are resolved and decisions arrived at. They must be attentive and passive during the meetings. Inherently although invited they are not even allowed to mix with the council of peace. They are grouped somewhere near the council meeting, where they can hear the discussions. In this way they listen and learn how to organize and operate council meetings. They are novices. Since they have given one goat they are called a council of commons. The next stage is the council of peace.

Council of Peace (*Matathi*)

After serving in the council of commons for a period of time, one is initiated into another stage. Now the second stage of councils is when a person gives another goat (second goat) to the elders[19]. It is after this goat that the person is qualified to join the council of peace[20]. It takes quite a number of years (15-20) between the first and second goat. In most cases one is allowed to give the second goat after the circumcision of the first born of the person undergoing the initiation

---

[18]There was no ritual performed at this stage, only animals were slaughtered and eaten in a general feast (Kenyatta 1938:107).

[19]This is when an elder is to be elevated into the council of peace (*Matathi* refers to special kinds of leaves that were used by leaders, once in this council his behaviour out to be different from the members of junior councils.

(Muriuki 1974:126). This means between the first and second goat, there are many years of training for leadership in the council of commons. With the second goat, the person becomes a fully recognized member of the council of peace. To show that this person has undergone the first stage of training, that he has given two goats, he receives two things: a staff (*muthigi*[21]) and leaves from a certain tree called *matathi*[22].

The two objects are for his office and show that now he has some power in the council of peace. Although the person is an elder, the training is not yet finished; he is still a junior elder. Now he is allowed to take part in minor cases and even to give his own judgment. As a leader he has a role to bring peace to the people. This is why the council is called a council of peace (cf. kenyatta 1938:107). In fact the stuff and the leaves are signs of peace. The elders of two goats are called elders of peace. They are supposed to keep the secrets of the council which, when revealed, could bring disharmony in the community. They conduct the day-to-day affairs within their villages without interfering with communities outside their locality[23]. The next level is the governing council.

---

[20]One may here argue that it is not the goat that matters, but maturity. The goat is only to signify that one has closed the floor. At this stage an elder has given two goats and utmost three.

[21]The Anglican Church actually recognizes leadership of a bishop by giving him or her a staff during an initiation ceremony commonly known as consecration. In most cases a bishop will have gone several stages, deacon, priest, rural dean, archdeacon.

[22]According to J. Middleton and G. Kershaw (1984:33) on the payment of a second goat, mostly when the child of *Kamatimu* is about to be circumcised, he becomes a full member of the *kiama* (council), he is given a stuff and is allowed to carry *matathi* leaves. The Church usually gives a cap or different robes to senior clergy like the canons.

Governing Council (*Maturanguru*)

This brings us to the third stage of initiation where an elder is required to give two more goats. This means an elder is now promoted into senior elders' governing council. The period between the two goats and four goats is also used for training. The person now becomes an active member of the Governing council of elders. Here an individual becomes a full leader, called *muthamaki*. Such elders are usually aged in years (70 and above). They are full of wisdom. The qualification here is the knowledge and wisdom that one has in leading and judging cases. Just like in many other communities there is an exception and a person who is not very old could be found in this governing council of elders. If the council found that there is a young man gifted in knowledge and wisdom, he is hurried to give the goats and fulfil all the necessary conditions in order to join this group of elders; for instance, one is ordained a priest or a bishop within the community[24]. The reason for this is to incorporate the young and wise leaders and such an election to the *muthamaki* grade lies entirely with the *athamaki*; if they see a young man whose prudence and knowledge has impressed them favourably they bring him on board[25].

While the council of peace manages the affairs of day-to-day life in their local communities, the governing council of elders manages the affairs of the whole of the Kikuyu community. They have no limitations as to their area of operation. They can even be called from far and wide to hear cases. They are learned in the Kikuyu form of government[26]. The governing council of *athamaki* (leaders) was frequently called

---

[23]G. Muriuki (1974:127) explains that, the junior elder could in special circumstances hear minor cases, which did not involve serious offences.

[24]C.W. Hoblely (1978:30) observes that occasionally one may see quite a young man, practically a youth, among the elders. This means that talented people could climb the ladder of leadership more easily.

[25]According to Hobley, (1922, New impression 1978:31) such young people had to have extra ordinary skill that attracted the elders.

in to assist in important or difficult civil disputes, particularly between Maasai and Kikuyu communities.

A Religious Council (*Kiama Gia Guthathaiya*)

The last and not the least of the Kikuyu councils and which very few people had a privilege of joining before death is the religious council. To be a member of the religious council one had all his children children's' circumcised, and his wife cannot give birth, and has become sexually inactive (cf. Kenyatta 1938:109). In order be initiated into the religious council, one must give a fifth goat. When accepted, the person becomes less active in the governing council in order to take on his new responsibility of a religious leader perhaps equivalent to the position of an Archbishop today. However doubles up as a strong advisor to the governing council.

The role of religious council of elders is to offer sacrifices and prayers to God for the community. They are the people who lead the national and communal sacrifices. The religious council takes sacrificial role because they are believed to be pure, having passed childbearing period. It is because they are pure and clean that God can hear their prayers. This is the highest and most honoured status that a person can have within Kikuyu community.

Finally one may ask what about women. Did they play any role in the society? The Kikuyu women had their own councils, *Ndundu ya atumia*, literally women's advisory council (Lambert 1956:95). In every mbari (clan) there was an institution of elderly women who were involved in all matters of the society. Kikuyu women are generally aggressive and they have never been left out whether in war or in any ceremony. Infact in most cases they conducted music. They also had their own leaders to manage their work. A part from helping one another in the *mugunda* (garden) and controlling children

---

[26]See H. E. Lambert who says that it is particularly this council which is empowered to deal with serious cases as murder and whose jurisdiction is regarded as extending beyond the boundaries of the individual own locality

in their homes, they also advised their husbands privately and individually and not as a group or in public. Therefore it is wrong for anybody to suggest that Kikuyu women had no public or official role of leadership in the Kikuyu community.

In case one is in doubt of this, one could check the role they played during liberation struggle. During the sacrifices both male and female were involved. Elderly women often acquired public status because they were regarded as part of the religious council. Kenyatta (1938:63) says that their ability to manage the economy has accorded them much prestige. So although they did not attend the initiation ceremonies for goat eating, they knew everything. Naturally women in Kikuyu society matured quicker than men. Therefore they were said to have no age grading system and they automatically joined the age groups of their husbands. So in Kikuyu society while men could not mature naturally women did. The political situation of both men and women during the liberation struggle threw the age grading system into confusion and gave the chance to women to become major leaders of liberation struggle. So what are the effects of political situation in Kenya to the Kikuyu society?

Modern Status of the Kikuyu People

The Kikuyu have always had a family-oriented government as explained above. They never had chiefs, but had a council of elders drawn from the senior elder age-set as you can see above. Such were commonly known as *athamaki* (kings). A spokesman would be chosen by consensus, but he would be removed if he were not cooperative. The Kikuyu are lineage oriented, considering themselves a lineage from one common ancestor, Gikuyu and his wife Mumbi as earlier explained.

---

[27]Louis Leakey 1933, J. Kenyatta 1938, Lambert 1995, Hobley and recently Kibicho 2006, Muriuki 1974 and others have all analyzed in details the political situations of the Kikuyu and the way they responded to colonial oppression.

The full-nine clans (meaning ten) of the Kikuyu are named after the daughters of Mumbi. As various peoples have joined the Kikuyu society, they have become part of the welcoming Kikuyu society, and taken on the language and mythical identification with Gikuyu. Much has been written by Kikuyu scholars and others on the legendary and historical origins and factors in Kikuyu history[27].

The Kikuyu have been traditional neighbours of the Maasai with whom they clashed once and a while, the Maasai often raided across the Kikuyu, Meru and Kamba areas and all the way to the Giryama areas of the coast. The Maasai would steal their cattle, though for the Kikuyu cattle grazing is not the focus, but farming. They helped the Masaai community with food during drought seasons. So the Maasai would turn to the Kikuyu for food and this made them friendly most of the time.

Therefore the Maasai and the Kikuyu had close ties and even intermarried with each other. During the Maasai civil wars at the end of the 19th century, hundreds of Maasai refugees were taken in and adopted by the Kikuyu, particularly those in Kiambu and Nyeri. This resulted to a kind of a semi group of people called wokabi's. This is a unique community in Kenya, which speaks the two languages. Until recently most of the Maasai national leaders were from this semi group community.

The church needs to adopt this age grading system to promoting leadership of both men and women. No goats will be required, but for a deacon to become a priest a ceremony is done. When one is made a rural dean a particular achievement is necessary. If the person has performed in the level then, one could be promoted to a deacon. Unfortunately the church challenges, the giving of goats but it is not transparent in the way it promotes its leaders. It has often been accused of nepotism and corruption and therefore, it cannot challenge the tradition of Kikuyu age-grading system.

CHAPTER THREE

Mapping the Transaction Between the African Culture and the Bible

Introduction

The transaction between the African culture and the Bible is a relatively recent development. It is a natural development of a church coming of age. Culturally it corresponds to the casting off of colonial rule and constraints, as nation after nation became independent. Perhaps most significantly it coincides with 'the rebirth of African culture' (Baur 2000:430). Therefore an important aspect of the Bible in Africa is the mapping of the transactions that constitute the history of the encounters between Africa and the Bible (West 2001:84).

It is interesting to note that a number of scholars, like Elizabeth Isichei (1995) and Ype Schaaf (1994), have engaged in this transaction but with little interest in the *kind* of transaction that has been taking place between the African culture and the Bible. However there are other scholars, like Vincent L. Wimbush (1993) and Nahashon Ndung'u (1997), who note that some African Independent Churches such as the *Akurinu* and Zionist churches emerged with a deliberate rejection of the beliefs and practices of the mission churches and gave the Bible a new interpretive approach, which helped them to identify their own teachings and practices in their transactions.

There were a number of initial impetuses to the development of the dialogue between the African culture and the Bible. One was the formation of African Independent Churches (AIC). As early as 1821, in Sierra Leone, an African Independent Church was formed because of discontent with white missionaries. In the 1890's these churches began being formed in Nigeria and today they are a major sector in African Christianity. Many have been formed in order to be independent and to express Christianity in ways more appropriate to their experience, even though not all may have been formed for noble reasons. This makes it clear that Africans do not transact with the Bible 'empty handed', separate from their experiences of reality, both religio-culturally and socio-politically. In their particular hermeneutic strategies for transacting with the Bible they are adept at using the full array of scholarly interpretive resources on offer, in order to engage the Bible in dialogue (West 2001:86).

La négritude, a movement initiated by Leopold Senghor, was the beginning of the transaction between the African culture and the Bible. Associated with him are Aimé Césaire and Léon Coutran Damas. These were part of a group of African writers (perhaps an organised group called African Writers) who began to challenge both the colonial system and missionaries. The *La negritude* movement called attention to what it meant to be African and began to establish the distinctive values of *African-ness*. This was an important reversal of the negative ways in which colonialism and missionaries viewed African culture and religion. From this movement came the study of African oral traditions. The publication of these studies resulted in a growing appreciation and awareness of the cultural wisdom and riches of Africa.

This writing and cultural movement was helped by the Black-consciousness movement of the United States of America (Black is Beautiful) and the magazine *Presence Africaine*. A number of African writers, including Wole Soyinka (Nigeria) and Ngugi wa Thiong'o (Kenya) were well received in Africa and the appreciation of African life and values was heightened.

The development and articulation of a distinctively African philosophy may be attributed to African original thinkers such as Senghor who began to describe African thought and worldview. The book *Bantu Philosophy* by Placide Tempels, a missionary priest in what was then Zaire, is regarded as a most significant development. This was first written in 1945 in French, with an English version published in 1969. Tempels analysed African culture and thought categories and has been called the 'Father of African Theology'. He concluded that the most basic focus of the whole African worldview and religion is 'life-force' (la force vitale). African thinkers have developed his ideas further. However the first African to write a philosophical study was Alexis Kagame, a Rwandan, who developed an African ontology based on the Bantu philosophy of Tempels: *Muntu* - God, spirits and men; *Kintu* - animals, plants and minerals; *Hantu* - time and space; *kuntu* - modality, such as beauty and laughter.[1]

Africans thinkers finally settled on three general areas of revolution against foreign domination: political, cultural (represented in the early stages by theologies of adaptation and inculturation), and religious (particularly in the theologies of inculturation such as the study of African Traditional Religions (ATR) and the call for selfhood). However, because for a long time African scholars were trained in the West in contexts where the historical, sociological, literary, and reader response methods were prevalent or still held sway, the development of African dialogue with the Bible was slowed down.

Important events in the development of the dialogue between African culture and the Bible should be highlighted. In 1955 there was a meeting on Christianity and African Culture in Accra, Ghana. During this meeting there came a call to use the language of African culture to communicate the Gospel. In addition, some presenters argued for the continuity between African religions and Christianity. This would be implemented by allowing the African religio-cultural heritage ('the myths, the stories and the proverbs') and the socio-

---

[1]Compare this with *Mundu*-person, *undu*-something, *kindu*-thing, plants and animals, *handu* -time and *kundu*- modality, beauty and laughter, which is the Kikuyu way of expressing their ontology.

political situation ('the meanings and the values') of Africa to interface with the Bible.[2]

The following year some publications came out from Francophone Africa, including *The Bantu Life-Unity* by Vincent Mulago and *The Rwandese Bantu Philosophy* by Alexis Kagame. A book of essays *Des prêtres noirs s'interrogent (Black Priests Question Themselves)* was also published, in which writers like Mulago, Kagame, Hebga and Mveng (students in Europe) began to express the need to get out of the shadow of Western Christianity and take genuine ownership for Christianity in Africa and its theological expression.[3]

In 1958, in Ibadan, Nigeria, a conference of multi-denominational African Church leaders gave expression to the desire for an Africanised Church and this eventually led to the formation of the All Africa Conference of Churches (AACC). At another conference, held in 1960 at Lovanium University, Kinshasa, a debate on African Theology resulted in a publication entitled *'Toward an African-coloured Theology'* by Tharcisse Tshibangu,[4] who was then a student at LU, Kinshasa. His view was that the Church in Africa must become truly African. His concern, at that time, was not so much to Christianise African Culture as to Africanise the church structure, rituals etc. His intent was to propose some preliminary conditions for an African theology, considering a truly African Theology could only be developed if theology was thought through

---

[2]See Knut Holter (1998:240-254), who puts it clearly, stating that African biblical scholarship would have a lot to offer to the western scholars were it not for the fact that Africans have been marginalized due to their economic situation, which hinders them from entering the academic biblical studies market place of current literature, data bases and conferences.

[3]See Wimbush (1993:88) who argues that African biblical scholarship has a unique hermeneutic style characterized by a looseness, even playfulness, vis-à-vis the biblical texts themselves.

[4]See African Theology, 183-194.

from within African categories and by means of African ways of thinking. Some of his thoughts include the following:

1. African theology presupposes the idea of revealed truth, since this knowledge is coming from God. Revelation is the starting point.
2. There is a human side. Every human requires 'logical rectitude' – a structure of thought that progressively leads to knowledge. He recognized the universality of principles of human reason, 'even at the level of scientific working.'
3. Since we are dealing with knowing divine realities, theology requires 'natural elements apt to express it analogically.'
4. The issue here is that we are really getting into epistemology: what does it mean to 'know' or have 'knowledge'? In particular with respect to God. How do we know God? Is it direct knowledge or is it analogical?

He noted three important issues: -

1. African theology must contend with the African mistrust of Christianity and Christian Theology as simply a tool of colonization whose purpose is to control Africans.
2. What is the relationship and comparison of Christianity and ATR?
3. The tension individual Africans feel between Christian commitment and their own culture.

It was then thought necessary to have preconditions for an African 'characterized theology' which would reject Western rationalism – a critical philosophy of doubt – particularly the idea that certitude in knowledge is achieved through active criticism or doubt until one reaches the point that one can no longer doubt. Instead, there is an African logic that is intuitive and synthetic, not rational and analytical. In fact African logic has full confidence (a 'spontaneous trust') in the truth of the senses (experience) and 'of the higher knowing faculties'. This refers to the spiritual senses. African logic is objective knowledge and certitude combined with common sense, which means the knowledge received from one's cultural heritage and ancestors: such a heritage 'formed an indivisible block of social, moral, juridical and religious truths.' Consequently, African logic has a foundation of knowledge from which it operates. These are not grounds for pure speculation leading to far-fetched theories.[5]

So African knowing is 'mystical', implying that one can know things intuitively, 'participatively' (knowing is through participation – not reflection). This participation includes identification of our being with life force and 'causality' (an interweaving of the metaphysical or religious realm with the empirical realm). Biblical scholarship must belong to the Church and the community, not only to the academy. In the African understanding there is no sharp distinction between the sacred and profane. Such are some of the elements of ordinary readings in African biblical scholarship, which surface in their own 'scholarly' reading processes. As West (2001:88) argues, Africa also has a wealth of other resources for reading the Bible, such as African art, which people use to exegete and comment on the Bible and which cannot be ignored.

This way of knowing is evidenced in the pedagogy of Africa, which is highly symbolic and uses symbols. It teaches using proverbs, legends and tales. A summary of the African way of knowing is as follows: It…

a) has spontaneous trust in the knowing power of senses
b) is naturally oriented toward a philosophy of common sense
c) trusts in intuitive knowledge
d) has a worldview that is global and dynamic, a vital vision of the universe (everything connected by way of life-force).

---

[5]This would result in an African biblical scholarship which concentrates on the correspondence between African experience and the Bible, locating itself within the social, political, and ecclesiastical context of Africa.

The next question was, 'How should the dialogue between the African culture and the Bible proceed?' It was possible to start with revealed data (the Bible) but rethink it in terms of a black mindset, then identify specific values in black culture and promote these through education. So the agenda and form of dialogue cannot be imposed by decisions or resolutions on what it should be. Rather we should pay attention to the reactions one experiences in the process of learning theology and reading works on theology. If a clash is experienced with African values one will have an opportunity to rethink Christian theology in concepts and categories familiar to Africa. Perhaps the common reactions to what is present will set the direction and agenda for a specifically inter-religious dialogue. Specifically reflecting on the transaction in a Kenyan context, Ndung'u (1997:62) puts it this way, 'even the illiterate members (of the Akurinu African Independent Church) take pains to master some verses which they readily quote when they give their testimonies'. To prove the transaction as an engagement with the Bible these very members carry copies of the Bible so that if called upon they can always request a literate member to read for them. So, the remembered Bible and the read Bible and African orality reside side by side.[6]

A challenge to this thinking came from Alfred Vanneste in an article 'A True Theology to Begin With' in *African Theology* (1995: 99) where he argued that Christianity is a universal religion and theology is likewise universal: 'African Theology is as unthinkable as an African physics or mathematics' (1995:195). He identifies two major approaches in theology in his context and situation: those who seek to rethink revealed truth (from a different perspective) so as to challenge and strengthen universal doctrine and those who focus on

---

[6]See Nahashon Ndung'u (1997:62), The Bible in an African Independent Church, where he explains how even the illiterate members of the African society confront and engage the Bible in dialogue. For Ndung'u, when listening to these people one may even not know that they are illiterate.

local needs and demands and thereby seek to develop a specifically local outlook. He says that some will even try to insert elements of tradition into the system. However he does not deny cultural and historical conditioning in the formation of doctrine, but insists we ought to seek to be true to the universal calling of the Church and doctrine.

He therefore concludes that Plato did not set out to develop a Greek philosophy or Descartes a French one. They were motivated to pursue universal truth. The theologian has even stronger reasons to pursue universal truth rather than a particular theology. The only way to seek such a universal truth in theology is to let the Bible dialogue with other cultures of the world, which are seen as a divine revelation, rather than to seek it in common human experience which is the starting place for the development of a philosophy. It is appropriate to accept the help of contemporary philosophy and wisdom in the pursuit of theological understanding and formulation. However this philosophy and wisdom is never definitive.

Absolute truth has priority over practical applications and use, but should one have to be reminded that scientific research is never of immediate, practical use? We first need to establish absolute truth. Practical use will follow from this. Vanneste also conceives of such application as a secondary, subsequent development from universal dogma. Looking for facile (lacking depth; easily obtained or understood) adaptation is therefore bad practice. True adaptation, in the deepest sense of the term, does not consist in descending to an inferior level in order to adopt the prejudices of the one who is talking. It is to ascend to a higher level, overcoming one's strictures and helping others to do the same. Such an effort will one day allow for humanity as a whole to meet together in full adherence to the purest, richest and most universal divine truth. He further cites an example of sacramental theology. In his time there was a rethinking and challenging of the traditional formulations. However, he can't imagine how 'primitive conceptions, closer to magic, could in any way be useful in this field' (1995:198). He also thinks that God's grace reaches us (all human beings) through our deep religious sense (sensus divinitatus). Through this religious sense, through the eyes of faith, God's grace secretly impels us to adhere to Christ. Thus it is not through culture or traditional religion that God draws us. It is through something that is universally present in all human beings that God's grace works. His challenge to Africans is that they should seek to contribute to the development of universal theology but if they opt for local, contextual theology they will be condemned to remain second-rate theologians. But he fails to realise that both the African culture and the Bible are the custodians of the universal truth.

Vatican II was in support of the transaction between the African culture and the Bible, calling for the development of African theology and the comparison of Christianity with traditional religion. It did so by calling for a plurality of theologies,[7] and by insisting on 'seeds' of divine truth in non-Christian religions. This gives the African theologian impetus to develop a specifically African theology. By 1969 Pope Paul IV had invited African Bishops to formulate Catholicism in terms 'congenial to (their) own culture' and to bring to the Church the original and valuable contributions of negritude. Another strong supporter for the transaction between the African culture and the Bible is Bengt Sundkler (1960) who, in his book 'The Christian Ministries in Africa', contended that if the sentiments of the Accra conference were true – that the Church is largely an alien institution in Africa – then it is because of the lack of conscious and creative theological reflection. In this book he offered what were regarded as helpful suggestions for western and African leaders in working together or dialoguing for harmony to produce a counterpoint. The impetus for African theology from the Protestant side seems to have come from this book.

Another famous conference was held in Kampala in 1963 where the All Africa Conference of Churches (AACC) was formally established. This assembly was the major impetus to the development of the dialogue between the African culture and the Bible (African

---

[7]Rather than the universal, one formulation view represented by Vanneste, Vatican II support diversity.

theology). According to Baur (2000), a major emphasis was put forward. The African Church was challenged to seriously develop a theology that does justice to African culture if selfhood was to be achieved. However many remained sceptical or cautious of 'bad elements' in African culture and the danger of syncretism (something Byang Kato made more explicit in the 1970's).

The second All Africa Conference of Churches was held in Ibadan, in 1966. This assembly was the first major consultation of specifically African theologians. Significant African scholars who attended this conference included Kwesi Dickson, Idowu, John Mbiti, and Sawyerr. The conference resulted in the publication of *Biblical Revelation and African Beliefs*, the first book on African beliefs in Anglophone Africa. The major breakthrough in this publication was that these scholars did recognise a certain dialogue was in existence between African cultural beliefs and the full self-revelation of God in Jesus Christ.

The third conference was held in Abidjan in 1969 where the African theologians recommended the indigenisation of liturgies and the Africanization of doctrine. However they strongly warned against syncretism, arguing that Christ must take the central role in all indigenisation. Another main theological conference was held in Lusaka, Zambia in 1974, where a strong call for self-assertion and self-reliance was made. Here Protestants issued a call for a moratorium on missionaries. In the same year, during the Episcopal Synod in Rome, the African Bishops called for the rejection of a 'theology of adaptation' and for a genuine African incarnational theology. They argued that Christianity must become incarnate in the life of the people, and also that the African Church should take responsibility for their own evangelisation.

In 1976, an Ecumenical Dialogue of Third World Theologians was held in Dar es Salaam. This was the first dialogue of its kind and could be termed as the last major step towards the genesis of a full dialogue between the African culture and the Bible. The planners and organisers of this conference were Mimwenyi (Zaire), Marmora (Korea) and Dussel (Argentina). The scholars who attended this conference evaluated the cultural and social political situation of each continent, the presence of the Church and the theological approach adopted. They ended up publishing a 17-page declaration called *The Emergent Gospel* (edited by S. Torres and V. Fabella 1976) and founding the Ecumenical Association of Third World Theologians (EATWOT). A year later another conference of the Third World Theologians was held in Accra (1977). During this conference it was concluded that African Theology was existing and in progress (in other words the dialogue had already taken root). This conference described the context, the various approaches, sources and prospects of such a dialogue for the future. Papers read in conference were published as *African Theology en Route* (edited by K. Appiah-Kubi and S. Torres). The conference concluded with the formation of EAAT, the Ecumenical Association of African Theologians.

In 1980, EAAT held another conference, in Yaounde, where much groundwork was laid for future theological work including the launch of the *Bulletin of African Theology*, which published works in English and French. In New Delhi another EATWOT conference was held in 1981. Here Africans were able to establish their own identity and make their own contribution within the community of Third World Theologians. The work of Engelbert Mveng demonstrated that African thinking on poverty and liberation was not just a sequel to Latin American liberation Theology. Those who attended broadened their understanding of economic poverty and liberation on the basis of the African contribution.

In 1983, EATWOT held a conference in Geneva. This conference is described by Baur as a very significant milestone for the dialogue between African culture and the Bible. For the first time, Western theologians were listening and learning from African theologians. They were entering into dialogue with each other as equals for the first time. At last, in 1991, the History of Theology of the Third World, published by Christian Kaiser, Germany, was launched. This is a multivolume publication on Third World Theology. Volume I by Parrat, which is useful to research information on the dialogue of African culture and the Bible. During this time Mbiye Lumbala published a large bibliography in *Revue Africaine de Theologie*, Vol.16, 1992.

One may here ask where the women theologians were all this time. In the 1977 conference in Accra, seven women took part, but the conference noted with concern the exclusion of women in this dialogue and declared that the future writings were henceforth to include the role of women in the Church. The women who were present in 1989 formed what came to be called 'the Circle of Concerned African Women Theologians' with a membership of 70 from throughout Africa. They then initiated the Institute of African Women in Religion and Culture that met regionally from 1989-1996.

Major Theological Emphases

The result of these many consultations among the African theologians enhanced the development of the African Independent Churches, which came to be seen as the first step of African theology or the result of the dialogue between the African culture and the Bible. These African Independent Churches were the first to express Christianity in their own terms.

Soon after the Africans developed the dialogue further into a theology of adaptation, in 1950's - 1960, an early attempt to incarnate the Gospel in the African cultural context was muted. The Jesuits in China first employed the theology of adaptation in the 16th & 17th centuries. This was novel and controversial. The standard approach was to assimilate converts to European Christianity. Eventually Rome prohibited the adaptation approach because it was felt the approach was built on dubious theological grounds.

Perhaps the earliest of African calls for adaptation came from the Francophone priests mentioned above (1956, Black *Priests Question Themselves*). These African students in Europe were critical of European perceptions and treatment of Africans. They argued for the 'adaptation' of the Church to the African context. Another approach that emerged is 'comparative', which looked for common ground with culture to which Christianity could be adapted and which could form a bridge for understanding. Such a move started within Church forms and structures, with the introduction of African hymns and instruments. This was followed by the indigenisation of clergy, and more and more the evangelism and pastoral work was shifted to Africans. That was followed by the search for beliefs, rites, symbols, gestures and institutions of African culture that corresponded to Christianity and could be utilized as a bridge to understanding the Christian faith.

One problem with this development was that the changes were mostly superficial. The underlying theology and practice remained largely Western. Replacing a white pastor with a black one who did exactly the same things in exactly the same ways as did the Euro-American pastor helped very little, if at all. It was noted that the doctrines of the trinity and Christological incarnation were originally Greek cultural formulations of a deeper theological mystery. This theology was closely followed by the theology of inculturation.

Theology of Inculturation

This theology arises out of and from within culture and flourished in the 1970's. It closely followed the missionary theologies of *tabula rasa;*[8] for Baur this theology is inculturation while Ian Ritchie calls it incarnation. However Baur's description fits that of incarnation. It was becoming increasingly clear that even the divine message of scripture was given in cultural garb. The African community needed to live the word of God in their own cultural milieu. Their life of faith would eventually lead to a new incarnation of the Gospel message. There was a need to use different terminology. As the divine message was incarnate in the life of Christ, so it must be lived. This was called inculturation.

The Roman Catholic Symposium of Episcopal Conference of Africa and Madagascar (SECAM) in 1974 officially rejected

---

[8]These theologies were instrumental in the founding of the Church in Africa, see Kä Mana 2002:90-91.

'adaptation' as a paradigm for theology and the Church and chose 'incarnation' instead. What African theologians were now in search of was a Church with African leadership, with truly African mind and spirit, and where Africans could feel free to explore the meaning of a true Christianity, without restrictions imposed from outside mission agencies, without Euro-American Christianity constantly looking over their shoulders. African theologians wanted the freedom to Africanise Christianity in a manner analogous to African Independent Churches.

Rather than starting with a pre-fabricated theology from the West or any other place, Christianity needed to be lived in the life and context of believers. The starting point for theology is Scripture and African culture rather than the reverse – starting with theology, doctrine and recognised practice and moving to adaptation in culture. It requires basic methodology, which is critical, and a continuous dialogue between African culture and the Bible as well as Christianity. The Christianity of the West is assessed in order to be assimilated to the African context. African religiosity is exposed to biblical criticism in order to conform it to the Gospel of Christ.

During this phase, serious research into African Traditional Religion was undertaken. In 1962, Idowu's *Olodumare: God in Yoruba Belief* challenged Western assumptions about the uniqueness of concepts of God in Christian monotheism. It also challenged Western views on African Religions. This research resulted in sharp criticism of Western anthropological assumptions, and descriptions of African culture as primitive, racial or inferior, and religion as animistic and polytheistic.

Ritchie described this phase of African Theology as 'rehumanization' of Africans. It did so by changing the way their culture and religion was understood and giving a positive evaluation of culture and religion in Africa. It also resulted in making Africans as a whole more aware of their cultural heritage. The study of African culture and religion became part and parcel of education. However we still had a few Africans like Ela and Bujo who critiqued inculturation for its focus on the past rather than the present. They claimed that its theology was done in the 'ivory tower' of academia and that such a concern for the past had little practical relevance for the present; people who were oppressed and deprived required a theology that could set them free. So, on such a basis, Justin Ukpong suggests that Africa can correctly be referred to as 'the cradle of systematic biblical interpretation in Christianity' (1996). He argues that the earliest attempts to structure biblical interpretation in Christianity are associated with the city of Alexandria and with such names as Clement of Alexandria, Origen, and others who lived and worked there.[9] This interpretation has resulted into the birth of theology of liberation.

Theology of Liberation

This is the branch of theology that flourished in the 1980's. In the 1960's missiologists began speaking of contextualisation: theology cannot remain abstract, it must be related to the context of the life situation of the people. Theologians began to prefer the term contextuality to inculturation. It came to be realized that the real life context of Africa was one of poverty, exploitation and oppression, through colonialism, post-colonial structures and relationships and, finally, by the African ruling class so that the common man or woman felt that the present was 'worse than in colonial days' (E. Fashole-Luke).

---

[9]For more information see West 2001:86, where he explains an interpretive history of the Bible in Africa.

Therefore at the Jos Conference in 1975 there was a call for a theology of liberation. At the 1976 Ecumenical Dialogue of Third World.[10] Theologians, Dar es Salaam, Latin American Liberation Theology made a big impression. Dedji says that the Pan African Conference of Third World Theologians in 1977 in Accra placed liberation themes firmly on the agenda.

During the Dar es Salaam gathering, a major and fundamental idea that came out clearly was the 'anthropological poverty' of Africa. The main issue wasn't material poverty and lack of opportunity, but identity. The views of the West, anthropological, religious and colonial, had denigrated the black person. So terms like primitive, inferior, animistic, and pre-logical came to be used of African culture, and, by implication, of African people. As a result, along with material poverty, the black African had lost his or her soul, which, according to Mveng, was a sense of identity and worth.

The most eloquent appeal for liberation came from the Cameroonian priest, Jean-Marc Ela, author of *African Cry*. South Africans applied the theology of liberation to their context of apartheid. This theology developed as a reaction to the dehumanising racial situation in South Africa. Mission theology failed to address this reality. Liberation theology was different from the North American Black Theology in that at first it refused to use violence and become racial. It simply sought equality with whites. The earliest significant voices in this theology are that of Buthelezi, Boesak and Tutu. The later phase of this theology is marked by the *Kairos*

---

[10]Today the terms 'Majority World' or 'Two thirds world' are preferred in postcolonial thinking to 'Third world'. The term 'Third world' was coined in 1952 by a French demographer, Alfred Sauvy, who noted a similarity between the nations gaining independence from colonial powers and the Third Estate in France. (The Third Estate comprised all those who were not members of the aristocracy or the clergy, and were the class who demanded freedom and equality during the French revolution.) He therefore used 'Third world' to refer to peoples who have been marginalized from the ruling class (Waweru 2005:15).

document of 1985 in which a younger generation of theologians became more politically confrontational. They spoke with a more radical look at Blackness, a greater use of North American Black Theology and a more resolute political engagement. Mosala and Chikane are major names in this phase: there cannot be a neutral theology; one must side with the oppressed or with the oppressors. In the third phase of liberation theology came the debate about the place of African women. So, women's and feminist versions also became a part of the discussion. Men dominate much of life in Africa and the Church in general. For a community to be complete participation from all sides was necessary; a theology of unity between men and women was paramount

Theology of Reconstruction

This can be said to be the fourth stage of the development of the dialogue between the African culture and the Bible. After the end of colonialism in Africa in the early 1990's, Africans saw the need to think differently. Valetin Y. Mudimbe (1988: ix) argued that the idea of Africa and the African was invented by those who wanted 'to serve as' the other of the West and the Westerner. He further emphasised that Africa which is 'reified in the colonial library' needs to be thought of anew, an idea which was echoed by Kä Mana (1993:21-39) when he called for 'a conceptual lift-off' as the only way to get Africa out of the miasma that its diverse problems provoked. This idea of rethinking Africa afresh also got a boost from Mabiala Justin-Robert Kenzo (2002:323) when he called for 'a new kind of thinking capable of mobilizing enough creative energy to fuel the reconstruction of Africa'. So, in the late 1980's and early 1990's, a paradigm shift in African dialogue with the Bible in terms of reconstruction theology was the obvious proposal.

In view of the above, one notes that the dialogue between African culture and the Bible had, since the 1960's, used the Exodus metaphor as its dominant motif. The dialogues metaphorically likened the African people to the people of Israel on their way from Egypt (read colonial regime) to the Promised Land. African Women's theology,

African Christian theology, and the Black theology of South Africa are examples of such dialogues which could now unite in a common theology of reconstruction, which was an all-inclusive approach.

Undoubtedly this paradigm shift is the brainchild of Archbishop Desmond Tutu, among others, who saw the need of a change from liberation to reconstruction after the release of Nelson Mandela in February 2, 1990. The idea of reconstruction theology was made clear by Jesse Mugambi, on 30th March 1990, when he was invited by Tutu, the then-President of the All Africa Conference of Churches (AACC), to reflect on the 'future of the Church and the Church of the future in Africa' to the General Committee of the organisation in the Nairobi meeting. Mugambi (1991:36), in his charismatic manner of presentation, called for an African theological articulation that would shift its theological emphasis in the post-cold war Africa from the common Exodus motif to a reconstructive motif. He strongly called for African theologians and other stakeholders to henceforth give priority to the reconstruction of African nations. Mugambi (2003:128) argued that it is the image of Nehemiah, not of Moses, which is the mirror through which we are able to strategise our mission to remake Africa out of its past history.

This call for a paradigm shift was supported by Brigalia Hlophe Bam (1995: xi) who argued that, with the collapse of Apartheid rule in South Africa in 1990, the Church had finally got an opportunity to share in the reconstruction of the nation. She voiced the need for dialogue in the 'new situation' when she observed that the Church had been in the forefront of resistance against oppression; now that the situation had drastically changed came the inevitable question, 'what now?' Resistance was no longer sufficient. People were obliged to ask how they could best share in rebuilding of the nation. The new context called for a new method. Such new methods were seen in South Africa through the integration of different apartheid educational departments into one single ministry of education, and also through the work of the *Truth and Reconciliation Commission* which aimed at the healing of the broken nation. More than anything else this jumpstarted the reconstruction of history and social relations as well as of the Christian spirituality of the people (B.H. Bam 1995: 45-52). This scholar also argued that as much as the Church was required to say 'yes' to reconstruction it must also learn afresh how to say 'no' to such acts of commission and omission by the state in its surfeit of freedom (1995:50).

The likes of Kä Mana (2002:90-91) also endorsed the theology of reconstruction by arguing that African theologies were climaxed in reconstruction theology. In particular, he sees the need for a theology of reconstruction as the fourth developmental stage in the dialogue between the African culture and the Bible. He acknowledges the missionary theologies of *tabula rasa* as the first stage in the dialogue since it is through them that the relationship between African culture and the Christian faith were conceived.

Therefore this theology of reconstruction saw the advent of free post-colonial African thinking, devoid of all the problems of pessimism and defeatism, emerging towards the construction of free and democratic societies in Africa. This is 'mirrored' by nothing else but New Testament scholarship. This in itself is the result of reconstruction. The text of the Greek New Testament has been reconstructed from thousands of manuscripts and fragments of manuscripts, a process that still continues. Equally, the Old Testament, commonly known as the Hebrew Bible, is also a reconstruction. The history of early Christianity must be reconstructed from widely scattered pieces of information and tradition found in the sources. The theologies of the New Testament writers must be reconstructed by critical analysis of the sources, because their meaning has been obscured by thick layers of later traditionalism and needs to be excavated to bring the original contours into focus.[11] So the question remains, 'where do we go from here?' It is our conclusion that any meaningful dialogue needs to be rooted in the reality of the local Church. There is a need for a specifically Evangelical reflection and engagement in the discussion. As Kä Mana

---

[11]Hans Dieter Betz quoted by Ukachukwu Chris Manu, *Intercultural Hermeneutics in Africa* 2003:2.

(2002:91) asks: 'How should Africans think and build the future of their content?'. He contends that there is a need for Africans to think differently and constructively. He sees a threefold mission for the church: to bring full awareness among Christian communities of the need to be fully engaged in enterprises of self-empowerment in every situation of slavery, oppression and dehumanisation; to bring awareness among Christians to grow structures that do not allow any temptation for tribal and ethnic domination; to teach alternative ways of living an active and genuine faith in Christ without falling back into types of religiosity that develop feelings of being enamoured with the invisible world at the expense of involvement in public and social life.

It should be noted that in the dialogue between African culture and the Bible Africans have been obsessed with identity, its history and culture. The result has been a loss of initiative and forward thinking. The situation in most post-independent African nations is dismal. We can't totally blame colonialism or neo-colonialism any longer. Much of the damage is Africa's own doing.

The situation of Jerusalem is a paradigm for Africa. The city was occupied and is now a shambles. There is a need to ask, 'where does Africa go from here?' We need to reconstruct our societies. What is the Church's role? We need also to note that liberation theologies were too caught up in specific political or economic ideologies. In short, Africans must accept responsibility for revamping and reshaping Africa. We cannot go back to the past (nor do we really want to). What is the vision for the future? How will we proceed? This is the call for a theology of social action (Manus 2003:5). There seems to be a growing interest in the social implications of the Christian faith. The question then is, 'why aren't our societies more influenced and changed by Christianity?' The problem is that authentic Christian experience has not persisted. We need to work for a genuine transformation in the Church and in the Christians. This is only possible through a genuine inter-religious dialogue between the African culture and the Bible.

Various methodologies have emerged within African biblical interpretation, as we saw in the historical overview. We should therefore outline some specific methodologies which are applied in Africa today such as comparative, inculturation, contrapuntal and postcolonial criticism; these are some of the genuine methodologies for transaction which do not place one culture over the other, perhaps apart from postcolonial criticism.

A Transaction between the African Culture and the Bible

CHAPTER FOUR

Methodologies for Transaction between the African Culture and the Bible

Introduction

Before attempting to juxtapose these two seemingly unrelated
– even antagonistic – texts (African oral culture and the
Biblical culture), it is important to indicate why and how I
propose to proceed. The proposed method of re-reading these two
different texts is as a result of several changes in both thinking and
living today. In the field of biblical studies, scholars are reflecting
upon the new modes or paradigms that are evolving or require to be
developed in the interpretation of the Bible. A common way of talking
about this change is to talk of a paradigm shift.[1] The general word
for the methodologies outlined here is intertextual criticism. The
term 'intertextuality'[2] would imply that texts acquire new meaning
once they are situated in the context of other texts (e.g. literary
text, social practice, cultural object and ideology) in a web of mutual
interference and illumination. So Miscall (1995:248) argues that

---

[1]Cf. Albert Nolan 1990/ 2:97, who describes this paradigm shift as a
new model for trying to conceive what we are actually doing when we try
to do theology, and especially Christian Theology, in our context.

[2]The term was coined by Julia Kristeva in 1967 to mean reading of
two or more texts together and in the light of each other. It is a theory of
considering productivity through transposition of texts in such a way
that readers and words are constantly made and remade in and through
the intertextual process (cf. Aichele & Phillips 1995:10).

intertextuality on a basic level involves a two-stage process: first, demonstrating or proving a basis for comparing the texts at hand (in our case African culture and the Biblical culture) through noting similar words, themes, structures and suchlike and, second, illustrating and assessing the significance of the parallels for understanding one or more of the individual stories in question.

One of the great problems of African biblical scholarship is that both the missionaries and their converts who established the churches in our continent were not practising theologians, even if they were committed Christians. This is the state of affairs that we have inherited as far as contextual interpretation of the Bible in Africa is concerned. Current church leaders are not biblical scholars and the few who claim to be biblical scholars, perhaps with the exception of South Africa, have not yet made much academic contribution to this field. Our pastors have little education, if any, and only a few can read or write Greek and Hebrew. This is the reason why, in the whole of Africa, very few biblical scholars are engaged in active contextual interpretation of the Bible.

It is important, therefore, to come up with a theory or a methodology that can be applied to the interpretation of the Bible in Africa by all, theologians or non-theologians. There are numerous ways of describing this paradigm shift in theology. We need a new model for trying to conceive what we are actually doing when we try to do contextual Biblical interpretation in Africa. Most African theologians have been trained in historical-critical exegesis, which heavily focuses on the Bible as the only true text, and interprets it by way of producing more texts (Biblical commentaries). 'Exegesis', as a word for interpretation, implies that the meaning is something hidden inside the text, waiting to be uncovered by the skill of the interpreter by careful 'objective' historical study.[3] In such an understanding there are two poles of interpretation, which stand in tension with each other: one is the situatedness of the biblical text and the second is the historical situatedness of the reader (cf. Draper 2003:13). Such poles obviously struggle to appropriate today's meaning and call for a paradigm shift.

We all know that Africa has entered a new era of postcolonialism, in which her biblical scholars are challenged to discern new approaches and insights to propel biblical scholarship into the twenty-first century. As Gerald West (1995:15) puts it, 'the older ways of understanding and practice, even experience itself, no longer work'. Therefore a new way of interpreting the Bible in Africa becomes necessary, particularly because African states have gained their political independence, creating a new context for biblical studies within our present situation. The task of this book is to formulate a theory for African biblical scholarship and then use it for biblical interpretation from a postcolonial point of view in dialogue with an African narrative. In the nineteenth century the Bible played an important part in the legitimation of colonialism in that it constructed a 'self-validating' world in which empire and domination appeared normative and permanent. While the Bible is 'reducible to a sociological current', it is equally important to recognise that it cannot be read in isolation from our (African) context. Therefore we seek a reading of the Bible within our own context of African culture. To achieve our goals, the following steps will be taken: first of all we will start by explaining methodological presuppositions; secondly we will explain a postcolonial theoretical approach for the contextual interpretation of the Bible using various Majority World scholars as

---

[3]Meaning, in fact, is not isolated 'inside' the text–'No text is an island'—but rather it is in the space 'between' texts (cf. Miscall 1995:257). So meaning arises from the subjective, or ideological, juxtaposing of text with text on behalf of specific readers in specific historical and material situations in order to produce new constellations of texts, readers and readings (cf. Aichele & Phillips 1995:14-15).

seminal thinkers (Dube, 1998, Sugirtharajah, 1998, Ngugi, 1981) and, in particular, Edward Said (1993), by presenting their views on postcolonial criticism in the most selective and condensed form possible; and lastly we shall then formulate our theory and show how it may be used in interpreting the Bible by using it to interpret a few passages of interest (e.g. Matthew 1 and Revelation 22:1-5).

Methodological Presuppositions

In the recent past, as African biblical scholars, we have come to realize that the Bible legitimated the imperial assumption of control of African culture (Dickson 1984:74-85). This has raised the question of how to deal with the Bible as a text that is so zealously taught and read in Africa. Such a question seeks its answers within the paradigm of contextualisation as the means for biblical interpretations within postcolonial situations. This involves taking time to investigate who we are, and our location and history in a postcolonial society. Draper comments that 'we recognize our specific location at the end of a long history of colonial domination, cultural dispossession and economic exploitation' (2002:16). We have come to recognize the need to affirm our culture and identity, especially in the field of biblical studies, and to study a text that has often been used as a tool of domination, and is largely accepted by the majority. As a result there is a danger that, in reading the Bible, Africans will continue to internalise and perpetuate their own oppressions. Hence we have undertaken contextual reading strategies and, with them, new methodologies. These have overshadowed the more traditional methods of research such as form, text and source criticisms which had absolutized the context of the origin of the text and simply omitted the context of the reader (Africa) as relevant for the meaning of the text. Recognizing the importance of the context of the reader raises the question of how to relate the two contexts—those of origin and reader— as both contribute to the creation of the meaning of the text.

No longer can biblical studies exist in isolation from the milieu of cultural studies of groups, practices and discourses found in, but not limited to, literary discourses in the colonised societies. This means that the process of Bible interpretation in postcolonial Africa is a 'conversation' in line with Gadamer's use of language as the medium of hermeneutic experience (1989:383-491). This is because two cultures will be in a conversation where each can interrogate the other. In African tradition, what has been going on for a long time (in myths and other narratives) has an important influence on what is happening at present. As African readers of the Bible, therefore, we have turned to methods common in our own contexts, such as 'postcolonial theories' of research, and practised them to interpret the Bible. Boer (1998), writing on postcolonial biblical criticism, states that:

> Biblical studies is itself a subset of religion, which belongs to the superstructure of the totality of society, sharing that space with art, culture, philosophy, politics and ideology...; it is then dependent upon the economic forms and social relations of that society, yet it may also anticipate possible future forms of social and economic organization (1998:43).

As a result of this new birth, many scholars in the Majority World have embraced postcolonial criticism, which has now spread across the academic world. Since biblical scholars in this World have turned to this mode of interpreting the Bible, probably for the first time in the history of biblical scholarship, the Majority World is placed at the centre of its dominant discourse. We need to read the Bible from the Majority World's perspective rather than from the Western World's perspective. This research has the potential to usher in another method of approaching the Bible, particularly in postcolonial Africa—a method developed within the context of a comparative approach to biblical interpretations in Africa and which has been in use in comparative religions (Dickson, 1984: 85). We therefore need to investigate the development of the comparative and inculturation approaches in order to be able to locate our approach within African biblical scholarship.

The Comparative and Inculturation Approaches

African religion and culture were condemned as demonic and immoral and it was therefore required that they be phased out before Christianity could take root in Africa (cf. Bewes, 1952:19-20). For Bewes, African religious life was similar to that great, vague and nebulous inheritance of animism, which needed to be replaced. In response to such an attitude to African religion and culture, a number of missionaries and some African theologians were sympathetic to the African cause. As a result, they were able to develop methods that showed a mutual correction between African traditions and Christianity. As Upkong (2000:12) argues, both these groups undertook research that sought to legitimize African religion and culture by way of comparative studies carried out within the framework of comparative religions and philosophy. The main purpose of this endeavour was to show continuities and discontinuities between African religions and the Bible, particularly the Old Testament (2000:12). Because many saw a close affinity between the Old and the New Testament worldview, the comparative method was also taken to be of value in the interpretation of the New Testament (cf. Dickson, 1984:180-182).

The major African scholars who have applied the comparative method such as Mbiti (1971), Dickson (1984) and Upkong (1987) were keen to illustrate the similarities in patterns of thought and feelings between the Bible and African religion and culture. They were aiming to demonstrate how both the people of the Bible and the African peoples have expressed certain basic notions. For instance, a West African scholar, J. J. Williams, in 1930 wrote a book entitled *Hebrewism of West Africa: from Nile to Niger with Jews* where he sought to show a correlation between the Hebrew language and the Ashanti language of Ghana, basing his comparison on similarities both in sound and in deity worship. Such comparisons were later seen as superficial and weak (Upkong 2000:13).

With the above understanding, African scholars moved to another kind of approach which aimed to make Christianity relevant to the African religio-cultural context and this gave rise to the inculturation approach, which has come to be associated with scholars like Upkong (2000:14). He has determined a preliminary condition and a series of components, which constitute an important aspect of this approach (2001:191). The preliminary condition is the commitment of the interpreter to the Christian faith and to the process of actualising the biblical message in the context of people's situation in life. Here the context of the reader of the biblical text is his/her actual situation, which may result in an interpretation that is dependant on the mindset and the concerns of the reader. Inculturation hermeneutics uses an African conceptual framework for reading, where the African culture is the subject of the interpretation (2001:191). This methodology seeks the continuity of African culture and its identity. So, through the use of an inculturation approach, one draws together the meaning from comparative analysis in a coherent fashion, at the same time showing commitment to analysing the message of the biblical text in concrete life situations (Upkong 1995:13). This means that the engagement of doing exegesis is a witness that the reader is involved in the community. For Upkong, 'the Bible is life-oriented' and its interpretation leads the scholar to be transformed and to transform the community in the light of the Scriptures (1995:13). During this process the reader seeks to actualise 'the gospel message' in the actual situation of life in so far as the actual context is intensified by the problem at hand.

From the material discussed here we can easily discover that what matters in interpretation is the aim of the researcher. A comparative approach will seek to show the continuities and discontinuities between African culture and the Bible in order to legitimize African culture (cf. Dickson 1984: 84). The inculturation approach will, on the other hand, seek to make Christianity a relevant religion for Africans (Upkong 1995: 14). The approach undertaken in this book is a further development of these approaches within a postcolonial context. So, while it can also seek either to legitimize the African culture or to make Christianity relevant to Africans, it does recognise both as two independent contexts, which can dialogue with each other to evoke a new meaning in a postcolonial context. The final methodology proposed in this book is similar to that of a comparative approach but it has an overt link with postcolonial criticism. We therefore need to look at postcolonial criticism and the way it has emerged.

Postcolonial Criticism

Postcolonial criticism has emerged as an alternative to liberationist and inculturationist readings of the Bible, which had sought to confront all forms of oppression, poverty and marginalisation in society (cf. Upkong 2000:14), and has staked a claim to represent Majority World voices. Once liberation is achieved, the prophetic voice in that context shifts to another context. Postcolonial criticism emerged in the Majority World with its theoretical underpinnings sketched out in the work of cultural critics Edward Said and Homi Bhabha (1994), among others, as an alternative voice. Said's (1978) evaluation and critique of the set of beliefs known as Orientalism forms an important background for postcolonial studies. In 1993 Said wrote another thought-provoking work entitled *Culture and Imperialism,* where he re-examines a popular mode of thought, and challenges our thinking about our cultures. Said turns a critical eye on the nineteenth century novel which, he claims, played an important role in legitimating Western imperialism, in that it constructs a 'self-validating' world in which empire and domination appear normative and permanent (1993:62). His evaluation and critique of culture and imperialism provide avenues for developing an approach to the study not only of African novels but also of the Bible. Said's approach is an attempt to question various paradigms of thought which are accepted on individual, academic, and political levels (1993: 32-33). Our interest in Said's use of the term 'contrapuntal' is not based on the way he applies it but on the meaning of the term, as a way forward in biblical scholarship in a postcolonial setting.

Postcolonial criticism is an interpretive act that is gaining momentum among scholars of formerly colonised societies. It means a resurrection of the indigenous people who were once marginalized and oppressed. According to Ruiz (2003:123), it is an act of reclamation, redemption and reaffirmation against the past colonial and present imperialist tendencies, which continue to exert pressure even after political independence has long been achieved. Said blamed European states for the creation of a body of knowledge known as Orientalism and urges a 're-thinking of what had for centuries been believed to be an unbridgeable chasm', to rephrase his words, 'separating the rich and the poor' (1978: 350). Indeed, if postcolonial criticism seeks to subvert the master narratives that have shaped the way societies are identified, Said's efforts are undoubtedly the roots of that postcolonial criticism.

Musa Dube (1998:228), following in the steps of Edward Said, takes the term 'postcolonial' to imply that we have all been thoroughly constructed by imperialism to perceive each other from a particular stance. Dube (1996:37-59), therefore, sees postcolonial criticism as a methodology for interpreting biblical texts for decolonisation of the same. She argues that, as postcolonial African scholars, we must now seek ways and means of understanding our past and present exploitation and develop new ways of encountering and respecting 'the other'. In this situation, she sees a postcolonial approach as the way the Bible is to be interpreted within our own African context, and as a means of struggle against cultural and economic imperialism. For Dube, postcolonial criticism in biblical scholarship aims to challenge the context and the contours of biblical interpretation and the existing notions and preconceptions of professional guilds and academies (1998:131). However, I think if we are able to bring our culture (African) into dialogue or conversation with Biblical culture and let the two cultures challenge each other, a better result will be achieved than positioning them against each other in a quest for domination. The cosmology that emerges in such a conversation will offer space for those once colonized. Today it is inconceivable that anyone will deny that the impact of the Bible in our own lives as colonised peoples is irreversible. In fact, we do not want to walk without shoes, if indeed the Bible was used to introduce them to us, nor regret the education that came along with the missionaries. What we need to do is to explore how to allow the culture of the coloniser and our own culture to interact and to move beyond the limitations of both cultures.

Postcolonialism is suspicious of the colonial imports, including the biblical text, which it does not exclude from the critical analytical gaze to which other colonial texts are subjected (Surgitharajah 1998:15). It differs from the liberationist tendency of regarding the Bible itself as the place where the message of liberation is to be found (cf. Pablo 1990:66). The postcolonial critics are keen to argue that the Bible arrived in the hands of the colonisers, who then used it as a tool to civilise the colonised. This leads us to another Majority World scholar who may also have been influenced by Said, Sugirtharajah (1998). He argues that if we turn our attention to the current state of biblical scholarship, we quickly become aware that this scholarship has been going through different phases, 'often described as pre-critical, critical and post-critical, sometimes as historical and narrative, or author centred, text-centred and reader centred' (1998:15-17). He sees these as phases of how biblical scholarship has been conceived by the West. He then proceeds to argue that those of us from the Majority World who have been subjected to colonialism are now struggling to present biblical scholarship in our own context of postcolonial criticism, while we term the rest of biblical scholarship as colonial.

He further argues that a postcolonial theory is able to challenge the context, contours and normal procedures of biblical scholarship. It is our history of oppression and marginalisation under the rule of the colonial powers that, more than anything else, calls for a re-reading of the Bible in the light of our own context. Sugirtharajah (1998:15) sees postcolonialism, therefore, as a discourse of resistance that tries to 'write back' and work against colonial assumptions and ideologies long established in cultural studies. Writing back or working against the past may not be of any help today, but how to move along with what was implanted and what we hold as that which ought to have been, is what is needed for today.

No matter how much we want to decolonise either the Bible or our languages, it will not be an easy task. Nevertheless it is a noble goal which any postcolonial critic can support, but I want to put forward a new argument: that in our efforts to preserve our cultures, sometimes we perpetuate a mixed culture (a hybrid culture that is produced by the mixing of different cultures) that is only a part of what we seek to challenge. If postcolonial criticism involves scrutinising and exposing colonial domination and power as they are embodied in both local languages and biblical texts and interpretations, looking for an alternative while overturning and dismantling a colonial perspective (Sugirtharajah 1998:16), then we need to note how much we are entangled with them. In a sense, postcolonial critics find themselves in a paradoxical position of purporting to defend their cultures and rejecting colonialism while, in fact, they succeed in sneaking into their discourse a disproportionate volume of colonial products; these are what I call 'backdoor inculturations'.

We may be preaching our cultures, aiming to legitimize them, while practising what we claim to be dismantling and overturning (colonialism). What do I mean here? Let us take a famous Kenyan writer as an example. Ngugi wa Thiong'o (1981), in his postcolonial criticism of Western languages in his book *Writers in Politics*, argues that African writers in foreign languages have not produced African literature, but foreign literature. I contend that Ngugi himself has lent legitimacy to this deplorable state of affairs by strengthening the foreign languages through his extensive use of foreign-language derived phonetics, which masquerade as vernacular. Ngugi (1981:64) argues that we cannot develop our literature and traditions through borrowed tongues and imitations, yet, in his recent publication of a vernacular (Kikuyu) novel entitled *Murogi wa Kagogo* (*Crow of the Wizard*), right from the beginning, where he makes his dedication,

Ngugi (2004) has words like 'humwaka' (homework), 'bamiri' (family), 'Njanuari' (January), and 'miriniamu' (millennium), just to mention a few (Waweru 2007: 30). One does not need to be a Kikuyu to realise that this is not Gikuyu language. In the same way, Ngugi rejects Christianity and the Bible while his novels are replete with biblical narrative and symbols (cf. Brown 1997: 30-36). This shows how as postcolonial critics we may fall into the trap of self-deception. If colonial objects (Bible, cars, clothes), institutions (democracy, church, school) or competencies (writing, maths, and chemistry) are there to stay, then we need to develop a way of dealing with them. In such a case, postcolonial critics need to formulate a method of study that will allow both cultures to interact side by side to allow a new world to emerge. This will help in integrating what is affirming, and in removing colonial ideologies that are diminishing African traditional culture.

Going a step further in postcolonial criticism, and being aware of West's (1997:322-342) argument that postcolonial criticism has yet to make its mark on African biblical studies, I could argue that postcolonial criticism is made up of research agendas that have developed with reference to the end of colonialism in the Majority World. Such agendas are still diverse and no strict consensus about what constitutes postcolonial criticism exists. I would, therefore, prefer to take a different approach in postcolonial biblical studies and demonstrate how many of the literary components and thought patterns of the Bible can be illustrated by those of our context (African culture) instead of raging against it, even though the Bible was used to legitimate domination.

In a context of postcolonial interpretation we have to appreciate that colonial oppression and marginalisation are gone (though this does not mean that colonialism as an ideology is gone). The new situation in which we find ourselves gives us a new context, a context of exploration of cultural identity and of a desperate need for social reconstruction and development (Draper 2002:16). Raging against the Bible as a colonial text, or against western languages as oppressive may not be of any help in overcoming our dilemma, not that we forget these issues (we should look critically at colonial interpretations of the Bible, since the Bible itself is open to various interpretations), since they form what today is the major concern of postcolonial critics. We need to realise, however, that postcolonial criticism is not only about fighting the past, but about making use of that past and letting it dialogue with our present to create new meaning. In fact Ngugi admitted, in an interview with Weekly Review magazine (1978), that the power of the Bible is undeniable, as he states, 'I have also drawn from the Bible in the sense that the Bible was for a long time the only literature available to Kenyan people that has been available to them in their national languages' (1978:10).

Ngugi had earlier stated that 'the Bible paved the way for the sword' (1964:57). Though this Kenyan writer does not draw the parallel himself, he is clearly emulating the Kikuyu seers whom he describes in *Writers in Politics* as 'Mau Mau' freedom fighters who '...rejected the culture of the oppressor and created a popular oral literature embodying anti-exploitation values. They took Christian songs; they took even the Bible and gave these meanings and values in harmony with the aspirations of their struggle' (Ngugi 1981:27).

What I see as important in postcolonial criticism is the need to recognise our context and then use it for a positive reading of the Bible in order to create a world to counter domination, drawing on elements of Kikuyu culture, which are also part of the context of the reader. These are two texts, one written (Bible), and one oral (our culture), which we must read without disregarding either. To do so effectively, we need to 'distance' ourselves from both our culture and the Bible in order to read them as two texts of similar importance. There is a need for interpreters of any text, whether oral or written, to keep a particular distance in order to suspend what they previously held as the real meaning in order to allow a new understanding (Draper 2002:17) that may result from the dialoguing of the two. In other words, postcolonial critics need to realise that what we call 'our world' or 'our culture' is not superior to the culture of colonial powers or, for that matter, to the culture of the Bible, but we need to read them side by side in order to allow a new world to emerge. This can only be done contrapuntally.

Contrapuntalism

To do so, I would like to draw on the theory of Edward Said, using the musical metaphor of counterpoint, which is seen as central in two major works of Said entitled *Culture & Imperialism*, and *Orientalism*. Said (1993:36) describes contrapuntalism as a connection or mutual consideration of otherwise disparate social practices, of culture and empire, of history and of the connections, not outside and beyond them. In other words, 'we must be able to think through and interpret together experiences that are discrepant, each with its particular agenda and pace of development, its own internal formations, its internal coherence and system of external relationships, all of them co-existing and interacting with others' (1993:36).

If one follows Said's method of approach in interpreting experiences that are fundamentally relational, coherent but separate and comprehensible to particular traditions, this will lead to a counterpoint. In music a counterpoint is the result of two voices and rhythms being played independently, but nevertheless ending up in creating a harmony. The method is similar to that of the comparative approach, which may also be defined as inculturation, in that it will also seek to work with materials that can create harmony with other different materials (cf. Upkong 2000:14). It will also be similar in that it takes note of a common context. Such a model will preserve what is unique about each culture, but will identify different themes and see how they can evoke possibilities of enriching each other. It is important that it also preserves some sense of the human community and the actual contexts that contributed to the formation of such cultures. Therefore, according to Said (1993:32-33), various traditions can be read and understood together since they belong to comparable fields of human experience. In that case we need to note that the African cultures and the Biblical cultures by their very nature are ways of life. They explain the style and objectives in form, meaning, value, goals, truth and reality. They are the products of prophetic creativity in the social order. As such, they are already legitimate, but they have to engage in a conversation as they play their own rhythms in order to create harmony. We, however, need to explain what we mean by a model before we formulate a contrapuntal model.

Within New Testament scholarship, the model of contrapuntal reading should be seen as one line of approach among others (e.g. Upkong 2000). It is a profoundly ideological model. In New Testament studies the term 'model' is often used rather loosely as a synonym for words such as 'metaphor', 'analogy', 'image', 'symbol', or 'paradigm' (Elliot 1983:3). Models allow scholars to compare factors more easily and they stimulate the imagination so that an understanding of the particular issues is more easily arrived at. A model is used in order to interpret and try to make sense of some social reality; on the other hand, it is an approach that is interpretive of social factors of life in a particular way.

The contribution of models in general to our understanding of the New Testament is quite significant (Tidball 1983:14). Models of such operations and reactions are basically models of interpretations, which equate to the historical critical, literary and contextual approaches. A model is a tool that moves to the level of explanation. According to Rohrbaugh (1996:8) models must be calculated to fit the level of abstraction appropriate to the data and adapted to regional and historical variations. A contrapuntal model looks upon cultural experiences from different origins, with a central task of criticism at a level of inquiry that allows the two to interact.

Models, which are constructed contextually, tend to simplify reality. Many scholars object to the use of models on the grounds that they impose alien concepts on unsuspecting data and oversimplify it. Esler however argues that:

> This objection is based on the mistaken notion that we can ever avoid employing models! Everyone uses models; for the most part, however, they remain at the level of unspoken, even unrecognized,

assumptions or prejudgments which are based upon our own experience and which inevitably shape our interpretation of the texts. Sometimes an exegete's model comes to the surface (1994:12).

We would argue that by using a contrapuntal model as an interpretive act we stand a better chance not only of understanding what John says about the future in the Apocalypse, but also of understanding how our Kikuyu myth about the past can influence the way we interpret John's view of the future and access its meaning for the Apocalypse community. The point to be underscored is that if interpretation of a text of any kind takes place, then some domain of reference will be used by the reader, rooted in some model of society and social interaction as formulated by the reader.

Models are a means that enable the interpreter to move from his own context to that of the text. They are heuristic tools which investigate, organize and explain social data and its meaning (Rohrbaugh 1996:8-9), hence models can explore social phenomena in a way that gives us more insights regarding the particular community under research, and they can test certain hypotheses which social theory has led us to expect. According to Richter (1984:61), the usefulness of models lies in their ability, for instance, to offer a systematic way of organizing information in order to focus attention on social structure and the dynamics of social process between apparently unrelated data from the same or different sources. A good model must always create space for the pre-conceived ideas of the interpreter to be re-examined.

The use of models is, however, not without dangers. Models should not be seen as mere templates that can be placed over any or on all data. They must be shaped to suit the data. Models must also take note of regional and historical variations, as Rohrbaugh (1996) states:

> A model offers the interpretation of a text from either Testament
> tools that are adequate for setting out the social systems that inhabit
> the world or the context behind the text under study. The best a
> contemporary biblical scholar might offer Bible readers is a way to

recapture/return to the domains of reference which derive from and are appropriate to the social world from which the biblical texts derive. All interpretation, it would seem, requires and ultimately rests on such models (1996:9).

Hence it is my argument here that the contrapuntal model ought to be applied in conjunction with other textual approaches to help build a profile of the community and the author under study. Nevertheless the researcher must avoid the risk of falling into the trap of what Bell (1992:46) calls 'interpretive slippage'. In such a mistake the analyst's argument becomes circular and the interpretive tool may even become part of the data one is trying to interpret. Being aware of this, we can then reformulate a model of contrapuntal reading.

It seems to me that an African contextual interpreter of the Bible should speak of the process of interpretation of the Bible as a "contrapuntal" reading of it (in the spirit of Edward Said's (1993) emphasis on 'contrapuntalism' as the medium of reading foreign texts with our own texts as the fundamental analogy. This is because a contrapuntal reading is a two way process, in which each of the texts involved can interrogate the other and create harmony. In African traditions, meaning is determined in the community by listening to different incidents that let a new meaning emerge. People talk about an experience that happened long ago and let it dialogue with a present one until harmony is reached. This is because it is recognized in African culture that what has been experienced before remains an important influence on what is to be decided and done now. The present, whether written or oral, needs to draw on the reservoir of a myriad of previous experiences. At the end of the story, what is it which 'wins the day? It is the performance aspect of oral tradition which is important. Above all, it is because the meaning of what we are experiencing (reading) is always linked inextricably to our context, to the real life situations of the community (reader). One may agree that the problem is not so much the Bible as a written text, but that the missionaries tried to promote it as a text that was supreme over our oral texts, particularly in confessional scholarship.

Parameters of "Contrapuntal" Transaction

The Bible is the Church's book and its final authority on religious matters in Africa. However, we need to remember that the Bible has no absolute or neutral meaning that is applicable from age to age, nor is it applicable to each age in the same way. The same text will have a significantly different meaning depending on the reader's context. Even if the Bible remains the same, the change of context will result in a 'paradigm shift', small or great, depending on what the new context requires for interpretation. This is true for any reading of a text for interpretation, not just the Bible. At the most basic level, words themselves only have meaning in particular contexts, in relation to that which the reader understands to be going on. We understand what is written if it agrees with what exists in our context, with what is being read, and with the conventions of the oral traditions of a given community. So we understand what we read or hear from the Bible according to what we think is going on in the text and in our own culture, according to what we conceive or comprehend and according to what kind of writing it is.

It is easiest to explain a contrapuntal reading as a contextual nature of reading in human understanding, if there can be any misunderstanding. It includes the discovery that the old methods of approach to biblical exegesis (e.g. historical) are defective. They overlook the fact that all knowledge is subjective, that the acquiring of it is not purely disinterested or an objective pursuit, and that it serves particular interests and concerns (good or bad). They also ignore the fact that ideas are not neutral, absolute and eternal but conditioned by the material circumstances, the context, that gave rise to them (cf. Nolan 1997:97). If the reader understands the context to be one thing and the community knows that context (story) differently, then we get either a comedy or tragedy! For instance, a person who has never seen a horse has no vision to help contextualise a reading from the book of Revelation about a red and a black horse; such a person may assume a horse is like a sheep, whereas they are two completely different animals. Such a reading can create misunderstandings as in a Kikuyu story of a child born in town who, when he saw a goat eating grass, wondered and asked 'what type of a dog is this that is eating grass?' All of us could give examples of failing to understand new stories that have no commonality with what we are used to. In such a situation contrapuntal listening implies listening to what you know and for what you do not know, letting a new meaning emerge. In such a practice, we need to read a biblical text with an African oral text, one on one. We have to listen to both texts 'contrapuntally' for harmony. Even if we just want to read the Bible, if we want to understand it we need to situate our context, because its context is different from ours, which makes explanations necessary.

We can only work out the biblical context from what we read in the written text, because the biblical writers didn't write to us as Africans, but to others. The writers were Jewish scribes and teachers writing to their own Jewish people who believed that God had promised them a Messiah, now present in the works of Christ. At that moment the writers were concerned with the meaning of God's covenant to the people of Israel in their new situation. They may have also wanted to explain the faith to those who were becoming new members of the Christian faith.

This leaves us with no option but to read what biblical writers wrote alongside stories from our own context, in order for us to understand what they meant. In that way we will be able to ask what is happening both in our historical setting and in the biblical texts. If we can place the biblical writers and their readers in a context we can recognise, and understand what the texts were to them, then when we consider a similar story of our own and locate it in that context, we can better understand the biblical texts. Of particular importance in the process of contrapuntal reading is the recognition of the master myths (oral narratives), which Miles Foley (1991: 1995) calls metonymic referencing which saves time and energy when we read. These are the one or two word expressions in a story which summarise a whole world of meaning, of common ground in different societies, without the reader in either case being aware of it. Examples today would be the word 'ancestors', which many people use favourably or unfavourably, even if they don't fully understand the reference, which is to those who died years ago! For Dube (1999:39) these are sacred beings who regulate the norms of the society and ensure their stability and health. If we miss these metonymic clues we may fundamentally misuse the meaning of the word. I say 'misuse the meaning' because my fundamental assumption is that the interpreting of the Bible requires harmony between two uncommon contexts, in other words, meaning is not located in the text or in the reader but between them. When readers shut out their own context there may be only misunderstanding, instead of conversation there may only be a monologue, and domination of the other culture occurs; this is really what happened with the arrival of missionaries in Africa (Dube 2001:145). As a result there is a failure to learn anything and usually a failure to grasp the meaning of the other text also (our cultural beliefs were considerably misunderstood by the missionaries). True reading consists of openness to the other text, in which there is a mutual willingness for harmony in order for a new meaning to emerge.

A Contrapuntal Model as a Dynamic Transaction Method

I have already referred to the contrapuntal perspective of Edward Said, which insisted on reading together materials, whether written or oral, from different contexts. Reading such texts together allows interpretation of the texts from a level playing ground. This approach insists on the particular nature of the Bible as a 'sacred text' and as the normative text for Christians. Contrapuntal analysis is not undertaken simply out of interest, but because both the Bible and the oral texts of the Africans impact on people's lives and also on the way the African Christians live in a society.

The problematic part of this comparative analysis model is in its assumption that human society is the same everywhere and always. This is a problem with the African traditional way of understanding society. Mbiti (1972: 52) at least is aware of the problem. He says that it is within the traditional thought-forms and religious concerns that Africans live and try to assimilate Christian teaching. He further argues that these traditional thought-forms strongly colour much of their understanding of the Christian message. These traditional thought-forms are sources that no doubt provide much material, which presents a great opportunity for trying to harmonize and co-ordinate a new meaning in contrapuntal reading. This is one of the tasks facing African biblical scholars, and it is in the performing of this rigorous task that we will probably be making our contribution to African biblical scholarship. Perhaps we will thus break the mould of past approaches to Bible interpretation and bring the benefits of contextual Bible interpretation to the front door of all African Christians. This is why we want to move towards a contrapuntal reading methodology for a contextual interpretation of the Bible in Africa. However, in any successful interpretive process the context of the reader/listener must be considered in order to avoid running the serious risk of self-deception.

Three Poles of the Contrapuntal Model

A contrapuntal reading needs to pay attention to three important areas of exegesis. Firstly, we must give priority to the *context*, not the reader, not because we doubt whether the Bible is a true word of God able to confront the reader with revelation, but because the readers and the listeners of the word are predisposed by their social, economic, political and cultural contexts so as to read and listen in a certain way. Secondly, the reader must *isolate* him or herself from the traditional approaches of interpretation and also create a 'critical distance' from the context of the Bible and the situational context of the reader in order to allow new meaning. The third pole is that of *acceptance*; there is need for the reader to own the text (Bible) and also accept the meaning discovered through the reader's context.

Contextual Pole

One of the things we learned in Africa during the colonial times is that there are no neutral readings of the Bible. The interpretations of the Bible by the missionaries fundamentally affirmed Western hegemony and imperial control of Africa (Draper 2002:16). African thoughts arising out of their own experience and situations were deemed to be illegitimate and often silenced as backward and ungodly. Our social context determines what thoughts we possess, what tools we use to interpret, and what counts as an answer from God!

We need to agree that all cultures are not static; they change from time to time. I am born and bred in Kenya and all my life has involved reading the Bible against the background of Kikuyu traditions. That particular context has opened my eyes to see many facets of the text (Bible) that I would never have otherwise seen. This has led to a new context of cultural identity and of a desperate desire to understand the Bible from my own African culture. The answers to the questions of yesterday, which have disturbed many African scholars, particularly how the missionaries interpreted or translated the Bible, may no longer offer help for today – not that they are lost, because they form an essential part of our on-going contrapuntal analysis and form the pre-supposition for the reading going on now (cf. Hermanson 1999:8). It is important, however, to recognize this because contrapuntal reading is not just a matter of running after every African story for comparison and defence purposes. It stands in continuity with the whole reservoir of meaning. Therefore contrapuntal reading involves spending time analyzing our context from the point of view of society and history. As Kenyans (Africans), we understand our specific context at the end of a long history of oppression, cultural dispossession and economic exploitation. There is a need to affirm our African culture and identity especially in connection with the Christian faith brought by the missionaries, often used as a tale of domination of our own culture.

Isolation Pole

I use this term because I think it is time to isolate ourselves from the hegemony of historical, critical study that emerged from the enlightenment, which gave special prestige to historical questions as 'scientific'. I do not see much value in giving such exclusive status to historical study. There are valuable methods emerging from literary studies such as structuralism, rhetorical criticism, and narrative criticism (Draper 2002:17). There are also new models available to Bible interpreters developed from social anthropology as well as cultural criticism. However, it is important for a Bible interpreter to isolate him/herself from both the Biblical context as well as the situational context in order to gain 'critical distance'. In this way the reader will have 'binary vision', and will be one who can see things both in terms of what is in the Bible and in terms of what is actually here and now (present context). In other words the interpreter needs to suspend what was held previously as the meaning of the text, in order to open up to new understandings, which may even contradict the previous pre-suppositions. It is that stage which I call the isolation stage in order to signal that the reader/listener seeks to learn anew from both texts rather than to discard them. This stage of isolation requires the reader to let the Bible be other than according to her or his preconceptions, to be strange, unexpected, and even isolating and alienating.

In other words, the text, whether written or oral, is not under our control or at our disposal. It has an integrity of its own which stands over against us; we need not take it for granted or think we control it; it is not an object but another subject which calls us into dialogue. In such a dialogue, we let the two texts play each other. We let them answer our questions, solve our problems, letting a new solution emerge. If the texts challenge us by their difference, then we also get insights coming from our particular contexts which challenge the texts to open themselves up as new, as texts of today.

Acceptance Pole
I use the term 'acceptance' because I see it as a process of 'appreciating' the text and really owning the meaning discovered in one's own context and community, taking responsibility for it. In other words, my accepting of this phase of the interpretive process includes the understanding that it results in changed behaviour, in action in and through the community of faith in society. It is not simply a question of interrogating the Bible for doctrine, but of relating

it to a lived tradition of the readers (lived faith). If one is to appreciate the full significance of a paradigm shift, then one must accept a radical conversion with its far-reaching consequences that cannot be fully appreciated all at once. We all know that interpretations have consequences and we need to face up to them. This is because the Bible is a particular kind of a book for those who are Christians. It is quite possible for someone of African traditional faith, or of no faith at all, to do historical critical study of the Bible from the point of view of respecting it as a 'sacred text' for a particular community of faith. It is quite possible for anyone to analyze their context, but a Christian reading of the text would understand her/his context with the intention of acceptance of the revealed interpretation. Perhaps it might be possible for someone of no faith to make some suggestions concerning the 'acceptance' of the Bible by a faith community, but this stage of process of interpretation is inherently emic that is, read from inside the community, rather than etic that is, read from outside, bracketing the faith question.

Locatedness of a Contrapuntal Transaction

In terms of the application of the whole methodology, I would like to argue that a contrapuntal reading of particular texts is also guided by an understanding of the fundamental nature of Christians and of who Jesus Christ is. In simple words, the interpretation of the individual texts is placed within the ambit of what the interpreter considers to be the primary axis or thread of the whole. Examples of difficult areas of interpretation are oppressive strands within the text, e.g. the story of the dispossession and genocide of people of Jericho, which accompanied the entry into the city (Js 6:2-7); stories of injustice, such as the rape of Tamar (2 Samuel 13:1-19), and many other violations of women in the Old Testament.

These we read against the fundamental axis of liberation, love and justice, which characterizes God's dealing with his people. Part of the harmony which takes place in the act of contrapuntal analysis involves listening to the Biblical texts and our own oral texts as they interrogate each other. We need to make choices in our contrapuntal reading of the Bible; just as in life, we may choose to read from the perspective of the oppressed, the grieved, and the marginalized – and we know our own stories to go with particular biblical texts. It is justifiable to do so, in order to understand in what way the stories of the Bible may contribute to our life and our faith in a hostile global environment. Biblical stories range over a spectrum from simple, unilinear, tightly plotted sequences (such as a joke) to complex, multilinear sequences wherein any number of possible connections between events may be inferred (as in epic). However before any meaningful dialogue can take place we need to reflect on what is popularly known as textuality and orality.

Textuality and Orality
Within the African context we have two groups of readers the educated who are usually referred to as the professional readers and the uneducated who are commonly referred to as ordinary readers.[4] While the professionals will use the available tools such as dictionaries, commentaries and lexicons, the ordinary readers will use orality as a tool. This means that the majority of Africans have an oral knowledge of the Bible as well as a read Bible. According to Itumeleng (1996: 43-57), most of the Bible information held by Africans comes from socialisation in the churches themselves as they listen to prayers and sermons. This reality does not rule out the presence of the Bible as a text because the text must have been present before the remembered version. So, even those who do not know how to read have a considerable exposure to biblical texts, which they later use in their dialoguing with the written text. Draper recently wrote an article on 'Confessional Western Text-Centered Biblical Interpretation and an Oral or Residual-Oral Context' where he urges scholars not to ignore the complexity of the dialogue between literacy and orality in biblical interpretations. His main concerns are the working relationship between these groups of readers. Draper starts

---

[4]Such a classification is necessary because all readers are not the same and their levels of reading or applying tools are different.

an interesting conversation, which calls for further investigations on how to walk the path from orality towards textuality. This is what we shall be doing in engaging in dialogue between the African culture and the Bible. So does this mean that the Bible is ambiguous?

Ambiguity of the Bible

The encounter between Africans (Kikuyu people) and the Bible is usually recounted in broad strokes, for example Ngugi wa Thiong'o argues that he quotes the Bible because he and the Bible have common grounds of interest and concern. Yet he denies his Christian faith: 'I am not a man of the Church, I am not even a Christian' (1972:31). So this brings out the dilemma many Africans face in dealing with the Bible. Whether or not they claim to be believers, the Bible occupies a central position in their lives; as Brown (1997:31) puts it, the Bible still serves a determining frame of reference in all works of Ngugi wa Thiong'o.

The Bible emerges in surprising and refreshing indigenous forms and traditions, playing a major role in both the construction and deconstruction of modern societies. Even when people try to be stridently hostile to the Bible, they end up using it all the more. So the dilemma of the Bible in the transaction between African culture and its culture is the way it was used during liberation struggles not only in Africa but also in Latin America. This religious transaction is our main interest here. Throughout, I seek to illustrate and assess the significance of the parallels for understanding the individual texts in question.

CHAPTER FIVE

Inter-Religious Transaction Between African Culture and the Bible

Introduction

It is important to engage in a transaction between our African terms and those of Christianity. There are numerous ways of carrying out this transaction in theology. We need a new way to try to conceive what we are actually doing when we try to do contextual theology in Africa. Most African theologians have been trained in historical-critical analysis, which heavily focuses on Christianity as the only true religion, and interprets it by way of producing more texts in support of it. In fact some of my students in Nairobi International School of Theology were confused and they did not understand that you are first and foremost an African before becoming a Christian. Some of them were saying that you have to be a Christian and then an African; this idea caused them to displace their context of doing theology. Every faithful Christian must practise Christianity within a particular context. 'Contextual' as a descriptive word for interpretation implies that the meaning is something hidden inside the context, waiting to be uncovered by the skill of the interpreter by careful 'objective' historical study. In such an understanding African religion and Christianity stand in tension with each other; this is because of the situatedness of Christianity in Africa and the historical situatedness of the African religion as part of our culture.

Since there are a thousand and one themes in the African culture, we shall here only reflect on a selection of these: ancestors, dreams, myths and dowry in African marriage. In African life these themes play a central role, as is evident both in African religion and in African Christianity. It is clear that the coming of Christianity has not erased the African reverence or respect for our culture. There is great potential for inter-religious dialogue between Christianity and African religion if the dialogue already taking place on the plane of culture can be developed. Key issues in biblical and African culture that will benefit from the insights gained by dialogue include intermediaries, inspiration (ancestors as the primary source of cultural innovation), and culture as a means of calling to specific ministries, Christology, Christian identity, cosmology and the experience and understanding of God. Such topics call for mature theological reflection. African theologians need to do research on ancestors and myths and their role in African Christianity in order to develop an African theology of genealogy. We now engage in a reflection on ancestors before re-reading Revelation 22:1-5 in the light of the Kikuyu myth of land.

Christ Our Ancestor

The major concern of African theologians is to find out the relevance of Christ to our faith, which has been an ancestor-based faith for a long time. There is no doubt that ancestorship is the subject which has been most talked of in today's African Christian theology. The theology of the ancestorship of Christ is incomplete without theological consideration of its link with us; for indeed, Christ the Head is incomplete without his body, the church, of which we and the Saints in the other world (including our ancestors) are members (Nyamiti 1991:13). This has resulted in an examination of the relevance of Christ's ancestorship to the heavenly saints. Those saints in heaven such as Abraham, Isaac and Jacob are ancestrally related to us by the fact that they participate in the ancestral status of the redeemer (cf. Mt 1:1-16). Among the saints are the African ancestors who died in friendship with God (Nyamiti 1991:12). The importance of ancestors can be understood by recognition of the belief that in Africa, all that we posses belongs to the ancestors as well as to the living community. Attempts to sell possessions such as land were regretted and in olden days such actions were impossible. This issue was the principal cause of an uprising in Kenya, when the settlers to whom land had been leased thought they had bought it. In confronting the Christian teaching on Christ and the ancestors with the African worldview, we have no option but to reflect on the biblical teaching about ancestors (cf. Matthew 1:1-25).

There is no doubt that African traditional religious practice has been exploited and perhaps misconstrued so as to promote Christianity. In Africa, the role of the ancestors is a critical question. Perhaps, as we stated earlier, the issue of ancestors is not problematic. Although there could be differences about how ancestors are understood in Africa, one thing in common is the unbroken chain of life stretching from the unborn through the living to the living dead. The ancestors are a power to reckon with because they not only represent the continuity of life, but also the force which maintains the community (Dube 1999:39). For this reason they are honoured in ritual, through the sacrifice of animals, the pouring of beer and through care of tombstones and through other acts of respectful remembrance. In times of trouble or sickness, dreams were used as the primary medium through which ancestral forces communicated with their descendants (Guma 1997:17). The relationship between the ancestors and Christ Jesus is often not clear to Africans and is not much discussed even though no perceived conflict exists between belief in the ancestors and belief in Christ.

However the missionaries problematized and rejected the ancestors, even, in one case at least, coining the phrase 'ancestor worship'.[1] As Seoka (1997:5) argues, it must have been in someone's interest to demonise African culture and religion in order to promote that which was appealing to some people (cf. Dube 2001:145-164). Interestingly, in Christian experience we have the corollary of Christ and the ancestors within the Christian calendar, when we commemorate All Saints' and All Souls' Days. On the other hand the Jewish culture is closer to the African culture. In the Jewish culture ancestors were important, perhaps more important than has traditionally been acknowledged. Not even once is God characterised as the Lord of faithful people who died long ago. Jesus insisted that those who died long ago, like Abraham, are not dead but living. Such a testimony from Christ should not be taken lightly, for he says 'the dead do not marry but live like the angels in heaven' and, as proof of this, cites the ancestors. 'Have you not read in the book of

---

[1] The Kikuyu had three major religious practices, deity worship (which is done even today in Christian churches), communion with ancestors and sacrificial practices. (The age of communion with ancestors and sacrifices is gone, though it may be there to some extent among some few people, though I have not come across it). The ideas underlying these religious practices cannot be adequately addressed in English, but in Kikuyu language the difference between the three is distinct. We have *gûthathaiya Ngai* (to worship God), we also have *gûthînjîra na gûitangîra ngoma njohi* (to sacrifice and pour out/sprinkle beer or whatever one is drinking) for communion or remembering those who are separated from the community. The essential difference between worship of *Ngai* and what is known as 'ancestor worship' is that the word *gûthathaiya* is never used by the Kikuyu in connection with ancestral spirits (cf. Kenyatta 1938:231-268). The ancestors are always invited to join whenever a sacrifice is made to *Ngai* on an occasion of national importance (cf. Middleton & Kershaw 1972:60), but they are never worshipped. So when one is using the Kikuyu language it becomes clear that there was no 'ancestor worship' in Kikuyu religion, but when one is speaking in English there may be no difference between ancestor worship and worship of *Ngai*. This underpins the importance of using one's language to articulate some ideas.

Moses, in the passage about the bush, how God said to him 'I am the God of Abraham and the God of Isaac and the God of Jacob'? He is not God of the dead, but of the living' (Mk 12:26-27). Perhaps in Kikuyu God is the God of Gikuyu and Mumbi, the first parents of the Kikuyu society. So, clearly, Jesus understood the ancestors as the 'living dead'. In fact the Hebrew name *Elohim*, which is plural, may have originated with the ancestor cult of Israel.

Moreover, Jewish elite families kept records of their physical ancestry and kinship, called *toledoth*. There was a belief that one's ancestry determined a person's nature and destiny. In Africa today it is commonly believed that, if a family had an ancestor who was a medicine person, a seer or a diviner in the olden days, today one can trace in such families a priest within the Christian ministry. In Jewish tradition, this is clearly formulated in the manual of the disciples from Qumran, where the catechist is instructed to teach all the members 'the *toledoth* of all the children of men according to the nature of the spirits; their signs according to their deeds in their lifetimes and according to the visitation of their afflictions together with the times of their peace' (1QS 3:13-14). In opposition to the *toledoth* of Matthew about Jesus, there is another *toledoth* of *Yeshu* in rabbinic writings, which depicts their perception of Jesus' illegitimacy. Clearly, the ancestry of any community whether African, Christian or Jewish is an important part of the self-understanding of that community. In African traditional religion the ancestors are the intermediaries, who plead with God to meet the needs of their families and communities and to protect them from evil forces and natural disasters (Dube 2001:146), a role assumed to be played by Christ in the Christian faith.

A Reflection on the Ancestors of Christ (Matthew 1:1-25)
Matthew seems to make a major theological point by starting his Gospel with the *toledoth* of Jesus. He begins by telling us that Jesus was a legal heir to the throne of David, by virtue of his lineage. This fact is immediately set forth in verse one, which states Jesus was the 'son of David, the son of Abraham.' His kinship to David is mentioned

before that of Abraham, the father of Israel. By giving us the list of ancestors Matthew affirms their importance. As in the African way of life, ancestors are remembered both selectively and schematically. They are always commemorated by pouring a drink, preferably wine (or beer); when the ground swallows up the drink this is a sign of acceptance. The whole African theology of ancestors is embodied in mythology. There seem to be correlations with the African theology of ancestors in every culture and the Matthew passage. It is certainly evident in myths of creation whether Jewish or African that ancestors are the foundation of societies, whether patriarchal or matriarchal. Matthew's structure is both Patriarchal and Matriarchal; he divides the genealogy into three groups of fourteen generations, separated by important historic points (Matthew 1:17). The three divisions of Matthew's genealogy are: Abraham to the reign of King David (Matthew 1:2-6), David's kingdom to the Babylonian captivity (Matthew 1:6-11) and Release from Babylonian captivity to Christ (Matthew 1:12-16).

Over the years, a kind of ancestor-reverence culture has continued in African Christian life, a deeply religious culture. It is an ancestor culture rich in spirituality, in responses and in understanding, with its own set of fears, joys, hopes, expectations, limitations and even a kind of eschatological expectation. This ancestor culture is subject to change and adjustments and is resistant against threats to its existence from both African religion and Christianity.

Matthew, in chapter 1:1, names two key ancestors: 'Jesus son of David and son of Abraham'. The naming is a strategic move by Matthew to acknowledge Jesus' solidarity with all the people of Israel. The connection of Jesus having Abraham as an ancestor gives Matthew the right of access to Jesus as a 'living dead', and to all those who descended from Abraham. The genealogy claims a specific ancestry in the royal lineage of David making Jesus the 'anointed one' of Israel. Matthew's arrangement of three sets of ancestors, each comprising 14 generations indicates the divine intentionality of the whole arrangement. It is God-planned for the salvation of his people. This genealogy does not tally with the list found in the Old Testament nor with that of Luke (cf. Luz 1989: 100-108), but that is not important. With the expansion of Christianity in Africa has come a meeting, an encounter, between Christianity and this ancestor culture. There is now an even more dynamic continuation of this with potentially rich dialogical insights. The important thing is that Matthew affirms the centrality of Jesus' ancestors by placing his genealogy at the beginning of his account. What is also important is who, out of a range of possible people, is named in the ancestry of Christ.

African Christians, as well as the followers of African traditional religion, seem prepared to place traditional ancestor culture alongside biblical accounts of ancestry, treating them sometimes interchangeably, sometimes contrasting them, finding a balance between similarity and difference. Does the African belief in ancestors easily transfer into Christianity? This requires the articulation of a theology of ancestors and of the culture of the living dead and a discussion of the issues raised. The issues in such a discussion include the living and the dead in a gender-balanced way.

It is not only surprising, but fascinating, that Matthew was gender sensitive, in that he mentioned a number of women in the list of ancestors, and all of them were problematic. This is in line with the African understanding of ancestors, where the judgement for sins on this earth does not (necessarily) fall on the descendant ancestors. The women mentioned are, first, Tamar, who in Genesis 38:11-30, is recorded as being Judah's daughter-in-law, who, after being denied a promised husband (the last of Judah's sons), had impersonated a harlot. She enticed Judah to lie with her and from that illicit union came two sons – Perez and Zerah; and from Perez sprung Boaz, David and ultimately the Christ. The second woman mentioned is Rahab (Joshua 2:9-13), a non-Jewish prostitute from Jericho who became the wife of Salmon and the father of Boaz. She is followed by another non-Jewish woman called Ruth, a Moabite who had followed her mother-in-law back to her country (Ruth 1:16). She later became the levirate wife of Boaz and the mother of Obed, grandfather of David. Matthew also refers to Bethsheba, the fourth woman in his list, the wife of Uriah the Hittite, who conceived Solomon after her first child, born as a result of the adultery forced on her by David, was smitten by God (2 Sam 11:2). Apart from Mary the mother of Jesus all the women mentioned in the genealogy were problematic and, more than anything else, these women appear to sully the purity of the genealogy of Christ, but also offer a way of allowing us to recognise our ancestors even if they died before the coming of Christ and his salvation. Nevertheless we can say that the first three women play an active role in fulfilling the divine will. Also, two Gentile women are mentioned and perhaps Bethsheba was also a Gentile, outside the ancestral clan. Their presence within the list is a signal that all the nations are included in the salvation plans particularly because the *toledoth* begins with Abraham, the father of blessings to all nations. This is a core point of the Gospel of Matthew, climaxed in the statement 'Go therefore and make all nations my disciples' (Mt 28:19-20).

Although Matthew's genealogy of Jesus is problematic since Jesus has no blood connection with those on the list, it affirms the importance of Jesus' ancestors whether through Mary or Joseph. Therefore despite those signals of 'irregularity' where women of faith are mentioned to maintain the covenantal purpose of God, the chain of biological continuity is maintained up to Jacob the father of Joseph (some scholars disprove the listing since Joseph was not a biological father to Jesus), yet with Joseph the chain is cut: 'And Jacob the father of Joseph the husband of Mary, of whom Jesus was born, who is called Christ (Mt. 1:16). We do understand that Jesus is not the biological son to Joseph but the son of Mary; even Matthew goes on to explain this: he suggests that Joseph, being aware that this is not his own child, intended to 'put her away quietly' but an ancestor/the angel was in time to instruct Joseph to take her as his wife (Mt. 1:25). Even though Matthew has laboured to set out his *toledoth*, he still breaks the chain he has so carefully put together, but this finds a resting place in the African understanding of fatherhood, in which is encoded that if a man accepts a child to be his, then the child becomes part of his generations. You may also call this a 'legal fiction' if you like but it is quite common in Africa: the majority of us even in the 21st century do not know our biological fathers. And this is how Jesus enters the chain of Joseph's ancestors. This may sound unconvincing to us, and the Jewish opponents of the Christian faith were also unconvinced of it, but in Africa a person can become our ancestor, our brother or sister, even if not of our own flesh and blood. It is in this respect that Jesus is the son of Abraham and the son of David.

Matthew may have understood this theory from his own Jewish traditions, but he sees Jesus as 'Emmanuel, God with us' (Mt 1:23), hence not requiring blood relation to be part of Abraham's lineage. So Matthew is 'within and without' in order to affirm the traditions of the ancestors and he also transcends the traditions. Matthew was adopting a 'master myth' of his own people, the *toledoth*, and accepting it afresh. The African understanding of ancestors and family relations is quite at home with such an arrangement. The conversation here brings out a number of things that are common to both the New Testament and in the African traditions. They demonstrate clearly that the area of ancestors is rife with dialogical insights calling for theological reflection.

Genealogy

It would not only be foolish, but also uncalled for, to say that the Jewish understanding of the importance of genealogy or the *toledoth* is similar to our African traditions or 'master myth' of the genealogy. However there are overlaps that cannot be ignored at any level. There is a need to look anew at the importance of genealogy in Africa, whose role the missionaries failed to incorporate in the Christian faith of Africans. So, in our dialogue, we have the space to revisit the question afresh.

It quite clearly emerges that Jesus stands within and outside a particular chain of ancestry. This is the paradox we must accept, just as we have accepted the Bible as our own, even though our texts are oral in orientation. As much as we value the significance of

Abraham, Isaac, and Jacob, as the 'living dead' we then need to affirm and acclaim the same for our ancestors. Recognising the fact that Matthew punctuates the chain of male ancestors with women of faith who 'broke the rule' in order to accomplish God's covenantal purpose, we equally need to recognise our African women of faith (Okure 2001: 42-63) as our ancestors.

Just as many African societies would claim, without proof of blood relation, that a particular person was a founder of a particular tribe, the true father of Jesus is not Joseph but God, through the Holy Spirit. This means that no community or tribe may claim Jesus as their own ancestor to the point of excluding the rest. This is the same way that African myths operate; one may find a common myth of origin among very different people in different areas within African traditional religion. Jesus is Emmanuel, God with us; he is for all nations. In Africa, ancestors are never personal; wherever you travel or live, there are your ancestors, even if they were buried miles away and perhaps even knew nothing of your recent migration. From this reading emerges the need for us to affirm the importance of ancestors and our right to honour or pay respect to them. For through them we gain our place in space and time in a way that affirms our own importance as human beings. It also emerges that any listing of ancestors that excludes women, because of patriarchal systems, or men in the case of matriarchal systems, is incomplete and unacceptable. Following the same line of thought, as Christians we need to note that affirming our ancestors does not exclude those outside the chain. The inclusion of those both within and outside the chain is the principal message of Christians' togetherness; we are a Church of a World Wide Web.

God

God is the ultimate father of all the ancestors. In traditional religious life, as well as in Christianity, ancestors abound in references to God as their creator and maker. He communicates to the living through the ancestors in traditional life, and there are uncountable references to ancestors in the Bible (cf. Hebrews 11). God lends a measure of authority to ancestors, where they are assumed to be living with him or within his reach. There are numerous texts in the Bible telling about the ancestors being concerned with the life of the living (e.g. the rich man and Lazarus), and even desiring to communicate with them. In particular the notion of the Spirit of God, or God as Spirit, is an area of overlap between Christianity and African belief in ancestors. Here questions concerning revelation and communicating through ancestors also await further consideration.

Cosmology

A new world begins to form when Christian understanding of ancestors comes into contact with the African experience of ancestors. This is evident in the genealogy culture, which is set in motion by the encounter of the two religious traditions. One of the indicators of this is the use of the Bible in African Christianity, in both mission and development. By the end of 1995 the Bible had been translated in full or in portions into 601 African languages (United Bible Societies 1996:4). The Bible in African languages provides a fertile ground for inter-religious encounter. Africans reading the Bible in their own languages do not have far to go before they discover that they are treading on familiar ground. So the biblical cosmology finds a friendly hearing within African soil. The biblical and the African world mutually revive, discover, complement and modify each other in an on-going and living process. This cosmology in dialogue is ingrained in the ancestor culture, in which it is received (perhaps without questioning, since our individuality does not either start or end with us), retold and given authority, especially among Christians. Thus, for example, it is reported that among the Zulu-speaking people a mutual relationship in the form of dialogue, discipline and punishment prevails between the living and the dead. The ancestors:

Are told of the needs of the community and of the family; if they bring unmerited suffering an elder goes into the cattle kraal and tells the ancestors that they are behaving foolishly or irresponsibly (Vilakazi , et al.1986:16).

This is similar to the Christian practice of informing Jesus about their daily needs, believing that God will assist or provide the desired needs.

Vocation

In and through ancestors many people are called to particular duties, professions or mission, whether of a short or long duration. One may be called to be a diviner, a seer or a prophet. A calling is a calling whether in Christian ministry or in African religion. On the Christian side we have men and women called to various careers and mission, such as ministers and preachers. Callings to areas of duty or ministry in the Bible and of African religion tend to parallel each other.

If the calling ultimately comes from God, is not God being active in both cases, whether in the Bible or in the African religion? Is it possible to talk of 'Christian obedience' as opposed to other obedience to a higher calling? So, an African who takes up his/her traditional calling through ancestors, as instruments or fulfilling the mission of God in the community, is the same as his/her Christian counterpart.

Therefore ancestors are not just individual phenomena, but also social and religious phenomena. They generate social and religious influences upon communities. An experience of one's ancestors may influence subsequent behaviour. Ancestors do not distinguish between Christians and non-Christians; it is more the understanding of different people which may result in a different meaning.

Therefore, it is one of the ironies of African Christianity that missionaries' resistance to the hegemony of African traditional culture, with which we began our study, resulted in the word ancestor being rejected in almost all African translations of the Bible (Dube 1999: 33-59). And, as Dube argues, where they are mentioned they are equated with demons rather than with the 'living dead' like Abraham, Isaac and Jacob. It has also emerged that although Africans have accepted the Bible as a 'sacred text' they still clearly value their oral traditions and require them to be included in modern translations in the right way. Perhaps this is a signal that their resistance to accepting Christianity whole-heartedly was not resistance to 'what is contained in Christianity' per se, but to 'what was taught thus'. Therefore we need to bring about a dialogue between the Bible and African religion in order to let a new meaning emerge. The missionaries' teachings in Africa had a price tag; there was the danger that Africans practised both their religion and Christianity together, failing to be one thing or the other. For us, establishing a dialogue will allow one faith to emerge, grounded and planted in both the Bible culture and our own African culture. We can also reflect on the issue of land as a newfound promise both in Revelation and in our culture:

A Reflection on the Future Hope (Revelation 22:1-5)

Our approach is based on the earlier discussion of contrapuntal reading method. The function of this approach is to bring to the fore the overlapping issues of our culture, which in this case would be the Kikuyu myth, and the passage of Revelation 22:1-5. The contrapuntal reading will enable us to interrogate the pre-critical reading practices of Christians and help us to interpret the Apocalypse in our own African culture and read it from our specific location of the Kikuyu concept of land. Extending our reading of the biblical texts in the light of our own contexts can do this. In this case, land and economics is a case in point, in order for us to be able to place John's idea of land.

Land and Economics
In the entire socioeconomic history of ancient Israel, and also of the Kikuyu, land was a fundamental means of production. This being so, ownership or non-ownership of land formed the basis of the wealth or poverty of both the modern Kikuyu as well as of Jews of ancient times. Norman Gottwald (1983) has given a well-researched analysis of the role of land in the enrichment or impoverishment of social classes in ancient Israel. The story of the exodus was more or less based on the struggle for land as

well as on ownership and the right to cultivate the land. Land is the key to every biblical reference to garden or vineyard (see Gen. 2; Isaiah 5; 1 Kings 21; Rev. 22:1-5). For the Kikuyu, no other issue qualifies better than ownership of land to represent the presence of the kingdom of God on earth.

The significance of the ownership of land as an economic power base defining the freedom or lack of freedom of the people of the Bible appears clearly in Micah 4:3-4. The struggle to free oneself from oppression caused by landlessness is an act of preservation of one's culture. This is so because the wealth of the coloniser, both in the Bible and in Africa, was also a product of cultural domination (cf. Gottwald, 1983:308f). This basic under-standing of land is here seen as underlying John's vision of the new heaven and the new earth, to replace that which has been taken not only by the Romans but also by the old Babylonian power. It is from this background that John writes his Apocalypse and particularly Revelation 22:1-5.

Revelation 22:1-5
The Apocalypse has been a favourite book of our communities. It is suited to the African context, not only because it emerged at a time in Israel's history when she had lost her sovereignty, but because this is where land, as part of the new creation, is taken seriously. It has a powerful appeal, which may tell us more about the original rhetoric of the text than modern historical, narrative or rhetorical analyses (Draper, 2004:251).

After the destruction of Jerusalem in 586 BCE, Jews were the subject of dispossession and oppression by successive empires, which readily gave rise to a perception of ongoing persecution from the dominant rulers who had taken over from the Jewish rulers. This in turn fostered the prophetic apocalyptic desire for a definitive manifestation of God's justice on the sinful nature of the pagan, and for a new garden for the Jews, a Utopia (Richard 1995:6). The vision of the new garden plays a significant and dominant role in the whole of the Apocalypse. Moreover, a cosmic finality for the new garden is also the symbol of deliverance and fulfilment. This is well reflected in Isaiah 35, where freedom and joy are promised for the ransomed of the Lord. The new garden, as the reign of God, is not in heaven but it descends to earth, for the faithful and the martyrs to enter and enjoy holy fellowship with God forever. The passage about the new garden is therefore chosen here as representative of the many illustrations of John's conviction that at last the justice of God and his grace will prevail against all odds. The positioning and the importance of this passage in the Apocalypse have attracted the researcher to the critical analysis of the passage.

The Apocalypse ends its visions with a significant vision of the final state of things. All things will be new for the old is gone and the new has come, a new earth and a new heaven. The writer portrays the new garden as an earthly city. The number already sealed to enter the garden, the 144,000 and the multitude from all over, give evidence of the importance of the garden to the readers. The passage of Revelation 22:1-5 has been represented as a phenomenon that can be interpreted in terms of a myth. For Morris (1969:242), there is need to understand the passage in symbolic terms. He explains that it is John's way of passing on to us the information that the ultimate state of affairs will finally be of great blessings to those who remain faithful, for his concern was the future life of his community.

Throughout the Apocalypse the prophetic formula of 'thus says the Lord' has been replaced with a new formula of 'he showed me'. The use of the Jewish traditions with respect to images and symbols becomes more marked. According to Caird (1984:264), Revelation 22:1-5 is the most important passage in the whole of the Apocalypse. The vision of the new garden is the real source of John's prophetic certainty, for only in comparison with the new garden can the beautiful Babylon be recognised as that destructive power which is 'an old and raddled whore'. The picture of the garden offered hope to the community more than any other promise that was made to them.

Therefore, we see the ideal garden set out by John as a source of hope to a community that was threatened by oppression and persecution. Hence the garden has inspired the believers' efforts for the betterment of humankind. The garden in this passage actually is the ideal set before Christians purposely to inspire them to be more faithful to God and to work for him, because the reward is entry into the new earth. Richard (1995:165) says that John utilizes the passage of Revelation 22:1-5 as a model of reconstruction of the earth, as a tool for constructing hope – Utopia, God's transcendent and eschatological design for all people. The new garden is fundamentally a re-construction of the collective consciousness of the Christians who are reading and hearing Revelation. A reading of Revelation would leave the reader with an awareness of how deeply one is mired in Babylon (life in this world), but it would also leave them more keenly seeking the new garden.

The vision of the new garden in this passage goes beyond the rest of the visions of the Apocalypse and deals with precipitating conditions and overt activity associated with the reign of God at the end (Caird, 1984:264). The idea of the garden restores the original plan of God for the human race (people will be back in God's original plan as described in Gen. 2:8); a new Eden is what the marginalized community dreams of. The new garden offers a contrasting political economy, a vision of another, better, world that shows God's liberating purpose (Rossing, 1999:161). The reader must take a step to move from the evil colonial situation to new lands which are to be desired, as opposed to neo-colonialism and imperialism, the destructive and arrogant ideologies. This fits our postcolonial objective, which is to understand how the two colonial powers (both colonial and neo colonial) contrast with each other. Keener (2000:508-509), argues that the new garden represents God's creation and what a reader needs to do in the midst of the dominant and the powerful coloniser is to adorn him/herself with righteous acts:

> The time for adorning ourselves with righteous acts (Rev.9:8) is now. Even though Revelation emphasises the New Jerusalem as a

future city; it is being built in the present. If the character of Babylon is evident in the world around us, the glory of God's presence among us should be revealed at least in the way we live (2000:508).

The new garden here is interpreted as that which we all need to achieve in this world of today, where the present experience of righteousness anticipates the future. The new garden of Revelation 22:1-5 is in the form of a myth from the beginning to the end. Here lies a potential dialogue which is concealed in myths. Hemer (1986:11) says that the importance of this passage is greater because the Apocalypse was addressed to people who lived in Asia Minor, a land of many cities. The important thing for John in the new heavens and the new earth is precisely its setting for the new garden of God. There will be no thirst, for in the middle of the city will be a tree of life straddling the river which flows from the throne of God, bearing fruit throughout the year to feed the 144,000, while its leaves will feed the multitude from the Gentiles and there will be no diseases, for these leaves have curative properties (Rev. 22:2). Reading this passage in Africa would open up an encounter between the biblical vision and an African culture of myths.

In Revelation 22:1 the angel now shows John the river of the water of life. John now recalls several Old Testament scriptures. The presence of the river and the tree of life make us think that the author has the Garden of Eden in mind. John draws his material from Genesis and Ezekiel. According to Genesis, the river starts from Eden and divides into four branches, while Ezekiel's stream comes from the temple rock and runs to the Dead Sea. This concept is both in biblical and extra-biblical literature. The Jewish teachers often circulated stories about Eden, for example Jubilees 3:12 mentions that there will be holy trees in Eden, others claimed to have dreamt of a river of fire (1 Enoch 17:5), while many also claimed to have seen the river of the water of life (1 Enoch 17:14). Such rivers became rivers of joy and love flowing from God's throne. God was believed to be making the last things as at the beginning. Beasley-Murray (1978:330) argues that this does not mean that the end is thought of in terms of its relation to the first things, but the first things are viewed as prophetic of the nature of God's purpose in history. However the last things supersede the beginning of all things. This river, which becomes the source of life, is more in accord with other Old Testament visions of it. Zechariah in his vision saw the 'living waters' flowing out from Jerusalem (Zech. 14:8). Ezekiel had a similar vision, of a river flowing out of a temple and pouring out into the Sea, becoming deeper as it went and giving life to all things everywhere (Ezek. 48).

Therefore what Zechariah and Ezekiel left unclear in their visions, John makes clear in his; the crystal-clear river in the city confirms the idea of brilliance. John's river is flowing from the throne, which signifies that God is the source of life, but it is flowing from the throne of God and of the Lamb; now for the third time in this passage John adds *kai tou arniou* (and of the Lamb) while referring to God. John does not want his Christians to miss the point of the Lamb's involvement in the final order of things. It is, therefore, important to note that the river is flowing from both God and the Lamb, which was based on Ezekiel 47: 'If any one thirst let them come to me, and let them who believe in me drink' (John 7:37). He wants us to understand that it is Christ who has taken the place of the temple in the New Jerusalem and who is now the source of the river.

In Revelation 22:2 the river now flows in the middle of the broad street, for it flows through the middle of it. The river in the vision of the prophet Ezekiel flowed from the temple outwards (Ezek. 47:12). The river may be circular since it does not flow out of the city but through it, supplying all. The river is not only for the purposes of satisfying God's people, but also to water the trees of life which were growing on both sides of the river. We have here to take singular for plural since one tree cannot be on both sides of the same river. These trees would signify that mankind has been allowed back into the Garden of Eden where trees of life are lining the river's bank. There could also be another way of interpreting this phrase. Beasley-Murray (1978:331) says:

> In the middle of the city's street stands a single tree, the tree of life, situated between either sides of the river. Such would then imply that the river has in its own course split into two watering the whole garden.

John wants to say that at last God in his mercy has brought all peoples to their original place, to enjoy in the Garden that which they had long desired and waited for. In this verse, one of the interesting exegetical observations is that, although both the tree and the river are said to be giving life, John does not portray them as life-givers. For John it is God who is the source of life through this river and the tree of life. The tree produces its fruits every month, and the words 'twelve manner of fruits', do not imply different kinds of fruit but rather signifies that every month a fruit was produced. The tree of life will bear fruit throughout the year. Jewish visions of the future involved supernatural agricultural abundance without any labour (Joel 3:18; Amos 9:13). In such an agricultural view rivers and trees occupied an important place (1 Enoch 24:4-25:7; 4 Ezra 8:52). Ezekiel 47:12 gives the best version of this view:

> And on the banks, on both sides of the river, there will grow all kinds of trees for food. Their leaves will not wither nor their fruit fail, but they will bear fresh fruit every month, because the water for them flows from the sanctuary. Their fruit will be for food and their leaves for healing.

John talks of a single tree of life, but with 'twelve fruits' each a month' to comply with the description of the original tree in Eden, which symbolically will imply that there is only one source of life, Jesus the Lamb that was slain.

Apocalyptic language is at work here, and John is speaking symbolically to imply through this mention of the month, without sun and moon (Rev. 21:23), that the fruits were in abundance continually. He also says 'the leaves of the tree were for the healing of the nations'; to make us understand the abundance of life in the land, the leaves of the tree will bring healing to the peoples of the world. This was the traditional way of treating people in Kikuyu land; various trees were used for healing. For the Apocalypse the leaves would only be interpreted to mean stimulation. They aroused peoples' emotions to maximum joy in their hearts. These leaves would be promoting the happiness of the nations in the land. Therefore the tree of life, with its fruit and leaves like the manna (Rev. 2:17), symbolises life at full capacity and delight. The river equally signifies a complete supply of all that is needed in an inexhaustible manner. Both the water of life and the tree of life are for the healing of the nations (Rev. 21:6; 22:1-2), but Babylon's wine makes the nations drunk (Rev. 14:8; 17:2; 18:3). The healing implies that the nations will be completely healed in the full sense of the word (Bauckham, 1995:316; cf. Lee, 2001:291).

In Rev. 22:3 the first section is actually a citation from Zechariah 14:11. From the point of view of intertextuality, we should also note especially the reference to Genesis 3:14-19. God's purposes concerning Babylon are to destroy it. He has both planned and done what he spoke concerning the inhabitants of Babylon. The absence of a curse must be seen here as a total reversal of the fall of man. Zechariah says that God's people will become a blessing instead of a curse (Zech. 8:13). The Greek word *katathema* (accursed) would mean that there is no longer 'anything cursed', it does not imply an act of cursing. John wants us to understand that, where the throne of God and of the Lamb is, there can be nothing 'accursed'. This is possible because where God is there can be no cause for a curse. God's original plan for mankind has been restored; therefore, it is possible for the holy God to dwell in their midst: 'the throne of God and of the Lamb shall be in it'. Due to the presence of God and the Lamb, their glory will be everywhere and only blessings will be known in this land. The presence of the throne in the midst of the land reminded John's community about the forum and theatre at the centre of typical Roman towns (see Keener, 2000:501).

It is the servants of God who will be giving service. The service is no doubt implied by the verb *latreusousin* which RSV translates as 'his servants shall worship him'.

Rev. 22:4 tells us that the people of God will receive even what Moses was denied. To see the face of God was something that was not allowed to mankind (Exod. 33:20, 23). Now, 'they shall see his face'. This will be the privilege of all the faithful servants of God in that land; they will see him face to face. Their joy shall be made complete by the bliss of God's presence. In similar vein, Jesus' beatitude declared that those who are pure in heart 'shall see God' (Matt. 5:8). This will be an emotional experience and the saints will now be free to see their redeemer without shame, while those who persecuted them will be denied the presence of God, and will be subject to his wrath because of their sins.

In Rev. 22:5 we are assured again that the people of God will not need lamps, for there shall be no night any more: 'God will be their light and they shall reign forever and ever'. This is a great assurance to all who have suffered under the power of evil. This kind of reigning is a special one in that there are no subjects to be ruled; rather it means that they will always experience exaltation in the presence of God (cf. Zech. 14). Therefore, they will all enjoy the royalty of the Almighty, because they are now face to face with his reality (Rossing 1999: 59). This is a realisation of the awaited promise made in Rev. 3:21: they shall now reign with Christ and God together. This brings to a close John's idea of a new land of God and the Lamb, leaving the readers overwhelmed by the glory that awaits them in future. The hope created by this mythical story of creation is similar to that created by the African myths of creation.

An African Story of a Garden Similar to that of Revelation 22:1-5
My thinking and subsequent investigation on the subject of African culture and the Apocalypse has led me to conclude that African spirituality is antecedent to, and the corollary of, biblical mythology. The supporting argument is based on the historical factors which point to the experience of the African people as believers in myths. We will here take the Kikuyu story of a garden of origin as representative of other African myths. In the Kikuyu story of origin we have a garden that provides all that people need; such a garden is the basis of the importance of land in African narratives. Therefore, land belonged to all the members of the community and also to individuals, but not as a commodity that could be owned or sold. It was an inheritance from the ancestors, to be kept and respected.

The Kikuyu religion, like Judaism, has various myths of origins. One of the most common myths, and that which is known by the people, recounts that one day, when mankind was increasing on earth, Ngai (God) called the man *Gikuyu,* the founder of the tribe, and gave him a vast land with ravines, the rivers, the forests and the animals. The land was naturally fertile, lacking nothing that mankind desired on earth. This land was for the man and the woman to rule and till and for their posterity (Ngugi, 1965:2). The most important feature of this land was the big mountain, which God called *Kiri-Nyaga* (Mount Kenya); this mountain would be God's resting place when he came to visit his people. *Gikuyu* was taken to the top of this mountain of mystery so that he could see the beauty of the land that God had given him, similar to the Jewish myth of creation, where God gave Adam the Garden of Eden, with all that the human race could desire (Gen. 1-3). So, when God was dividing the world into territories and giving them to the various races and nations that populate the globe, he gave the Kikuyu people a Garden full of good things of nature (Kenyatta, 1938: 23; cf. Ngugi, 1965:2).

At the heart of the land was a forest of fig trees, and *Gikuyu* was then commanded to go down and establish his homestead on the selected forest spot, which he named *Mukurwe wa*

Nyagathanga (first home-cf. Ngugi, 1965:21); the trees would provide fruits to satisfy the people. The Kikuyu social organisation within the land consists of a strong bond of communal relations governed by a family system of clans named after the mother of the family and age-set affiliations. The land must be reclaimed from those who came and occupied it (colonialists or African elites) either by force or by pretence. The average rainfall in this land ranges between 40-110 inches. This rainwater drains into a considerable number of streams that irrigate the whole land. It is correct to state that there is no valley which is not watered by a river or a stream in Kikuyu land. The sources of these rivers and reservoirs are Mt. Kenya and the Aberdare Ranges: the former with its glacial-snows, and the latter with its forests and steppes, which, like an enormous sponge, retain the moisture through the whole year. The vegetation is most luxuriant and often gigantic, of a stature only found at the Equator. Although the pattern of correlation between the Bible and our culture seems to be everywhere, it is certainly evident in the stories of creation and particularly in promises of land.

A Contrapuntal Reading of Revelation 22:1-5 with a Kikuyu Story of a Garden

We have here the possibility of a conversation between Revelation 22:1-5 and the Kikuyu story of a Garden, which has the aim of creating hope and challenge, in order to motivate people to work towards a future life, or to open themselves to the possibilities of the new world which emerges as a result of Utopias created by these Gardens. It is quite pertinent to analyse the passage (Rev. 22:1-5) and the Kikuyu story contrapuntally in order to expose the dynamic encounter between the two; here we listen to the two texts for their harmony.

The Blessedness of the Garden City (Rev. 22:1-5)

Two important factors surface in this section: the throne of God and the Lamb, not mentioned in the preceding chapters, now dominates the scene. This is comparable to the Kikuyu Mountain, which is the throne of God among the people. The paradise of Eden is also brought in for the first time, with the intention of joining the end of human history with its origin; in other words back to that original Garden of Eden. This is echoed in the Kikuyu belief that God gave the Kikuyu a good land with ravines, rivers, forests, game and all the gifts (cf. Kenyatta 1938:3). This is a blessed garden to the faithful people of God. In the Apocalypse of John, as well as in the Kikuyu story, the garden belongs to *andu a Ngai* (God's people); through the blood of the Lamb they will be inheriting the salvation as is expressed in Revelation 22:1-5.

At the centre of the gardens are the trees of life being watered throughout the year by a river? However, it is clear that those who will not remain faithful will be judged; the whole of the Apocalypse is a challenge to make sure that the believers make right decisions, otherwise their lampstand will be removed (Rev. 2:5). In the Apocalypse, the judgement takes place in the future, as also does the entry into the blessed garden city, but it has finality for us because it determines the quality, the mood and seriousness of our present time, that is to say, it transforms the present moment into a particular kind of *kairos* document or a moment of time (see Nolan, 1987:64). Unbelievers, or those who compromise themselves with Babylon (oppressors of any kind), will automatically be excluded both from the blessed Garden city and the Kikuyu lands on the basis of their compromise.

To the Kikuyu people, the land creates an expression of the need for an attitude concerning the urgency of regaining *Ngai's* blessedness in the present time. They will have to reclaim land which has been taken from them by the rich, when the right time comes; otherwise fighting at the wrong time would mean a total annihilation of the whole tribe (Kenyatta, 1938:43). The Apocalypse community was equally unable to fight back (the Roman rulers were beyond their power); deliverance is through Christ who has overcome death. To the Kikuyu, deliverance comes equally from *Ngai* (even though they will have to fight for it) and domination will be no more in their lands. Then there will be plenty of land for the people, including the cities that are now in those lands. Both John's community and the Kikuyu community will first have to co-exist, and yet not to compromise, with the oppressors; they have to treat them 'with courtesy mingled with suspicion' (1938:43; cf. Rev. 2-3). Both the Garden city and the Kikuyu story express the urgency of the present moment as one is faced with the present reality—hence the need to respond to it urgently. This discovery makes the Kikuyu reader of the Apocalypse more open to see the Garden city as the good life to be expected and which must be achieved.

The remembering and significance of the Garden city and the Kikuyu story are climaxed in the blessedness of John's city in the garden. In both stories fruit production is highlighted and communities will not lack anything in those gardens. To the Kikuyu/African Christians the blessedness of John's Garden city becomes a symbol of that expected good life, when good governance is available in Africa; but when that fails, the risen and glorified Christ becomes to the Christians an alternative kingdom (an inspiration to work for it and wait for it, that means 'to work patiently'), where they partially experience and also wait for the final fulfilment of that blessedness (cf. Mbiti, 1971:60).

Common Elements in this Transaction

The significant transformation brought by the new garden is that God's new world excludes the oppressor, as Satan's present socio-political manifestation (imperialism). While for John's story Rome must be excluded, to the Kikuyu it is the exclusion of the colonial forces from the Kikuyu land that matters. This exclusion is evident in virtually every detail of the Kikuyu understanding of land, as well as in the story of a new garden. It unfolds into a new vision for Africa (see the discussion below of issues emanating from our contrapuntal reading). The new vision of a garden is what we require in order to persist in the struggle for justice and prosperity in our poor Africa. The source of the rivers and trees in both gardens is God; the rivers and trees are also the source of the fulfilment of the needs of people who will live in the land. The water and the vegetation make the land habitable. The land is also a gift to God's people. The new life is emphasised by the description of the vegetation of life (cf. Gen. 2:9; 3:21-22; Rev. 22:2).

The above similarities attract the Kikuyu people to read the Apocalypse afresh, as a result of the light thrown on the Apocalypse by the Kikuyu experience of land. Kenyatta and Ngugi, among others, recall ancient material, just as John recalls the material of the Old Testament to formulate the vision of a Garden city. The Kikuyu people were either suffering persecution or living in fear of it. Kenyatta (1938:47), argues that they were put under the ruthless domination of European imperialism through the insidious trickery of hypocritical treaties. The descending of the Garden city becomes a real comfort to John's community as well as to the Kikuyu who now read it to create their own Utopias.

Revelation 22:1-5 offers new insights in place of the present spiritualised explanations of this Garden city, which at times have proved to be more frightening to the people than offering them the genuine salvation of land which is here and now. Since biblical interpretation and preaching must strive to make sense of the present life situations within the individual's context, contrapuntal reading may be used for the propagation of the gospel among our African people. Such a reading then becomes the pillar of imparting cultural norms and values to the African people, derived from the Apocalypse of John or any other biblical texts.

Discordant Voices within the Transaction

The apocalyptic vision of the Garden city differs from the Kikuyu story of land in that it anticipated a total destruction of the present, while the Kikuyu story of land anticipates a radical transformation of the present, characterised by transposing some future events into the present. The Kikuyu expected the present to endure and, therefore, expected no spectacular change in future. This would then imply that the deliverance expected at the end of the colonial domination of the African lands is a near future, which is not radically different from the present in the sense of what the ruling powers will leave behind. So, while the Kikuyu expectation is for the present world to remain, the Apocalypse's vision of a Garden city is at home with 'apocalyptic eschatology', where a total destruction of the world we live in today, as Babylon, is imminent.

Such a concept is non-existent within the Kikuyu eschatology and this makes the two stories radically different from each other. This radical difference between the two is also expressed in the view of the dead. While in the Apocalyptic vision the dead are brought back to life to enter the garden city, in the Kikuyu view, life continues with the present generation while the dead move into the past.

Issues Emanating from this Transaction

The two kinds of stories have one thing in common: a theology of land. The search for a theology of land for Africans takes place in the context of the historical struggle of our brothers and sisters to wrest back their land from the hands of their colonial guests. We have experienced and even seen tears flowing uncontrolled down the cheeks of our grandparents when they remember the blood of our people that was shed in the defence of ancestral land. So the story of land is a pillar for imparting cultural norms and values both in the Apocalypse and to the Kikuyu. Such a transmission aims at ensuring cultural cohesiveness within the two communities. This is a theme which is highlighted in both stories. Our analysis reveals that both are coherent revelations and offer theological expressions of their own worldviews through the various symbols and metaphors that have been employed in creating the stories. The power of symbols and images in these stories are both a challenge and a hope to their communities.

They contain insights which bear much significance both for the churches in Asia Minor and for the African community setting in which the respective stories of land are narrated. They are both capable of providing reasons for human behaviour and praxis. The commonality, therefore, in these stories provides opportunities to unlock the Apocalypse to African Christians in general. In this concluding section I wish to show how both narratives could function and how they could bear on the social contexts to which they are addressed. They are equally open to different interpretations. As we said earlier, interpretation is an ideological, theological and a philosophical activity determined by the interests, concerns, presuppositions and the traditions of the interpreter. The way John, Kenyatta and Ngugi reconfigured the stories of land gives a clear-cut direction of what they wanted their people to do. They saw the present as the time of God's intervention. Also they regarded the future in these stories as a visible state of affairs. For them, the stories refer to the life of their communities in general or to those whose lives need liberation. This is why we can reclaim the stories in a new dimension following John, Kenyatta and Ngugi, as a response to the oppressive experience in the perspective of active resistance. Reconfiguring both the stories of land will allow different meanings to emerge. A conversation between Revelation 22:1-5 and the Kikuyu story of creation brings out various issues. Such issues show clearly that the stories are rich with insights calling for a biblical theological reflection.

Inspiration as a Way Forward

It is clear from our contrapuntal reading that both narratives are instructions with inspirations that are able to create a desire in people to acquire the land they need for their sustainability. The new idea of land that emerges here is to inspire the people to move forward in our postcolonial African societies, just as John's and the Kikuyu communities required inspiration to survive the challenges of their times. So, while the Kenyan society today cannot escape the influence of the present political system around it, the community must be inspired to fight for their rights, or made aware of the contradiction inherent in that political system. I say contradiction because the Uhuru (independence) Utopia, whose basic doctrine of love and equality inspired people originally, has never been achieved. Hence they need to be encouraged and challenged to move forward. In other words, the present political system in Kenya is still a child of colonisation that needs to be challenged.

God is Ultimate

In both these two stories of land is the fact that God is the ultimate point of reference. We realised that in the Kikuyu way of life, as well as in the Apocalypse community, stories abound with references to *Ngai* as the Almighty being. The Kikuyu concept of God is that *Ngai* is one and provides the needs of the people through the creation of land. Here the Apocalypse acquires a new positioning: it is now approached in openness and its meaning is embraced within the Kikuyu concept of God, and the Kikuyu people see it as speaking to them. The same God, who was the ultimate point of reference in Revelation 22.1-5 and in the Kikuyu narrative, must now also remain our point of reference even as we work out our second liberation, which is a new African ideology. In short, we conclude that the African community, or the Kenyan community for that matter, will continue to rely on *Ngai* to intervene in situations that are still oppressive in their life.

Eschatology as a Concept

We may start by stating that the issue of eschatology is a complex one, and we cannot deal with it in detail in such a short section. We will, therefore, only reflect on it as an issue that has emanated from our contrapuntal reading. Although the Kikuyu people expected an end to the present situation, their concept of eschatology is rather different to that of the Apocalypse community. The Kikuyu people's eschatology is concerned with issues of here and now in particular situations. This implies that the Kikuyu has no concept of universal eschatology. This calls for a paradigm shift from Western thinking of eschatology (in terms of *chronos)* to African thinking of eschatology *(kairos)*. In fact the word eschaton in Kikuyu is *muico,* which does not refer to time as *chronos* but as *kairos* (cf. Nolan 1987:61-69). According to Mbiti (1969: 159), African eschatology in terms of time is a composition of events which have been realised or actualised or are about to be realised in the immediate future, within a generation or two. Mbiti's argument, then, means that African eschatology conceives time as qualitative rather than quantitative. Nolan agrees with this African eschatological understanding of time when he states that 'the eschaton is a future act of God that has finality for us because it determines the quality, the mood and seriousness of our present time, that is to say, it transforms the present moment into a particular kind of kairos' (1987:64).

So, to the Kikuyu, *muico* (eschaton) is indeed one of the constituent elements of their divine time *(ihinda riria riamure)*, because you cannot have *ihinda riria riamure* without an eschaton. The Kikuyu world for the departed is not different, therefore, from the present material world. That world is not better than the present Kikuyu *bururi* (land). They conceive it as the same as the present world with the same day-to-day activities. For that reason, there are no desires and wishes in Kikuyu culture to leave this world and go to the next world to enjoy a better life, as in 'apocalyptic eschatology'. This makes the Kikuyu understanding of escaton *(muico)* radically different from that embodied in the vision of the new garden, where the destruction of anything that opposes God's plan for creation takes place in order for the new world to descend from heaven (burned into ashes 'in the lake of fire' cf. Rev. 21:8). For Mbiti (1969:160), 'if the future becomes remote, for example, some years [hence], then it is hardly thought of or spoken of and has little or no impact upon the people'. This justifies the Kikuyu concept of *muico* of the world as kairos other than chronos.

However Decock (1990:76) argues that the main obstacle with regard to eschatology lies in the fact that the eschaton is understood in a chronological sense as last, coming at the very end of history. The question is, 'Who understands it this way?' It is, of course, people whose concept of time is chronological, but African concept of time is not, so Africans do not have terms like 'the very end of history'. There is no time when African history will come to the very end.

For the Kikuyu, it is the individual who comes to an end through physical death, while their land remains. They have no concept of 'new heaven and new earth'. The Kikuyu world must continue with its days, months, years and festivals uninterrupted. Equally, there is no concept of final judgment, since the Kikuyu cannot lose contact with *Ngai* at any time, where such a thing would result from judgement. In the vision of the new garden such judgement is key, and comes upon the unrepentant at the end of human history, when this world is brought to finality by God and the Lamb (Rev. 21:1-8). In Kikuyu traditions the judgment or condemnation comes in the present life to those who compromise with the oppressor. It is said that Kikuyu liberation fighters killed more of their own, who were thought to have compromised, than they did of those whom they were fighting.

Similarly, if resurrection refers to the state of blessedness and the life of bliss that God shall dispense to the faithful Christians in the hereafter of the Apocalypse (Rev. 22:1-5), then such a notion is not found in the Kikuyu eschatology. The Kikuyu have no element of spiritual redemption or a close contact with *Ngai* in the next world, other than that of being an intermediary. So the idea of another physical life in resurrection is not only unknown to the Kikuyu but also unintelligible (cf. Mbiti, 1969:166). Decock (1990:79), who seems to advocate a universal eschatology, argues that rejecting a chronological sense of eschaton brings with it the danger of absolutising particular eschata, and the particular struggles that go with it. He does not think that seeing the day of liberation, whether from our sins or other circumstances, as final and ultimate is a true way of understanding eschatology. But this is the way eschatology can make sense to Africans. So, since the Kikuyu myths strive to make sense of life in the present context, eschatologies that stress the 'present' may be proper weapons to use in the propagation of the development of a garden that emerges from the contrapuntal reading of John's desire for a new garden and the Kikuyu desire for land. Kikuyu eschatology qualifies to be eschatology because it deals mainly with things taking place at the end of the present domination, giving birth to a realised eschatology. The hereafter is of no hope and promise, quite contrary to 'apocalyptic eschatology', where a new, better world and better social status are promised.

Though different, therefore, both the new garden of Revelation and the Kikuyu myth espouse a kind of eschatology. While John's community anticipates 'apocalyptic eschatology', which, when embraced by the Africans, causes them to interpret the new garden in a literal sense, and expect it to happen in the near, near future in line with the time perspective of African eschatology, the Kikuyu has a different kind of eschatology: that which is actualised or experienced in the 'here and now'. That means the end of things happening at present; things prophesied in the ancient past (myths) will become fulfilled in the present. This also ought to be the Christian understanding of the risen Christ, through whom we have experienced salvation (cf. Mbiti, 1971:42). The Kikuyu people saw themselves as the fulfilment of their myths (cf. Lonsdale, 2003:58). They were in the *muico* period and they had to resist domination and then acquire and continue to develop that which is theirs 'here and now'.

This kind of Kikuyu eschatology calls us to a new emergent vision. We must relate the eschaton *(muico)* to our present situation here and now, so we need to advocate change as a way forward, not only for Kenya but also for Africa in general. This brings the desire to conquer the evil, poverty and corruption that are now dominant in Africa, as a way of achieving the new garden.

In summary, we have engaged in a contrapuntal reading to demonstrate that, although we can study the Bible in the light of the African concept of narratives, there are similarities and dissimilarities between the two. Having brought Revelation 22:1-5 into a conversation with a Kikuyu story that is similar to those found among most Africans, we can conclude that a new understanding of a garden/city has emerged. Both Revelation 22:1-5 and the Kikuyu story can be seen as an effort to demand that, in spite of the oppression against Kikuyu/Christians, they need to remain faithful to their *Ngai* and must not be overcome by Babylon's seduction. In the light of such insights, its implications for modern Christians, especially among the Kenyan community, can be better appreciated by African Church leaders and faithful, contemporary, preachers. The Apocalypse through African stories then gains new meaning to the African community/church of faith. It unfolds as the expected achievement of the new garden, where farming and working will be improved, and sustainable development implemented, and those who will remain persistent both in work and faith will finally be ushered into those new lands (cf. Rev. 22:1-5).

We have observed that both texts uphold a belief in one God. It also became clear that the Kenyan people rediscovered the notion of land easily from their familiar point of lands, once they had an encounter with the garden city introduced by the arrival of the Bible in Kenya. We also noted that since the two stories are different, both in space and time, reading them together needs care. Such differences could feature in the sense that, while destruction is a major theme before the new garden of John descends, in the Kikuyu story destruction of the colonial development is not their aim, but their departure. We also noted that though there are discordant voices between the two stories, such differences couldn't nullify the fact that John's garden/city makes sense to and appeals to African religiosity. So, while the two cannot be the same, the Kikuyu story helps land-minded Kenyan communities to understand the Apocalypse. This means that the African narratives could be a basis for African biblical scholarship in the context of preaching and explaining the book of Revelation among the Kikuyu and Africans in general. The ultimate conclusion of this kind of contrapuntal reading lies in the view that the Apocalypse and the African narratives refer to the expectation of all time that may only partially be realised in the risen Christ, offering utopia that keeps people going. We therefore now need to look at dialogue between the African culture and the Bible in terms of worship and mission.

A Transaction between the African Culture and the Bible

CHAPTER SIX

African Culture and the Bible Transact in Worship and Mission

If it is to make sense, the subject of African worship and the dialogue between African culture and the Bible should be approached from the point of a common understanding of what worship is, in both the African culture and in the Bible. The subject of worship is the centre of theological scholarship in African Christian Theology as well as in African mission and scholarship. Here, African Christian Theology is taken to mean the study of African Christianity and the people who practise it, while African mission and scholarship is taken to mean propagation of Christianity in Africa. In both areas, spirituality is a matter of concern. In African religion, as well as in the Bible, worship and spirituality are enshrined in a belief in the concept of a being whose potency is locked up in objects, other beings or in energy, a force which is immanent in all things; something as intangible and pervasive as 'the other'. It is everywhere, it flows through all things but it draws itself to a node or focus in conspicuous ways. This is what we may mean by Christian mission and scholarship.

The meaning of spirituality in the Bible, particularly in the New Testament, has largely been influenced by the Greek worldview in which the term *pneuma* was used to refer to wind, breath, life, soul, mind, power and spirit. Spirituality is the source of worship. The word 'worship' is derived from the Anglo-Saxon *weorthscipe,* honour. So, in Revelation 1:10, John says, 'I was in the Spirit on the Lord's Day, when I heard behind me a loud voice like a trumpet.' With these various connotations, spirit appears to be a subtle and uncontrollable element of the material world whether in the African way of life or in the Bible. It is the beginning of worship; no worship exists without the Spirit whether in African religion or in African Christianity. Spirit as wind is a component that is physical and can be experienced in our midst, while as breath it has the power to drive human beings to higher grounds of spiritual experience during worship. The constitutive factor of *pneuma* in the Greek understanding is always its subtle and powerful reality in various components. In the Greek material world the character of *pneuma* is never spiritual in the strict sense, as in the New Testament. *Pneuma* is taken as distinct from *nous*. The latter is regarded as a state or an activity of contemplation of things and the former as a dynamic power that nourishes not only for mission but also for worship. While *pneuma* is common to both human beings and animals, *nous* is something peculiar to human beings. The presence of this spirit in human beings may account for the experience of the breath that inspires *(mantikon pneuma);* for Africans this may relate to the ancestors, and their visitation is what inspires for mission and worship.

Africans value life as a gift from the creator; community forms the natural context for experiencing the power of the spirit, and ancestors are the link. The African 'mantra', "I am because we are, and because we are, I think I am", becomes the 'master narrative' for mission in the community. It is expressed within the African spirituality, which has a close affinity with the Bible. The New Testament speaks not only of *pneuma theou* (spirit of God) but also of *pneuma hagion* (gift from God). Holy Spirit is not a concept found in the Greek world, but it is common in the Greek of the New Testament to indicate the different characteristics embodied in *pneuma* as a biblical term. In African terms we talk of good or bad spirits *(ngoma njega na njuru).* So here lies the interface between African spirituality, worship and the Bible.

African Worship: the Corollary of the Bible

My understanding and subsequent investigation into the subject of African spirituality as worship, and the Bible, leads me to conclude that African spirituality is antecedent to, and the corollary of biblical mythology, where we experience Spirit as the power of God for mission and worship. The spiritual world of Africans is densely populated with ancestors, spirits and living dead (Mbiti 1969:75; Loba-Mkole 2005:82). The evidence supporting this ideology is based on historical African concepts of God. The African people believe in *Murungu,* the one whose appearance cannot be described, the Ancient of Days: *Mutura Muoyo*; the God, the great one: *Ngai*; the one who is able to penetrate and to permeate all being: *Mwene Nyaga*; the source of being: *Mumbi,* whose origin is beyond that which African mythology can describe, whose essence is unknown. For Nyamiti (1996:41-47), this essence is expressed in Christ who is our ancestor. So within Christianity the father becomes "exemplar of His divine Son, who is His perfect image in being and activity" (1996:47). God is the creator of all things and the spirits can do both good and bad things to the people and as a result, altars for worship were developed. The spirits are an integral part of the religious heritage for African mission, where people are deeply aware of the spirit world as affecting life experiences for better and for worse (Mugambi 1992:74).

In their spiritual life, the Africans had no structured worship (communal prayers or religious ceremonies) such as morning and evening prayers. So long as all was well, it was taken for granted that the spirits/ancestors were pleased with the general behaviour of the people. In the case of serious illness the ancestors were communicated with through a diviner or a medicine person, and, lest the illness resulted from the bad behaviour of the community, causing offense to God, a sacrifice was offered and the sick person recovered (Kenyatta 1938:239). One of the main aspects of African worship and spirituality was that the people were daily in contact with nature. Thus worship was/is essentially a way of thanksgiving and praise. The thunder and lightning, sun and moon, rain and drought, day and night, were all regarded as direct manifestations of God and his works. More often than not, people would call upon the ancestors to intercede for them in case God was upset and decided to strike them in these manifestations. This is the fundamental basis of African worship as the means for mission.

These are therefore the abiding African concepts of worship and are amazingly biblical. In the Bible, God is Almighty, Most high, Holy and the King of kings (cf. Gen 1-3; Rev 2-3). In African spirituality the understanding of God in these terms predates the arrival of the Bible in Africa. However a number of African people lack such understanding; more often than not they think that the Bible is superior to their own culture. According to Ndung'u (2003:262) this shows a lack of Biblical interpretation, but Africa as a whole is sick, starved, bleeding and a physically-challenged continent. Perhaps Mugambi (2003:8) is right to think that Africa is now, more than ever before, subjected to internal violence and destabilization, and this is more likely to affect African culture than anything else. If this is the case, rethinking African worship as a way forward for mission and reconsidering the way it relates to the Bible is a noble task (an area of scholarship) that we cannot afford to ignore. If our African Christian worship has any basis, then such a basis is to be found within the African culture.

Amazingly, if one reads Luke 1:46-55, one learns that the incarnation took place in a cultural context similar to that of the African understanding of ancestors as a point of connection between the living and the dead. The one who was there before is to be born of woman, and he who was present when all things came into being, and who had spoken to our forefathers (ancestors), comes to live among the people. More than anything else the incarnation of Christ qualifies him to be an ancestor after death and resurrection. The incarnation story is also closely connected to the African way of naming children: amongst the Kikuyu of Kenya, children are named after the grandparents of both sides of the family, e.g. if the first child is a son he is named after the father of the husband, and the second son will be named after the father of the wife; all other children born within that family will be named after relatives from alternate sides. It is believed that the child takes the character or the spirit of grandparents, uncles and aunts. This is an element of African worship and mission: worship in the sense that ancestors are venerated through naming in later generations, and mission in the sense that they continue to live among the people.

African Sacred Groves: a Place of Worship and Mission

In every village *(rugongo),* there was one sacred tree set aside as a place of communal worship of God, where sacrifices were offered to God. Around and within the area of such trees, bushes, shrubs and other smaller fig trees were also allowed to grow alongside, so that the altar was actually a sacred grove (cf. Ngugi 1965:19). It is interesting to note that no branch of any sacred fig tree from such a place of worship, nor any of the surrounding shrubs and bush growth could be cut down, nor were goats or sheep allowed to go near. Any person who desecrated such a place was subject to dire punishment. This had much in common with the old Hebrew idea of an altar.

The Hebrew covenant code was in particular specific about the materials for the construction of altars. The altar was considered as the holiest part in the place of worship. Two materials are mentioned in particular: 'altar of earth and stones' (Ex 20:25). So both to the Africans and to the biblical world, altars were part of worship and mission. In the case of mission, sacrifices were offered on altars for healing of the community in times of drought or famine. Today we offer worship in churches while seeking healing for our communities from God. So here worship is taken to mean expression in corporate gatherings around an altar to adore the creator, and give praise and thanksgiving to God. Worship around an altar may be verbal or silent depending on one's culture

Mythology: a Tool for Mission in African Worship and in the Bible

If Africans take a walk through the Bible, they will not go beyond the first three chapters of Genesis before they receive a command for mission, not only for keeping and tilling the earth (Gen 2:15) but also for a spirituality that is familiar to them. It is an African belief that human beings came from the earth, first as spiritual beings. The Bible (Gen 1 - 3) teaches that human beings were created from the earth, and unto earth they will return. One interesting thing in African mythology is that there is no speculation as to how God went about his business of making people and neither is there speculation on how many days God took over his whole creation. Africans appreciate God's power of creation through the spirit without speculating about how long it may have taken God's Spirit to complete creation. So the African understanding of creation is more scientific than the biblical story. It was just a big bang and people came from the ground and unto the ground they shall return, that is all.

However, in general the African stories of creation are in agreement with the Biblical story of creation, where God's Spirit is referred to in terms of *ruax, neshamah* and *nephesh.* These terms can mean wind, breath, air, life, or spirit with reference to God. They find harmony in the core meaning, like two rhythms played together in a counterpoint. The mythology enables people to understand where they came from and unto whom they will return, but through the spirit. Such myths also help people both in Africa and in the Bible to understand the environment in which they live and their relationship with the rest of creation that belongs to their God.

So, in both stories of creation, there is a divine order and a design beyond human understanding, yet perceivable through the spirit of myths. The phrase *ruax 'elohim* in Genesis 1:2 might be interpreted as involving some manifestation of God, either as wind or spirit. Hence the comprehensive belief that God made human beings from the soil and soil is no more than a part of the earth. The consequences of this counterpoint lead us to conclude that human beings are incurably spiritual, whether they know it or not, and this attribute is expressed in worship. Their understanding of the nature of God's spirit comes from the myths and is practised in worship within sacred groves (altars). Therefore, the belief that things do not just happen but are planned and caused is very strong (cf. Lk 1: 46-55; Gen 1-3). Therefore *ruax* applied to God shows the inner nature of God characterized by incorruptibility and sustaining power (Isaiah 31:3), that we require for mission and scholarship.

African worship and mission, as in the Bible, has various myths of origins. Such myths conclude that one day, when mankind was increasing on earth, God created the people, the respectful founders of their tribes and gave them each a vast country with ravines, the rivers, the forests and the animals. These countries today make up Africa. Such countries were naturally fertile, lacking nothing that mankind desired on earth. Africa was for the man and the woman to rule and till for posterity. For the success of mission and worship in the Bible, altars were regarded as important. These involved religious objects, used either for the construction of the altars, or for burnt offerings. The altar was the exclusive domain of the priests. The Hebrew word for the altar is *mizbeah,* appearing more than a hundred times in the Bible. It comes from the root *zbh* 'to slaughter', 'to sacrifice' meaning that the altar is the place where animal offerings were slain. At the altar liquids are poured out and grains burnt. This is the heart of mission and worship both to the Africans and in the Bible.

Mission as Moral Teaching in Worship

If mission is a way of humanization, then the morality of the Bible and that of African worship have teaching in common, such as the spirit of togetherness, love for others' relatives, neighbours and God, care for parents as well as the elderly (cf. Ex 20). The relationship between family members is enhanced in the teachings (Gal 6:2) and is extended both to the living and to the ancestors (Mt 1:1-16; Heb 11). It is in this context that moral value systems are taught and nurtured by the philosophy of *umundu,* 'you are because I am and because you are I am', which is embraced in the context of African worship systems. If one member misbehaves and annoys the community, he or she attracts the wrath of the ancestors. Discipline is maintained through the values and norms of the society, which determine the way that worship is conducted in a community. To this end, those who have gone before the living are acknowledged as mediums through which faith experience is expressed, particularly through dreams. So for Africans, worship is not limited to Sunday, but is for every moment of life even when one is asleep.

Therefore Africans who become Christians find no contradiction between their acceptance of the new faith, and the continuation of their traditional beliefs (Mugambi 1992:80, 93). African worship is based on spirits being constitutive parts of human beings, or as spiritual beings that live in a different world but interact with people through dreams. Moreover, the phenomenon of spiritual beings is not peculiar to Africa since the Bible also attests to the manifestation of God's Spirit in dreams.

African Dream Culture Expresses Mission and Worship

Therefore, for Africans, dreaming has been seen as part of worship within their religion. Dreaming is a universal human experience; it is an experience of worship that is recognized, in retrospect, to have taken place at night while one was asleep or in a spiritual world. For Ngugi (1998:17) the phenomenon and interpretation of dreams has intrigued human beings from time immemorial. It is assumed that a dream has the same sense (truth) as that of waking thought; it is a real spiritual experience, which in retrospect we acknowledge as a dream world. Some dreams in African spirituality are straightforward while others are rather complicated. Dreams are paramount for mission in biblical life and a common phenomenon in African peoples' spiritual life, as Chinkwita (1993) puts it:

> Many African societies believe that dreams can guide them to their destiny and to a large extent help to shape their cultural relationships with each other. Unfortunately very few of their dreams have been recorded. People have relied on oral tradition as a means of preserving culture. There is a prevalent view among many African societies that dreams occur at a particular time when the gods intend to reveal something, which is unknown to human beings (1993: 55).

In Kenya people are said to have received worship songs through dreams. Among the Tiriki both traditional and Christian hymns have been inspired by dreams or revealed to the musicians in dreams:

> Hymns, both words and tunes, are frequently first inspired by the dreams and visions of members of the congregation (of the Dini ya

Roho); and after review and perhaps modification by the elders, they may be accepted by the congregation at large and become widely sung. The elders also receive visions and insights from dreams, which they, too, must evaluate for Satan's influence.... several women compose hymn melodies from divine insight granted through dreams (Sangree 1966:187,203).

This kind of worship has been experienced through dreams, which have been used to convey messages pertaining to a community's future. It enhances their spiritual experience and an understanding of their God. This calls for a rethinking of our dreams as a way of exploring our worship in our modern society. Although Kenyatta in 1938 was one of the earliest African writers to document dreams as a point of worship for his people, for a particular mission, other African scholars such as Mpier (1992) of Congo has, 60 years later, explained the role of dreams as worship and spiritual manifestation among the *Yansi* of the Congo:

> That dreams occupy a prominent place in the life of the Yansi is evident from a stroll around a village in the early morning, as people are rising from sleep and recounting and discussing the dreams of the night. Prior to some undertaking, such as going on a hunt in the forest or going to the farms, people recall their dreams to assess their chances of success. When someone is ill, their dreams, as well as those of kinsmen, are carefully examined. All of which suggests that dream experiences are for the Yansi as important as, perhaps even in some circumstances more important than, those of waking life (1992:100).

Thirty years after Kenyatta's realisation of the Kikuyu mission through dreams, and thirty years before Mpier, Professor S. K. Kibicho (1968) similarly discovered that the mission of his people needed to be voiced. So he cited a dreamer whose worship experience had made him warn his people of some future events:

The message about the impending doom came to Mugo wa Kibiru while he slept one night. Apparently he had also gone through some mysterious struggle in his sleep because he woke up that morning full of bruises all over his body and he was trembling... unable to speak (1968:24).

So African worship had advanced to prophetic experiences and such prophets communicated through dreams from God, and their voices were loud and clear. During this period dream voices were also recorded from Eastern and Western Africa, thereby affirming African worship according to Professor Sundkler who argues that:

> One misses an important aspect of what is understood as constituting a vocation to the ministry in Africa if the dream is overlooked as a channel of God's call. This is a stage of development. Some have reached a level of intellectual sophistication or of Christian experience in which dream-experience is rejected as a source of guidance. The Bakole revival movement in East Africa is a case in point. Here dreams are frowned upon not only by the leaders but also by ordinary village elders, and this, as far as I can see, is an important indication of the Western influence in this revival (1960:25).

African worship is also rife in West Africa where people have been reported to engage in learning to worship in dreams as Christian 'spiritists'(Turner 1967:122-123). Some churches in Nigeria are reported to have experienced dreams during their services; such may be seen as the climax of their mission. They always gathered to pray and sleep in order to have spiritual experiences to recount and to be interpreted in a special service (Peel 1968:168). In parts of Africa dreams are regarded as of significance in the therapeutic process, such as voices from South Africa among the Western Cape people *(abaNguni)* reveal:

> The experience of dreams in this society constitutes complex forms of healing in which manifold and ingeniously artful ways of embodying wholeness and social justice are integrated. Ithongo dream experience among healers is their whole philosophy of

life, including ideas about causes of illness, intentionality, aesthetic in self-presentation, and moral validity (Guma 1997:13).

For Guma (1997:12) dreams among the *abaNguni* are understood as a meeting of subjective and objective reality. This is the backbone to African worship and mission for healing among Africans. This is the meeting point between the spiritual dimension of reality and the social-material conditions of Nguni existence. Last but not least we have the Anglican canon and pioneer of African theology, Professor John Mbiti from Kenya, who argues that:

> One thing is very clear: dreams are a major dimension of life, which has formed into a dream culture, otherwise they would not be discussed daily, they would not be taken into consideration in decision making, they would not make some people seek God's intervention to stop them from dreaming, nor would they be taken so seriously in health matters (1997:512).

Therefore dreams are undoubtedly the starting point for any discussion of African worship and mission, ranging from those interested in dream discussion 'every morning', to those who have rejected such ideas and no longer care about their spiritual dreams. When the Bible was translated into various African languages, African people were given the opportunity to encounter the Old Testament and the New Testament dreams. These were generally understood to contain images from God, particularly the dreams experienced by kings, priests and apostles; here lies the interface for a dialogue between African worship and biblical mission. There are some 130 references to dreams, and about a hundred references to visions, in the Bible. Dreams and visions are closely related as they are at some level identical spiritual experiences. Such a large number of references in the Bible concerning dreams proved to the Africans that God did certainly communicate with his chosen people through dreams. The translation of the Bible into African languages enabled them to discover prophets like Daniel, Jeremiah and Ezekiel, in particular, who are known for their worship and spiritual experiences in dreams (Dan 7:1; Ezek 1:1; Jer 23:25). Having the Bible in African languages legitimised a dialogue between the biblical dreams and the African dream narratives as means for mission.

It is clear in the Bible, as in African traditional religion, that there is virtually no distinction between a dream and a vision in terms of worship and experience. An interesting phenomenon within the biblical dreams, similar to that of Africans, is that there is always a spiritual encounter with God, an ancestor or an angel. Dreams are of great importance both in the Hebrew and in African worship. African worship and mission for liberation are embedded in dreams. Therefore dreams are a source of belief among the Africans. Such a source of belief is rife with insights calling for a theological dialogue between African worship for mission and the Bible.

Source of African Worship and Mission

The African 'Bible' was in oral form, enshrined within their traditions. They were not able to read and write in modern terms, but they were able to experience God in their own lives. It can, therefore, be postulated that their knowledge of God was based on revelations or on dreams as part of their worship. Such revelations are something very spiritual because they cannot be explained but must unfold to be captured and retold through narrative such as dreams. I believe this is the reason why African worship has no symbols or statues which they claim to be representing God (cf. Acts 7). There was nothing comparable to God; not even a son born of woman could equal God. However, there were many experiences to explain God within their communities.

Through observable historical events, God had revealed God-self in the wonders of creation such as a snow-capped mountain along the equator (Mt. Kenya), or rivers watering every valley. These he desired to be a revelation to humankind. It is within these historical sites that African worship draws its strength. Taken seriously, African worship has absolutely nothing to do with other religions of faith. However, the teachings of the Bible find similarities with African worship, particularly in the Old Testament, as argued above. Africans' worship experience as people is that there must be something beyond creation and beyond our explanation. This can only be the God who is the source of their being. This living power is beyond human comprehension and it transcends and permeates all being.

African worship was able to naturally and easily relate to biblical mythical stories within their own context, once the Bible was brought to them. The creation myth was not problematic as a source for worship activity to the Africans. The essential ingredients were already available within African spirituality for religious practice. In other words these people already worshipped God, they had experienced God in all their ways of life, before the arrival of Christianity in Africa.

Belief in Spirits

The African people believed in spirits as the source of their worship. Some spirits were seen as good and others as bad; this means that worship is also in both dimensions. The natural creation of God was the usual habitation of spirits in Africa. Thus certain trees are considered sacred for being indwelt by the spirits (cf. Ngugi 1965:19). So creation had a spirituality of its own kind, calling for worship. This belief and practice involves a certain power, which draws people's interest towards the spiritual world. Africans made offerings and sacrifices to show respect to the spirits. The spirits had no names and therefore it was rather difficult to know what types of spirits were being worshipped. For this reason there is bad worship as well as good worship. There were several types of spirits; human spirits, animal spirits and nature spirits. The human spirits were dead persons older than ancestors, which included both good and evil spirits *(ngoma njega na njuru).* There were also feminine spirits in Africa and these were known as *ngoma cia aka,* literally 'spirits of women', which would come and cause illnesses and havoc through powerful winds; at times a goat had to be sacrificed to appease them if they were very violent (cf. Kenyatta 1938: 231-241) and this was an expression of African worship. These spirits included the rejected spirits of people who died through cursing and created the spirits who lived in the bushes and would at times riot.

One thing I want to say here that would perhaps attract the wrath of some African scholars is the fact that, in African worship, many Africans could not differentiate between their ancestors and bad spirits.

In fact some of them have no words that can be used to distinguish demons from ancestors. The line between these spirits and the African ancestors is very thin. Therefore, one would not be able to explain explicitly that African worship could not be an act of worshiping the ancestors, particularly when one views some African practices. In other words, in African worship, I do not think that people were bothered so much about the difference between ancestors' spirits and God, when they came to worship. What was important was the sacrifice to be offered or perhaps the encounter with a deity, as a particular mission may have required of them.

Hence African worship as a means for mission is not just individual phenomena, but also social and religious phenomena, very similar to that of the Bible. This worship generates social and spiritual influences (mission) upon the people. The behaviours of the people are influenced by this mission activity either from the Bible or African traditions. Worship does not necessarily distinguish between 'African religion' and 'Christianity'. Rather, it is more the interpretations of worship or images and symbols in it, which may be given different directions labelled either Christian or heathen, and the subsequent actions may be done ostensibly in a Christian way of life by perhaps the missioners who want their worship to be seen to be above that of the others. African people participated wholeheartedly in African worship as a means of mission and women were in the forefront of this mission. We can only reflect on the African women by first looking at the place of women in the ministry of Jesus, particularly in the Gospel of John.

CHAPTER SEVEN

The Place of Women in this Transaction with Reference to John's Gospel

Much has been said about the dramatic changes in thinking and practical ways of living today. A number of thinkers and writers are reflecting upon the new modes or paradigms that are emerging in almost every discipline from sociology and economics to theology and religion. One way of refer-ring to this change is to speak of a 'paradigm shift'. The Gospel of John has recently been read in new ways such as narrative and ethical readings. Robert Karris (1990) has written a short book on the poor and marginal-ized in John's Gospel. No other group within Jewish culture may have been so marginalized as women; small wonder that John finds it appropriate to narrate women's stories at such great length (Jn 4:4-42; 11; 20:1-18). John portrays women as true ministers of the Kingdom, married or unmarried.[1] This chapter is a dialogue and conversation that seeks to reflect upon and express the faith of the women represented in John's gospel as well as that of women in African Christian communities, where they have, more often than not, been regarded as good only for marriage.

---

[1] In order to pursue such a noble course, African women theologians need to be encouraged to establish groups of ordinary women Bible readers in order to participate in oral theology, music, song, story telling and Biblical interpretation within their context, and also in written theologies as a way of encouraging them to come out into the open and into self-realisation.

Marriage was an important rite of passage in the Old Testament as well as in traditional African society. From the cultural perspective it was regarded as a communal concern. However, John does not show a major concern for the issues of marriage and ministry.[2] Professional male theologians who are opposed to the ministry of women usually anchor their arguments concerning women in ministry in the Pauline epistles. For Okure (2001:46), the belief in man's innate superiority and woman's innate inferiority resulted in the exclusion and marginalisation of women in all walks of life. Some of these men hold Paul's restrictions to be normative for today, while others feel that women's relevance is limited because they have been conditioned by tradition and culture to fulfil certain roles.[3] With respect to the Bible, a patriarchal reading restricts the public ministry of women by appealing to texts such as 1 Timothy 2:11-12, 14 and 1 Corinthians 14:34. Those who emphasise such readings forget other texts that do not restrict the ministry of women such as Galatians 3:28, Romans 16:1-3,6,12, and Philippians 4:2-3 all portraying women as active in ministry which includes the rearing of children, as demonstrated by the mother of Jesus, and Timothy's grandmother and mother (2 Tim 1:5). Therefore, as there is so little consensus

---

[2]Cf. Kenyatta (1938:163) who makes a similar observation - that the most important purpose of marriage was not sexual enjoyment but procreation. Hence John's concern was not for status but for participation in ministry.

[3]Showing a concern for the marginalized in the South African social struggle, Albert Nolan's book God in South Africa makes it clear that the time of conjecture is over, the issues are clear and to be a bystander is unacceptable because, as with our prophets' warnings of the past, God has spoken. Now is the time for action. In this regard men can no longer sit and watch women struggle alone for their social liberation.

about women in the Pauline writings, the answer is to turn to the Gospels for guidance.[4]

The debate in this chapter will therefore focus on the Gospel of John to dis-cover Jesus' concern with the ministry of women. It is clear that John is not directly concerned with the subject of women in ministry in his gospel. Nowhere within the Gospel does Jesus explicitly teach about the roles and nature of women (whether they should be married or not as a prerequisite to the ministry). Rather, we reread the Gospel with new eyes, noticing for the first time the contributions of women as recorded by John, who portrays women as active and innovative ministers. Reading with an implicit emphasis on the reality of women within the discourse restores and ensures the rightful place of women as ministers of the Kingdom.[5] Although we only see Jesus' attitude toward women indirectly, as it is revealed in his recorded words and actions, the Johannine Jesus affirms women in roles that were unusual and often unacceptable within that culture (cf. Jn 2:4; 4:21; 19:26; 20:15). Jesus' approach to women was in such contrast to his traditions that we can assume he was demonstrating a deliberately new way of dealing with women. Surely such a move is as valid as explicit teaching.

So I believe that John's story reveals a certain sensitivity towards and a deep honour of women, which is manifested in his selection and portrayal of incidents in Jesus' life. The Johannine Jesus is not

---

[4]Here we can certainly say that African women are the only people who can in the end define and articulate their priorities and experiences with regard to the Gospel of Jesus and to the other aspects of life. In this regard they undoubtedly have a major role to play in mak-ing a real claim to be involved in ministry. In John we do not see Mary, Martha and the Samaritan women being encouraged by male friends to join the ministry, but out of their own endeavours they have positioned themselves for roles of ministry.

[5]Mugambi (1989:27) asserts that the Gospel is understood as the mission of the good news of Jesus Christ to the world. According to the New Testament, mission is understood as 'going out' into the entire world to proclaim the good news of Jesus (Mk 16:15) - by either a man or woman.

presented as seeking to modify the feminine role prevalent within Judaism; rather, Jesus seems to view woman as altogether anthropologically superior and calls them to public ministry. He affirms their humanity right from the womb and throughout the ages, in the face of male opposition. He did so by engaging women in three great conversations.

Women in John

Jesus kept the reality of women in focus in the discourse to ensure a contrast with his culture rather than conformity to it, so that we may be exposed to his revolutionary new attitude towards women.[6] Many times we read the stories of Jesus' encounter with women without realizing the implications of his actions within the context of Jewish traditions and perhaps those of African societies today. However, the accounts would have had a very radical impact on the original readers familiar with the culture Jesus was challenging. It is therefore necessary for us to be familiar with the Jewish attitudes towards women that characterized the cultural milieu in which Jesus proclaimed his message. This helps today's readers to understand the message John intended.

The first-century Israelite culture provides the primary basis for defining women's hermeneutical focus in life as being the bearer of their husband's offspring and as a sexual release for their husband. In the Jewish culture it was enough for men that they had women who were keen on rearing their children and delivered the men themselves from sin through being good sexual partners (Hurley 1981:69). This emphasis on life is, understandably, the special concern of Jewish men although one can be assured that not all men and marriages were characterized by such assumptions. However, the abundance of statements such as these shows that the worth of

---

[6]When dealing with the Gospel and culture we need to consider the way in which Jesus Christ dealt with cultural issues in redemption. Jesus became a human, a man in a culture with a cultural name, who spoke a local language, received cultural education and conformed to the morals of his people (Neibuhr 1951:12).

women was generally defined by their biological function. This valuation of women as bearers and pro-moters of life was part of their mission already present within Jewish culture.

The Jewish people tended to characterize women as lower beings and as sexual temptresses. The Talmud describes a woman as 'a pitcher full of filth with its mouth full of blood, yet all run after her' Swidler 1976: 3). In this view, men's desire for women (lust) was thus considered unavoid-able due to the attractive nature of women; normally contact between men and women was to be avoided. Because women were held responsible for male temptation, they were barred from public life lest they cause a man to lust for them.

Intellectualism and innovativeness on the part of women should not be entertained according to Rabbinic Judaism. They should not be encouraged to study the Torah although this must be a man's highest priority. Rabbi Eliezer said, 'if any man teaches his daughter Torah it is as though he taught her lechery' (Swidler 1976: 93), and 'it is better that the words of the Law be burned, than that they should be given to a woman' (Hurley 1981:72). Due to a woman's lack of intellectual ability, she was also barred from the role of witness. Josephus explains in his *Antiquities,* 'the testimony of women is not accepted as valid because of the light heartedness and brashness of the female sex' (Swidler 1976:115). For this reason we are called to heed Schussler Fiorenza's (1983:45) clarion call for a reconstruction of the history of early Christianity to include women's visibility and contributions.[7] So we reread the teachings of Jesus

---

[7]Yes, reconstruction is what the New Testament interpretation is concerned with. Indeed, the narratives in John about women themselves are the result of reconstruction. The narra-tives have been reconstructed from various manuscripts, a process that is always continuous. The history of women in the ministry must be reconstructed from widely scattered pieces of information and tradition found in several sources including the Gospels. Of course we have to swallow our pride and agree that thick layers of Patriarchal prejudices have obscured many of the women's roles in the ministry, particularly in Africa, which need to be excavated to bring the original contours into focus.

about women with new eyes to notice for the first time Jesus' major concern for them as recorded in the Gospel of John but which patriarchal interpretations have often ignored.

Although Jesus did not precisely spell out his teaching on women, the way he treated women demonstrated his personal attitude towards them. Such an attitude implies that he expected women to assume an equal role with men as equal partners. Jesus' attitude towards women identifies the Bible as God's life-giving and empowering word for all peoples regardless of race, sex, colour and creed. The Gospel of John records the greatest encounters and conversations Jesus ever had with women. Firstly, Jesus engages in a theo-logical discussion with the Samaritan woman to whom he reveals that he is the long awaited Messiah. Secondly, Jesus has a searching talk with Martha concerning the resurrection. Thirdly, Jesus chooses to send the message of his resurrection to his disciples through Mary Magdalene. These three great encounters with women call for our attention and will now be examined.

The Samaritan Woman

In the story of the Samaritan woman, Jesus engages with both social and religious traditions by encouraging discussion with a woman. It was against both his culture and the Samaritan's to do so. Human culture serves, even if unconsciously, as the inevitable filter of and mark of all we do as humans, but Jesus overcomes such cultural barriers (John 4:4-42). While much hermeneutical concern has been paid to this aspect of the story, few have pondered the value of Jesus' conversation with not only a Samaritan, but a Samaritan who was a woman.

Jewish society frowned on the concept of men conversing with women, particularly in public. Conversations were particularly uncommon between Jewish men and Samaritan women, who were perpetually thought to be unclean. For Daube (1950:137), the daughters of the Samaritans are declared menstruants from their cradles by the laws of purity.[8] The Samaritan woman's surprised reaction to being addressed by Jesus is evident (4:9). She questioned his presence there and why he would ask a Samaritan for a drink of water (Sylvia 1984:165). The latter part of the verse may mean 'for Jews have no dealing with Samaritans'. The verb *sugchrontai* alludes to the religious code, which forbade a Jew to eat or drink from a container of an unclean person such as a Samaritan (or a Gentile), and especially of a Samaritan woman who is considered to be a perpetual menstruant. The Samaritan woman's shock is understandable when Jesus requests a drink from her vessel, not only because she was thought unclean but also because Jews did not usually come through Samaria.

When the disciples came back, they could hardly believe what they were seeing: Jesus conversing with a Samaritan woman. From the Greek point of view the disciples' shock was not at the fact that Jesus was talking to 'the woman' but rather to 'a woman'. Schnackenburg (1968: 54) argues that 'the disciples are not taken aback ... to see him disregarding the barriers of race'. They are aware of the restriction imposed on all Jews, and particularly a rabbi, with regard to the female sex. It was the idea of the religious leaders that one does not speak with a woman on the street, not even one's own wife, and certainly not with another woman, in order to avoid gossip (Haenchen, 1984, 1:224).

Jesus convinced the Samaritan woman about the true water of life. Conviction that Jesus could give her water led immediately to her believing in Jesus as Messiah. Just like Peter and other fishermen who, after the call, left their fishing boats, she left her water jar and went to the village to give witness to this great revelation. For a woman to leave her water pot and go to call others to come and witness this revelation is no less a call than that of

---

[8]Ngewa (2003:73) puts a question to us: 'what are the reasons behind the African church leadership's sometimes-negative attitude towards women? Does it originate in the Bible or in African culture? One can easily say that both of them isolate women in a very frustrating way.

other disciples, which involved leaving fishing boats and tax booths.[9] Many responded when they heard Jesus' message and also believed in him. Here we have a version of the standard Gospel formula for responding to the call to apostleship that is relevant for African women, namely to 'leave behind all things'.[10] The cultural and natural bonding of the woman with the Gos-pel of Jesus has a corollary in this basic biblical calling of women into the ministry (Okure 2001:52).

The concluding verses tell of the Samaritan woman's ministry in her village (4:39-42). The importance of her ministry is explained by Jesus to the disciples, 'I sent you to reap what you have not worked for. Others have done the hard work and you have reaped the benefits of their labour' (v. 38). The use of the apostolic language of sending *(apesteila)* by Jesus as he invites the disciples to join the Samaritan woman in the evangelistic ministry which she has already initiated makes it clear that the woman, who is clearly a single mother, is called like any other apostle. Thus, the Samaritan becomes a model for evangelistic and apostolic activity. The Samaritans believed because of her witness *(dia ton logon)* (v. 39). This expression is significant because it recurs in Jesus' ministry. Later that year, 'at the feast of Tabernacles, Jesus urged people to come and drink of him if they thirsted' (Sylvia 1984:166). Jesus said that he who believes in him shall have rivers of living water flow from his belly (Jn 7:37-38). The Samaritan woman's ministry tells us that when we drink Jesus as the living water we will not only satisfy our deepest thirst, but the living water will then flow from us to reveal him to others. As Ngewa (2003:71) puts it, the content of their knowledge changed after drinking the water and they knew that Jesus is truly 'the saviour

---

[9]For Ngewa (2003:73), there is great spiritual potential among the outcasts in our societies who, once they have accepted the Gospel, have the capacity to turn around and improve the spirituality of our societies.

[10]African women have attempted to construct a counter-world to what was asserted in the African culture of their time, sometimes constructing their own new essentialist readings from the oral culture.

of the world'.[11] So through the word *(dia ton logou)* many will come to Christ. John describes the Samaritan woman's work of evangelising that village in precisely the same language as he uses to describe the disciples' ministry. No one can on scholarly grounds dismiss this single mother's calling into the ministry as invalid. The second encounter of Jesus with a woman is that of Martha of Bethany.

Martha of Bethany

This encounter of Jesus and Martha of Bethany highlights the second greatest conversation Jesus had with a woman (John 11). Whilst the most important incident in this story is the raising of Lazarus from death, what John gives prominence to is the conversation between the two sisters and Jesus throughout the story. Their message to Jesus 'Lord, the one you love is sick' (11:3) was not mere information but a request for him to come over and heal Lazarus. Therefore our focus here will not be on the whole passage but rather on the way the author portrays Mary and Martha.

In verse 1 the passage introduces the three characters involved in the miracle. It is of great importance to note that John describes Lazarus in terms of his relationship to Mary and Martha. For John, it appears that both Martha and Mary were more prominent than Lazarus in this narrative. Although we, in the twentieth century, have little to do with the feet of another person, John obviously expects the story of Mary's anointing of Jesus to be of importance to his readers since he refers to it in 11:2 although the event itself comes later (cf. 12:1-8). John names Martha, Mary and Lazarus as objects of Jesus' love in verse 5. The mention of Martha first implies that she was the older sister and the hostess who went out first to meet Jesus. Witherington (1984:108) feels that the mention of the disciple

---

[11]They responded to the woman who had come to invite them by saying, 'we now believe not just because you told us but because of our personal experience'. They said 'we have heard for ourselves, and know' (4:42).

by John implies that Mary and Martha, as well as Lazarus, were disciples of Jesus. This is confirmed by Martha's affirmative answer 'yes Lord, I believe that you are the Christ, who was to come into the world' (11:27b).

Therefore in verse 3 the narrator intentionally calls us to see Mary and Martha as true followers of Jesus. The message they send to Jesus telling him of Lazarus' illness hints that they had faith in him and believed that only Jesus could handle their drastic situation (Witherington 1984:109). This impression is strengthened when we read that Martha got up and ran out to meet Jesus when she heard that he was approaching Bethany and also by the way she tells Jesus that if he had been there her brother would not have died (Sylvia 1984:194). Martha's response in verse 23 to Jesus' assurance that her brother will rise again is a clear indication of her theological awareness, and a portrayal of the belief of Pharisaic Judaism in the resurrection of the dead at the last judgement (Ellis 1984: 186). It is at this point that Jesus shows a paradigm shift from traditional eschatological expectations to a realization that he is the one who fulfils Jewish expectations.

Here we have Jesus using one of his 'I am' sayings to a woman, where Martha responds with a climactic personal confession of Jesus as 'the Christ, the Son of God, who was to come into the world' (Jn ll: 27). This personal confession is similar to that of Simon Peter in Matthew 16:15-19, which has often been associated with his position of leadership. In fact, this great confession of Martha is the closest parallel to Peter's confession found anywhere in the Gospels.

What is involved in providing hospitality, as any woman knows, is that it obviously takes time and preparation to entertain even the most casual guest. The next encounter and conversation is that with Mary Magdalene.

Mary Magdalene

This is no ordinary woman, she has been mentioned on at least nine different occasions in the Gospels, both as a woman from whom Jesus cast out seven demons, as well as the first one to talk with him following his resurrection. So, the goal and apex of John's Gospel is reached in chapter 20:1-18 where we find the ultimate revelation of Jesus' identity as the resurrected Christ, the Son of God, first shown to Mary.

It is interesting to note that Mary's personal relationship with Jesus continued, even after everyone else had given up, when she went to the tomb of Jesus in the early morning hours. Here, after discovering the empty tomb, she shared a moment with him in history that no one else can claim. This is the woman who then runs to tell Peter and the Beloved Disciple. Both Peter and the Beloved Disciple also run to the tomb and only after viewing the empty tomb did the Beloved Disciple believe (v.8), although this is difficult to reconcile with verse nine, 'they still did not understand from Scripture that Jesus had to rise from the dead'. Minear (1968:127) helps us by arguing that the belief of the Beloved Disciple was not in the resurrection of Jesus, but rather that, having seen the evidence, he finally trusted Mary Magdalene's report. Since in the Jewish culture the witness of a woman was not considered credible, it is possible that John wanted to highlight the Beloved Disciple's belief in the report of a woman.

Mary had the unique privilege of meeting and conversing with Jesus between his descent into the lower parts of the earth and his ascent to the Father in Heaven (John 20:17). Upon encountering the resurrected Jesus, Mary, unlike Thomas, did not need to touch Jesus to recognize him; whereas Thomas, even though he had walked with the master for three years, still needed assurance of who Jesus was. Jesus then commissioned her to tell Jesus' brothers the news of his resurrection. Mary becomes the first to announce Jesus the proclaimer as the proclaimed by giving the message of the risen Jesus to the disciples, and the disciples believed Mary's testimony. This is consistent with the Gospel's portrayal of Jesus' appearance to the disciples in verse 20 where no record of surprise or shock on their part is shown. So, what is the cultural and literary context of the conversations of Jesus and the women?

The Cultural and Literary Context

Traditional exegetes have made much of the Samaritan woman's sinful marital situation while neglecting her role as the first person in John's Gospel to whom Jesus clearly revealed himself as Messiah, and as the first missionary calling people to come and see Jesus. The revelation of Jesus Christ to the Samaritan woman is remarkable when one considers that she led a highly irregular life both as a person from a rejected minority group and also as a woman. Jesus did not discriminate against this woman but revealed himself to a person considered unworthy of receiving such a revelation and incapable of understanding it. Jesus was not limited by the Jewish culture of his day but addressed the Samaritan woman as an equal with men and a potential sharer in the kingdom. Culpepper (1983:137) argues that the calling of this woman was a model of female discipleship which Jesus used to modify the proposal that only male disciples were important figures in the founding of the church. The Samaritan got an apostolic role; she immediately went out, calling others in the model of Jesus' calling of the disciples: 'Come and see' (4:29, 1:39), and many believed 'because of her word' (4:39,42; 17:20). While the people who heard the woman refer to her words in verse 42 as *lalia* or 'common talk' (cf. Ngewa 2003:71), John himself refers to the woman's testimony in verse 39 as *logos* or the 'Word'. Here John offers a perspective that is not tied to any traditions, customs or theological hang-up which are uncomfortable with having a woman become a great evangelist or 'minister of the word' (Stagg and Frank 1978: 237). For John the hour is already come for even women in the Jewish cultural setting to be messengers of the Kingdom. From this narrative we can see that Jesus gave the Samaritan woman important theological teaching and engaged in dialogue with her seriously, by responding to her comments. The Johannine Jesus did not require her to stop being a woman, nor did he require her conversion from being a Samaritan to becoming a Jew, but viewed her primarily as a person in need of the revelatory truth of the kingdom of God.

On the other hand, the account of Martha and her family in John 11 is the longest narrative found in the Gospel of John apart from the Passion account. It is also the climactic sign of Jesus' ministry since it immediately precedes the account of his own death and resurrection. The story is paramount in the Fourth Gospel, for it makes a woman the recipient of one of Jesus' most profound revelations about himself, in which a woman responds confessionally to his declaration. According to Ketter (1952:287), the conversation between Jesus and Martha becomes one of the most magnificent revelations of Jesus God ever made to humankind, and Martha gave one of the most unreserved confessions.

John explains to us that Martha is an ideal of discerning faith. Her confession is only comparable with, and perhaps even more satisfactory than, the Petrine confession in John 6:68-69. It is Martha who serves as the Johannine model of discerning and steadfast faith rather than Peter. For a culture which placed little or no value on the word and witness of women, John portrays Martha as an exemplary model of what it means to confess the historical Jesus. Jesus transcends the cultural and the traditional mould of his day and sees Martha as a person capable of a perceptive and discerning faith. Witherington (1984:109) says that the story illustrates the Fourth Evangelist's conviction that women have a right to be taught even the mysteries of the faith and that they are capable of responding in faith with an accurate confession. In other words, they are capable of being fully-fledged disciples of Jesus. For Sylvia (1984:194) the fact that it was in Martha's home that Jesus and his disciples met for dinner just before his triumphal entry into Jerusalem is another confirmation of the kind of respect Martha had attracted from Jesus.

Last and not least is the fact that, in traditional scholarship, priority has been given to the male-oriented tradition of Jesus' resurrection appearances as preserved in 1 Corinthians 15:1-7. Paul says nothing regarding the witness of women to the empty tomb and the resurrection. However the Gospels make their witness prominent and affirm that women were the ones to find the tomb of Jesus empty (cf. Stagg and Frank 1978:144). The resurrection is foundational to New Testament faith (1 Cor. 15:12-19, 1 Thess. 4:14 and Rom. 10:9). The fact that Jesus decided to entrust a woman with the most crucial message of his earthly mission, the message of victory over death, shows how much he respected women. So we can observe that, although Peter and the Beloved Disciple are at the tomb (John 20), they did not encounter Jesus. Rather Jesus was encountered by a woman whom he chose to appoint as his witness, despite the fact that the testimony of a woman was of no account to those within Jewish culture.

It is possible to ascribe to Mary Magdalene a quasi-apostolic role. She should be described as 'the apostle to the apostles' (cf. Brown, 1975:693) since it was she who went, just like the Samaritan woman, to call the disciples. Essential to the apostolate was meeting the risen Jesus face to face and being sent to proclaim him (1 Cor. 9:1-2, 15:8-11 and Gal. 1:11-16). The story in John 20 clearly affirms Mary on both counts. She immediately goes forth to proclaim the message of Jesus to the apostles with a conviction that equals any other apostolic announcement, 'I have seen the Lord' (Brown, 1979:189). Whereas within Jewish culture women were neither rabbis nor were given a position of teaching men, the Gospel of John explains that the risen Christ commissioned a woman to teach his 'male disciples' the most basic tenet of the Christian faith. If we compare Peter and Mary in terms of apostolic experience 'both of them received the first appearance of the glorified Jesus and the foundational apostolic commission' (1979:43). John the Evangelist portrays Mary Magdalene as having a claim to apostleship not unlike Peter and Paul's. She discovered the risen Lord and received from him the commission to go and preach the news of his resurrection just like her male counterparts.

African Women
In the African culture (specifically that of the Kikuyus of Kenya), 'the word of a woman is believed on the morrow'. The connotation of the name given to the first African woman *'Mumbi'* (cf. Eve) was that she would become the mother of all the living (cf. Gen

3:20) and for us this name suggests that from then on the African man, as well as Adam, saw his wife more as the mother of his children than as his partner in a conjugal relationship. The unity of the couple suffered a blow in this understanding of who and what a woman is.

On the other hand, the Bible is a contextual book greatly influenced by people's way of living. The original manuscript, which was written in Hebrew, was a male-centred document. For that reason, starting from Gen 3: 20 through to Revelation its subject matter is largely male. The emphasis all the way through is the bearing of sons and their succession. Eve bore Cain and Abel; Cain married a wife and bore Enoch; to Enoch was born Irad; to Irad Mehujael; to Mehujael, Methushael; to Methushael, Lamech (Gen 4: 17-18). There is no emphasis on where the generation of women who bore these sons came from.

It is only in chapter five that it says, 'Adam lived 800 years and had other sons and daughters' (v. 4b). Women have a minority role in biblical accounts of lineage. Even in land inheritance a father who had daughters could not give them a share but instead had to distribute it to his brothers, as in the case of Zerophahad's daughters. These daughters demanded their right to have a share of their inheritance in order to prevent their father's name from disappearing. This case calls for God's intervention for them to have their share, but it was still only on account of the father having no male child. The story doesn't end there. It is continued in Numbers 36 which gives conditions for daughters who inherit their father's land. They must marry within their tribe so that the inheritance is not given to another tribe. They were forced to marry their cousins to safeguard family property. The Lord spoke to Moses and gave this order to the children of Israelites. This rule continues to heighten gender inequality in our society even to this day. In the African setting, family property was also normally handed down through sons, with special provision for the eldest son. The absence of a son as a male heir is seen as a serious disadvantage (Mbiti 1969:110).

Although African culture portrays women as instruments of creation, meaning that their most important role is procreation (Kenyatta 1938:163),[12] if we reflect on the role African women play in imparting living faith as they bring up their children, we are bound to compare them with the women of John's Gospel. As Okure (2001:44) points out, African women's unwritten theological contributions did not start today. We can mention a number of African women who were as much committed to the Gospel of Christ as these women in John's Gospel. Monica made unrelenting maternal prayer for Augustine, so Augustine without Monica is inconceivable. Another group of African women who cannot be forgotten are those wives of the pastors and catechists in the first missionary era in Africa. They were also like the women disciples of the Johannine Jesus. They spent themselves in supporting the missionary pastors, the catechists and their husbands; in teaching children (both their own and those of neighbours); in counselling other women and men; and in building up their faith. African women were also strong in leadership as evidenced by the Gikuyu woman chief called Wangu. She was the chief of Weithaga location of Murang'a District. She had been imposed as Chief by Chief Karuri in 1903 and was highly commended for her authority and dignity by the missionaries who came into contact with her (Cavicchi 1977:112)[13]

We have to say here that the task of remembering these African women and their faith, as John did for those women mentioned in his Gospel, has yet to be undertaken (cf. Oduyoye 1986). This should be our concern and should feature more prominently in the discourse on African theological biblical renaissance. It is as a result of such

---

[12]Cf. Mbiti 1969:110, who explains that a woman without a child in the African context was not accorded any dignity: 'her failure to bear children is worse than committing genocide. She has become the dead end of human life'.

[13]Cf. Kabira and Nzioki 1993:4-12, who strongly argue that the African belief that women must be seen as lacking in leadership qualities such as wisdom, command of respect and impartiality needs to be discarded.

an understanding that we undertook to explore the Johannine women as a way of trying to locate African women in such a discourse. So, together with women of the past and with those mentioned in the Gospel of John, one must remember also 'the contemporary African women, ever increasing in number, who are founders of churches (especially the Pentecostal and spirit type churches, dotted all over Africa), and the women leaders of prayer ministries and charismatic movements within established churches' (Okure 2001:44). This is only possible when we consider the fact that Jesus met people where they were, whether men or women, and perfected his image in them (Hunter 1978:27).

Alongside these women involved with various ministries stand those who are not professionally engaged in religious ministries; the many who are faith-filled in the rural areas and who are what West (1999) would perhaps call ordinary women, such as wives in patriarchal and polygamous traditions. These women work for a daily living for themselves and their families, yet they are full of hope. Theologically, such women have biblical convictions that govern their lives and those of their families on a daily basis. They regularly spend time drilling their children for the purposes of the gospel and socializing them into church and society. Many times they form pious groups to support one another or to help them to try and find a place in the church. Our greatest evangelists, these so-called ordinary women, are an untapped resource that can be reached through contextual Bible study. They are the closest to the grassroots. They see themselves in the lens of the scriptures and respect them as God's binding word, although sometimes too literally, and in ways that oppress rather than liberate them. So the stories of the African woman and the Bible cannot fit in any book, but in our minds, culture and traditions we must always appreciate them.

Therefore, African culture, like the Jewish culture, provides the primary basis for women's hermeneutical focus on life. Africans value life as the highest good and society forms the natural context for experiencing this good. 'I am because we are, and because we are, I am' becomes the mantra of the African World View (Okure

2001:44). In many African proverbs, myths and narratives, the woman features prominently in the births of nations and in their victories over enemies that threaten their destruction. Such valuation of women as bearers and promoters of life is part of the gospel that was already present in Africa before the arrival of Christianity. Women of this nature were evangelists of God in our traditional setting, proclaiming good news for their people. So even today, the average African woman, like the women in John, spends most of her time looking after the children, preparing, cooking and serving the community. The stories of both the Johannine women and those of African women need to be remembered as an integral part of life, especially in traditional settings where vital information was, and still is, passed on orally.

Reflections on Women in John and in the African Context

It is through John's portrayal of Jesus relating to women that we come to appreciate women in ministry. Here we are able to encounter Jesus' and the Evangelist's attitude towards women. Both African and Jewish cultures assume all women have similar characteristics and tendencies, and have set rules designed only for them. However, the Johannine Jesus treats them as unique and valuable individuals. Jesus does not have room for those who flatter women, but rather he places women in the same position as he does men. Therefore, John's approach to women is revolutionary considering the cultural norms during the time of Jesus. In the African concept of humanity God does not give the man the right of government, separate from the female, nor does he give to either of them the right to ownership, exploitation, or absolute and autonomous rule. In the African context both are stewards of God, they are to be conservators and trustees in the stewardship of God's bountiful creation (Shorter 1995:172).

Apart from a few women such as Mary the Mother of Jesus and Mary the wife of Cleopas, no woman in John is described in relation to men. Interestingly, John does exactly the opposite as he narrates the terms of the relationship between Lazarus and his sisters. So, rather than viewing women in terms of their common roles: wife, mother, cook, and server, as is common within African culture, the Johannine Jesus portrays them as persons capable of handling important tasks. Jesus views women, even today, not in terms of their sex or marital status, but in terms of their relationship to God.

Unlike pastors of today who avoid the company of women for fear of scandal, Jesus associated freely with women. He worked closely with women not related to him, like Mary and Martha, and even held an extended private conversation with a Samaritan woman of ill-repute. Jesus, unlike the Pharisees, does not blame women for male lust, but proves that it is men's responsibility to discipline their thoughts and feelings rather than denying women access to public life and ministry.

One of the most radical actions of Jesus towards women is his willingness to teach them. While rabbinical traditions considered it inappropriate to engage women in intellectual instruction, Jesus goes ahead and personally offers women instruction. For Jesus, women are capable of learning and understanding the theological truths of the Gospel and are capable of en-gaging in any theological debate. Jesus is not afraid to risk public scandal for the sake of teaching women. It is from such boldness that John further affirms women in their intellectual capacity as valid witnesses of the truth about Jesus, particularly that of the resurrection. Therefore, through the witness of the Samaritan woman, Jesus is revealed to the people of Sychar. More concretely, it is a woman of Mary Magdalene's reputation who is entrusted with the truth of Jesus' resurrection and instructed by the risen Christ to be a witness of that truth to the disciples.

In conclusion, we can argue that John in his Gospel presents women in a positive light and recounts their intimate relationships with Jesus. On the other hand, we can find numerous examples among the men who followed Jesus of individuals' lack of comprehension of women's re-lationship to God (cf. Thomas in John 14). This makes John's accounts of Jesus' encounters with women all the more amazing. Women in this Gospel are positively portrayed for comprehending the teaching of Jesus as well as for responding in an enthusiastic and appropriate manner. The Johannine women are bold to take the initiative in their relationship with Jesus; something our African women can learn from. So John presents Jesus as affirming these women in their unconventional roles. Hence we can conclusively put it this way: if leadership is a function of creative initiation and decisive action, both African women and the Johannine women qualify well for the role. Jesus pays no attention to the Jewish traditional views on women and I am sure he would not bother with the African worldview on women either. Rather he enters into theological dialogue with women, calls them into public ministry to reveal his revelation and values, and chooses them to be witnesses to the truth of his resurrection.

Jesus and African Women Today

This contextual use of the term 'Johannine Jesus and Women' also needs to be analysed within our own context if we are to do theology as a reflection upon the African experience. In the light of this investigation of the way Jesus related to women in John, it is appropriate to ask what relevance this study has to our African contemporary situation. Although the Johannine Jesus does not show direct interest in the subject of women in the ministry, his teaching, words and actions imply several principles that governed his relations with women.

First, he held them to be people. He did not view women in terms of sexual temptation or sexual gratification, as many men would do. He neither avoided nor pandered to them. He did not single them out as women by creating new categories or rules for them, but rather approached them as responsible and capable individuals within the community.

Second, Jesus viewed women beyond their culturally-defined roles. He never assessed their value in terms of their role in marriage or in child-bearing, but viewed them in relationship to his ministry. Jesus took the initiative to redeem humankind by coming among the people as a human being (Bate 2000:38). The Gospel message was that of the reign of God, which was exemplified in the ministry of Jesus not only to men but also to women. The ministry of the early church that was motivated by the 'Great commission' of Jesus Christ was for all (Mk 16:15).

Third, Jesus encouraged women to be active in the ministry to the best of their ability. For that reason he never specified certain areas of ministry for women and other areas of ministry for men. Rather he affirmed them as they took initiative in the exercise of their particular ministerial gifts. For Hunter (1978:27), Jesus met people where they were and perfected his image in them regardless of their gender status. So the arrival of the Gospel in the African continent must affect our cultural practices; it must be like the Good Samaritan who came to where the wounded, oppressed man was. A bearer of Christ's healing must meet African women where they are. The more the African church knows about the condition of women, the better able it will be to serve and involve them in the ministry.

Fourth, Jesus' approach to women highlights the norm of equality in the kingdom of Christ. He was willing to sacrifice his cultural norms in order to remain true to the kingdom vision of allowing all to participate. Here I would echo the sentiments of Van Engen (1996:11) that, in order for the church to be able to communicate the Gospel meaningfully, and serve effectively as God's prophetic agent by calling for conversion and transformation of people, societies and cultures, it must know the social and historic contexts in which it lives and ministers. It is through such an understanding that a paradigm shift can bring unexpected surprises and radical social, economic, physical and structural changes.

In Africa today the question remains: how can Africans live out the principles Jesus models for them in the Gospel of John? We live in a patriarchal community, which is somehow different from that of Jesus. Or is it really that different? Is it possible for us to allow women in the church to be individuals as well as women in an African context? Should the church avoid ordaining women for pastoral duties because of the sexual temptation they may represent to the male clergy? The right thing to pursue is to call upon our male staff to be responsible for their own sexual desires. Therefore we in the church must henceforth assess the value of women only in terms of their ability to function within the role of ministry, rather than in the role of wife and mother. The church should no longer focus in its teaching to women's groups only on their roles as wives and mothers, but also proclaim how they can participate in ministry; while at the same time put much greater emphasis on instructing men about their roles as husbands and fathers. We must then immediately allow women to serve to the best of their ability and avoid the African assumption that all women are inclined to a domestic bent, an artistic eye and a 'way with kids'. In this regard we require a quick admission into theological institutions of women who exhibit special theological insight or have the gift of preaching. The church needs to equally affirm all women as they take initiative in exercising their spiritual gifts. Without any limitation by our church subculture, we need to appeal to the kingdom norm of equality in Christ. This last suggestion requires further clarification before we can begin to adopt it.

In summary, we have to note that Jesus was not afraid to defy cultural prohibitions when it came to relating to women. However he did not completely overstep his cultural norms in implementing his kingdom vision. As much as the Gospel writers present testimonials of Jesus having women followers, the fact remains that Jesus did not allow women to be part of his special squad of twelve disciples. Nevertheless, this does not imply that women are forever barred from leadership roles within the church. Here I see Geddert's suggestion that Jesus was part and parcel of his real world, as he prepared the soil for the full implementation of his kingdom vision, as meaning that he avoided instituting all the radical changes that the implementation of that vision would entail (Geddert 1989: 12). Perhaps Paul's words in Galatians 3:28 are fitting here: 'There is neither Jew nor Greek, slave nor free, male nor female, for you are all one in Christ Jesus.' The death of Christ on the cross brought with it equality for Jew and Gentile, but only with time and with extreme struggle and sacrifice on the African church's part can this part of the vision be realized. Perhaps the African proverb 'a child is a child no matter the gender' is in line with the Pauline teaching 'there is neither Jew nor Greek'.

The problem in our African church today is that of implementing Paul's understanding of the kingdom vision in Christ: 'there is neither male nor female'. The question is: has the time come in Africa for us to allow Paul's thinking to become a reality within our present context? The answer is simple. We can no longer refrain due to cultural considerations, because women in leadership have become acceptable in almost every sphere of our African society except in the church, and here I mean top leadership of mainline churches. Is it possible that we have created our own church subculture that renders us incapable of implementing Pauline understanding of the kingdom vision? I think it is time for the African church to free itself from self-imposed bondage and allow the vision of Jesus to break through to the reality in all its fullness.   The African church has to borrow from the model of Christ given in John and apply it to its situation. However, any discussion of women in Africa, particularly with regard to family life, is incomplete if the issue of dowry is not addressed.

A Transaction between the African Culture and the Bible

CHAPTER EIGHT

Dowry: African or Christian?
Another Inter-Religious Transaction

A hot issue in African Christianity today is how, as Christians, to deal with the whole issue of dowries. Many Christians have not properly understood the reason why one should or should not pay dowry; some see it as buying or selling a woman to a man. Such a misconception is the main reason as to why quite a number of Christians feel they do not need to negotiate or give a dowry to potential in-laws. The topic of gender equity is becoming a common phenomenon in Africa and activists of the same are now seriously questioning the morality of giving a dowry to the girl's parents. In this book a response to such questioning regarding the true meaning of dowry in an African setting will be addressed. Theologians, scholars or civil society who argue against dowry/bride wealth or bride price have erred not only in their arguments concerning dowry but also in their own understanding of the real meaning of dowry within their African society. Such groupings have other interests apart from marriage, so they fail to understand what they mean by a Christian or a gender context in opposing dowry since they often fail to define what they mean by the term. If they engage with the subject of dowry as part of culture they should be able to follow the sense of it. Such an engagement will emphasize the culture of the people, making it the primary factor in the method of doing African Christian Theology. The many views aired within Christian circles are from a Western orientation and engage with

African experience only as an afterthought. So, those who oppose dowry do so either as a result of frustration with their marriages or because of failure to have enough to give. This kind of frustration causes fatigue and, as a result, many Africans have mistaken Christianity as a way of abandoning their culture, rather than letting their own culture dialogue with the Bible culture for an ultimate purpose of enhancing Christianity. Hence a new way of transacting with the Bible in Africa becomes necessary (Waweru 2007:23).

In traditional African marriage customs, Africans establish a close link between families through the interchange of visits and gifts popularly known as dowry negotiations and payments. For Africans, marriage is core in life; it is through marriage that the genealogy of a people grows and therefore they are expected to practice it, in order for a particular community to continue thriving. There are regulations that need to be followed as people continue to marry and be married. It is these regulations that many activists are opposed to. This approach has to a very large degree handicapped the development of African Christian theology and spirituality. In John's Gospel (1:1-4) the incarnation is fulfilled in the Jewish cultural context. As a lecturer of the cultural World of the Bible, I can affirm that African dowry is unique and it is here to stay. In any case the so-called committed Christians in Africa practise it more than ever before. The language, thought form, traditions and cultures which inform human values are embraced in the whole exercise of receiving/ paying of dowry. This culture of receiving or paying of dowry is the license of owning a family within the African institution of marriage (Mbiti 1991:104-115).

While the critics of dowry think that marriage in an African setting involves transmission of property in the form of bride price or bride wealth, in a real sense marriage involves two persons and two families with dowry or without dowry. Dowry is not the first step in the African marriage; the first step is the visit and negotiations that culminate in a bond which then results in the giving or receiving of tokens from either side. In other words, dowry helps in developing the bond without which marriage will not be properly initiated. In fact, the family of the bride spends more wealth during negotiations in the first stages of marriage preparation than the bridegroom's side. Only at the signing of the bond may the bridegroom's side be expected to give more. The definition of dowry in the *Oxford Advanced Learners Dictionary* (2005:442) is completely contrary to African culture. It defines dowry as 'money or property that in some societies a wife or her family must pay to her husband when they get married' or vice versa. In the Kikuyu culture *Ruracio* (dowry) is an exchange of gifts between two families and it is a continuous process that may remain up to the point of death and it may even involve many other families. For example, the property my paternal grandparents received when a daughter of theirs got married was directly passed over to my mother's parents. In this case my father's parents did not use that property but used it to create a new bond with another family. In short the Kikuyu people believe that for a man to get a wife what is needed is only a *Mwati* (a female sheep that has not sired) and a *harika* (a young female goat that has not sired), so the dowry is standardized in Kikuyu culture. Therefore a dowry is a fellowship that should be used by Christians to enhance their relationships with others.

Is African Marriage Real Without Dowry?

In Africa, marriage is looked upon as a sacred duty, which every person must perform. Failure to do so means discontinuing generational growth and hence the diminishing of the community concerned. Such continuity of a race is made possible through dowry. My thinking and subsequent investigation on the subject of dowry within African culture and Christian religious practice has led me to conclude that African marriage is antecedent to, and the corollary of, a biblical understanding of marriage. The supporting argument is based on the historical factors which point to the experience of the African people as people who practise marriage. God initiated marriage in the Garden of Eden, and Genesis clearly says it is not good for man or woman to be alone (Gen. 2:18). So, what is marriage whether in African culture or in Christianity? It is a legal union between a man and a woman as husband and wife. It is also a ceremony at which a couple is married (Mbiti 1991:106). It brings two people into a very close relationship, but this closeness is a clarion call for both to live in harmony and happiness. This kind of happiness does not come naturally; it must be worked out by creating a bond between the families of both sides and also with God's help. Unhappiness in married life causes other troubles in the family and the children are the worst affected. Without any doubt I can state that marriage can be the most happy and satisfying relationship, but it can also be the most miserable relationship between two people. This has made divorce the best option for many.

Marriage is an important rite of passage in African society. It is a matter of communal concern. Therefore it was never an individual affair but one for the whole community (cf. Oduyoye 1997:112). It was always planned and arranged by the elderly people of the society through various negotiations. Marriage is therefore the union, by intention, of a man and woman for the purposes of procreation and rearing of children and mutual companionship and assistance. Hastings (1973:27-28) argues that children were the most important result in marriage, rather than the inter-parental relationship. This is true in any African marriage. In fact, Kenyatta (1938:163) argues that sexual relations were only important for the purposes of procreation. The larger the family of a man, the more prestigious he was. A woman was equally respected if she had borne children in her family. The children in a family played different roles. Boys were the future heirs in their families while girls were the future stewards of their future families. And only a dowry could seal their relationships in future. The word *Kugura,* which has been translated literally as buying, means to exchange one good thing with another. Slave trading was never practised within Kikuyu culture, therefore you could not exchange human beings with property. But during marriage, gifts exchanged hands, not because of buying and selling of the woman but to establish a relationship. That is why the word *kuhikania* (marrying) is more commonly used for marriage, which means two persons being joined together in a ceremony.

In some African cultures, parents are the ones who choose marriage partners for their children after birth. This makes marriage a community affair rather than an individual affair. In other cultures the young men and women make the choice as they interact with each other in their respective societies. However, no matter who makes the choice, both families must gather around a table to negotiate and perhaps exchange gifts at various meetings. So, in Africa, marriage cannot be called a marriage unless the whole community is involved. When such a community is involved, there is eating and drinking and therefore gifts must exchange hands. Such gifts have obviously been labelled as bride wealth, bride price, dowry or even worse: some use derogatory terms such as buying a wife.

So, one may ask, what was the importance of the dowry and how did it affect the social, economic and political life of the people? It is in this that I think many people have misunderstood the issue of dowry.

Dowry: a Tool for Relationship

Marriage as found in the African tradition and marriage as found in biblical stories have factors in common such as respect for creation and continuity of life in a given community. The role of marriage, as I indicated earlier, is a communal activity rather than an individual one; therefore it is very critical in the social formation of a community and particularly for the unborn, the living and the living dead. It is in this context that marriage creates a strong bond between the two negotiating families and the clans of both the boy's side and the girl's. Therefore the issue of bride wealth in many African societies is understood as a way in which not only the couple is joined together but the two families are joined together. It is the obligation of the man's family to give and the girl's family to receive; the gift serves as capital for setting up the new wife's household. So, one must understand that the bride wealth goes to the new family rather than to the old families. Although it was given to the father or the brother of the girl, she is to receive that which came from the other family where the sisters of her husband got married. So it is a circular process, where property rotates within the clan. Hence the bride wealth from one family is used as a gift to the family of a wife, for the father or for the brother (Goody and Tambiah 1973:61).

Among the Kikuyu people, *ruracio* (bride wealth) was never given in full, the reason being that it was supposed to help in creating a long-lasting relationship between the two families. In this case bride wealth legitimized the children born in that marriage. The bride wealth in the Kikuyu community varied from one clan to the other (but the young goat and sheep were compulsory). It ranged between thirty and a hundred goats or sheep. The bride wealth also indicated the respect of one's family towards the other, hence the relationship.

The Meaning of Dowry

Marriage is a religious practice within African culture. Here religion is nothing more than human beings' spontaneous awareness and response to a living power, 'wholly other' and infinitely greater than him/herself or any other creation: a power mysterious because, although unseen, it is a present and urgent reality. To an African, this mysterious power was, is and shall always be present in all that they do. So the exchange of valuable gifts in marriage was and is a religious practice in itself, a sign of agreement, which boosts community pride. It is a way of initiating the new wife into the lineage of the husband's clan.

According to Canon Gideon Njuguna Numa, a strong Christian in the Kenyan Anglican Church and a senior Kikuyu elder, 'it is perfectly clear that to the Kikuyu mind, the word *kuuracia* (to give dowry) had nothing to do with buying and selling as such, but signified the making of certain payments for definite purposes other than the mere enrichment of the family of the girl who was to be married. The chief aim is to make the contract legally binding; the second, to make the children of that marriage legal members of the family which gave the *ruuracio;* and the third, to stabilize the marriage. It is best,' he argues, 'to translate the word *ruuracio* as 'marriage insurance', for above all else it acts as a guarantee of good faith on the part of the contracting parties'. So anybody who gives another view of dowry may have misconceptions. For Mbiti (1991:108), marriage gifts are outward symbols of a serious undertaking by the families concerned. For a covenant to be binding, vows have to be exchanged, and symbols are necessary as a reminder to those who have been bonded together.

Therefore, bride wealth is sacred and gives the woman freedom to even remarry within the same clan upon the death of her husband. Bride wealth, as Kirwen (1997:10-13) argues, is an indication that the children born within a marriage belong to the father's lineage (cf Matt l:lff; I want to believe that gifts also exchanged hands for this lineage). Bride wealth is not a source of wealth to the family as generally thought by many critics. It is only a gift of appreciation from one family to another and then to another. It is not intended to remain with a particular family. This would only happen if a man has only daughters. In such a case, a man would be requested to marry another wife who could bear sons so that the bride wealth could keep on rotating. This was a major cause of polygamous marriage.

Therefore, exchange of bride wealth is clear evidence that the woman has moved to another clan in a religious manner. She can then become the steward of the property of that family. For Mwaura (1996:253-269) women are in charge of all food supplies for their families, which includes storage and marketing. The ability to manage the economy gains them much prestige, as Kenyatta (1938:63) puts it. So contrary to the belief that a woman is bought, she religiously receives the right to establish a new homestead, which will eventually become a clan under her name, in the case of Kikuyu society. So bride wealth becomes a token of love from one family to the other and the ancestors are always invited to witness such an exchange. No single marriage in African understanding is legally binding without the slaughter of a goat or a sheep to be shared between the two families.

Both Receiving and Giving Dowry are Signs of Friendship

There is no doubt that African traditional religious practice has been exploited and deliberately misconstrued so as to promote the Western religious practice of marriage. The missionary experience was that Africans were firmly rooted in their traditional ways of marriage. Therefore, if they were to promote their system of marriage in Africa they had to undermine local experience and push the Western system, which is based on individual ethics such as the emphasis on celibacy being superior to marriage. This was one of the significant departures of Christianity from African traditional religious practice. In reality, missionaries did not have to do this by shunning bride wealth. They should have looked at parallels in these religious practices, using the common ground as a foundation for a more constructive approach to evangelism.

Instead, we find that the methods used were harsh and, to some extent, brutal. Thus, many Africans have sought to maintain their traditional ways of religious practices. This has been best expressed in the receiving and giving of the bride wealth. Despite what a number of feminists and neocolonialists have thought, Africans did not buy or sell women as I have argued above, but insisted on showing them the reverence which they had for them before marriage. Therefore, what the Western missionaries interpreted as buying or selling was to the African religion no more than the passing on of gifts from one clan to the other as part of a sacred rite of passage. In some cases bride wealth would be passed over to another family on the same day it arrived in one family. If a girl was married and her brother was marrying, the bride wealth would move immediately to the other family.

The consequences of receiving and giving bride wealth are evident in African settings. The bride wealth gives status to both the husband and the wife and dictates the place of each in the home. While the man would appear to be in charge, in a bona fide sense the woman is the real steward. Kikuyu families are both matriarchal and patriarchal, which implies that both man and woman have their roles to play in a marriage. Therefore, bride wealth is not replacing the girl, as Nthambua (1987:104) observes, but is creating a fellowship between two clans. However, as Kirwen (1997:10-15) notes, bride wealth legitimizes the children born in a marriage to the lineage of the father. This makes bride wealth very important to any African marriage. So, failure to give bride wealth will affect a whole generation of an African society. Such a generation will require redeeming in the future through an African system whereby the wife will be expected to give what her husband failed to give.

Dowry is not a source of wealth to the girl's father as many people assume, because in the African setting the poor would marry from the poor and the rich from the rich, though not as a requirement *(muiritu muthaka ahitukagira thome wangia).* This seems to be the tradition even in our contemporary societies. But, in one way or another, bride wealth may help the girl's parents to cover some expenses that they incurred while bringing her up (Vicchi 1997:60); this is a general assumption. Therefore, this is a gift of appreciation to her parents. It also acts as compensation to her kin for the children she is expected to bear and who will reinforce the husband's group (Price, Thomas 1954 :5).

Bride wealth was and is clear evidence that the wife is a complete member of the family she has joined. From henceforth she is treated as such. Bride wealth is the token offered to her parents who will forever miss her. This empowers the woman to be the steward in her new setting.

It is important to note that the parents of the man who is getting married are also busy arranging the preliminaries for the ceremony. Canon Numa says that the first stage of this ceremony is purely religious and consisted of making a sacrifice to God and also communing with the ancestors for blessings. The young man's father orders a small quantity of beer to be brewed on a given day, and in the afternoon of that day he takes a small ram or a small he-goat (which had not also sired, separate from the one mentioned above for a young woman), which is slaughtered in the courtyard in front of the hut of the mother of the young man who is going to get married. The goat is to be strangled and the father of the young man comes and pierces the chest for blood to spill out on the ground. The blood is collected in a small gourd and, holding it, the father prays to Ngai (God) so that his son's wife will become a blessing to the family. So the whole process of marriage is a complete religious practice that cannot be reduced to the issue of bride wealth.

The Implications of Failing to Give or to Receive

The failure of any man or woman to give bride wealth has far-reaching effects for the married couple. The family lacks moral authority to receive future bride wealth from their children. The main purpose of marriage is procreation rather than sexual gratification as we said earlier. It is through children that the lineage of a family is kept going even long after the death of the parents. For this reason many children have a myraid of problems if the system of dowry was confused within the Kikuyu system of marriage. Thus bride wealth in several African communities is held to be a child-price rather than a wife price. It is to be exchanged with the parents of the girl as she moves to the groom's home. In this case the bride wealth empowers the children to inherit from their fathers' family even if the mother goes back to her original parents (cf. Thomas Price 1956:15, 19). Due to the special importance attached to children, any childless marriage is seen as a bad omen. In such a case a man is to marry another wife but the first wife remains as an administrator in that home. Today such couples opt for adoption.

Barrenness is therefore not accepted; one is thought to have contravened the traditional laws. As Mbiti (1969:110) states, a wife's failure to bear children is worse than committing genocide. She has become the dead end of human life, since no bride wealth will exchange hands. Lack of such bride wealth means that no new friendships between clans will be initiated. This affects the family continuity. In such a marriage a man has to remarry and give bride wealth to another family so that his family will continue. So, bride wealth is not a simple affair in an African marriage, it is paramount. The idea of bride wealth therefore ties both woman and man to their respective families in case one dies. It also legitimized remarriage of the woman within the clan, to one of her husband's next of kin. Such a marriage helps the woman to get emotional and economic support from her husband's next of kin. It is good to note that widows of an African marriage have always been taken care of, unlike in contemporary societies where they are left alone.

It is interesting to note that even some churches have tended to discriminate against widows. In fact, in the Anglican Church, a young window who was not married in the church before the death of her husband is most miserable in that she cannot even become a full member of the Mother's Union for a number of years. So, bride wealth remains the only comfort so that no one can shake her from that family. In other words, it has legitimized her. So does bride wealth then violate Christian principles? It is failure to give bride wealth that violates the Christian principle that giving is better than receiving. What does the Bible say about bride wealth?

The Biblical Value of Dowry

When reading the Bible we understand what is written if it agrees with what exists in our context, what is being read and the conventions of oral traditions of a given community (Waweru 2006:334). In the Hebrew Bible the word dowry is derived from the word *mohah* meaning 'paying price'. The Israelites termed it as wedding money paid by the bridegroom in compensation for the bride. To the English it is the property the woman brings to her husband in marriage. To Africans it is the gift given to one's in-laws as a token of appreciation for giving birth to a good girl and bringing her up. This is in agreement with some scholars' argument that bride wealth was never a price but a gift in appreciation. Compare this with Genesis 34:12 where Shechem was ready to give anything to the parents of his lover. It is good to look at verse 9 where the exchange of girls was the first option (cf. Laird 1980:492). Here the man offers the parents any kind of gift in order that they may accept him as their son-in-law.

So gifts are given once the girl's parents have accepted the relationship between themselves and the boy's family. In Genesis 34:12 we encounter a man who is not acceptable to the girl's family and he urges them to 'make the price for the bride and the gift I am to bring as great as you would like and I will pay whatever you ask me; only give me the girl as my wife'. It is good to understand this urging as a sign of the great love that Shechem had for his love. Gifts and rewards were given for accepting the proposal of marriage but wedding money was given in addition to this (cf. Rebecca's case in Gen. 24:53; Gen. 29:24; Josh. 15:18; 1 Kings 9:16). Therefore, the Hebrew word *'mohar'* does not strictly mean bride wealth in terms of money but the equivalent of wealth that exchanged hands during marriage. In any case it may refer even to the wealth that was given to the girl on marriage and on leaving her parents.

Some other examples from the Old Testament could be cited such as the services Jacob paid for his marriages to Leah and Rachel, but he also became rich through these services. I do not know what marriage in Africa would look like without bride wealth. It would only result in a culture of divorce where one man or woman could jump from one person to another. Bride wealth helps to solidify marriage.

Bride wealth was not only common to the Hebrew people, it was a universal practice, although the meaning of it could differ from one culture to another. In Babylon the man was required to give to the girl's family or to the girl herself. One must note that if you give the girl you are marrying the *tirhatu,* which in Hebrew means a sum of money varying from one to fifty shekels of silver, it would still come back to you once married. So it is not a matter of who spends what but the key thing is the relationship.

For Palestinian Arabs, a husband gives *mohar* (bride wealth) to the girls' parents (Laird 1980:492). This is practised to the present day. However, this does not justify the argument that they buy or sell the girl, it is a cultural practice that has survived against the odds. The Middle East tradition is similar to the African tradition of marriage. In Malawi, among the *Chewa* people, it is the girl's family who gives the bride wealth to the boy's family. It does not mean that they buy the boy, but they create a relationship between the two families.

God's Intention in Marriage

Marriage goes back to myths of creation. In every society there is a story of how man and woman were originally created to satisfy each other. In Genesis chapter one, we encounter God who created man alone and then later saw the incompleteness of man and created the woman to make man complete. So exegetically, in parallelism or parenthesis, or perhaps both, God made male and female: 'he created them' (Gen. 1:27). While it is arguable that this does not directly refer to marriage, it directly refers to companionship between man and woman. The process of making that companionship complete and legitimate is what can be termed as the foundation of bride wealth.

God created not a wife or husband but two people who could be attracted to each other because of their sexual distinction. This may definitively be seen as the background to marriage, which was a later development. Man and woman are equal and both reflect the image of God. Marriage maximizes singleness by bringing together two different characters and making them one whole. The differences and conflicts among married couples are only signs of singleness, and resolutions are only signs of togetherness in marriage. Therefore bride wealth is a way to express the coming together of man and woman in terms of marriage. Bromiley puts it this way: 'possibly the existence of two distinct beings, man and woman, who are both generically man, reflects in a loose way God's own beings as three persons, Father, Son and Holy Spirit, who are all equally God. If so, Paul's argument in 1 Corinthians 11:1-12 takes on a deeper significance. But whatever the connection, God obviously planned and created human life as life within this distinction in unity, and by associating it with his own being, he conferred on it a high ranking and dignity' (1980:1).

With such an understanding, bride wealth becomes the only way to celebrate the union between these two persons. It is within marriage that distinction in unity forms an integral and inescapable part of human reality. It denotes the broader relation of the sexes in which no male can exist without the female and no female without the male, demonstrating a principal of coherence in creation. Bride wealth becomes key in bringing these two different persons together, but not as animals do, without consultations. So bride wealth makes *marriage* unique in Africa. When people marry it does not mean that singleness is gone, they are still single individuals who remain so even when married. Yet they operate as single people with strings attached to other relatives. God has a purpose for man as man and woman as woman. They both share the commission to have dominion over the rest of creation. God appoints them his stewards and they must cooperate to fulfill this commission; it is in such cooperation that they marry and exchange those things that they were commissioned to dominate as part of their joy. Therefore, God had commissioned them, blessed them and given them the power to be fruitful and to increase in number, but only if they are able to subdue the earth (Gen. 1:28).

Dowry Brings Equality in Marriage

In Genesis chapter two, marriage is laid out as part of God's plan. God makes the male first. Later God observes the male and notices his inadequacy in the solitary life (Gen. 2:18). As a result of man's loneliness God brought animals to Adam as helpmeets, but to no avail. They offer friendship of a kind, because animals are definitely friendly, but not an authentic friendship because they lack the necessary ingredient of equality (Gen. 2:19f). So God then decides to provide man with an authentic friend and true companion, being distinct yet equal, as part of humanity, and man said 'bone of my bones and flesh of my flesh' (Gen. 2:23). This acceptance of the woman by man is in terms of equity. However, only when the woman offers the fruit to the man as of part bride wealth do they come to know each other properly.

Therefore, the coming together of man and woman in marriage and being bound together through bride wealth constitutes a unity whereby they become one flesh (Gen. 2:24). This is where full companionship and fellowship is being experienced. So bride wealth was not meant for compensation as many African Christians may assume, but it was a way of bonding the two so that those whom

God has joined together no man or woman should separate. Thus cultural practices, which are helpful and educational, should be given preference within African Christianity. Giving or receiving bride wealth is one such cultural aspect that needs to be enhanced. This does not mean that it has not been abused, but those who abuse it do it because they have lost track of its importance. In that case, what is needed is not to discard it but to correct the wrongs that may have penetrated into it.

Therefore God is the author of marriage, and anybody planning to alter its institution by way of either avoiding bride wealth or demanding it in excess is interfering with God's plan of procreation. One must note that marriage corresponds with God's will for the human race. This includes relationships within the entire human race.

Dowry is the Seal of a Family

God created man and woman and gave them the right of government, ownership, and stewardship. They were jointly to continue the creation of the human race; they were to multiply as conservators and trustees. The command to multiply is not merely as an end in itself, but is to be obeyed in an orderly way and this was to happen through marriage in which bride wealth was part of that process. To deny bride wealth is to deny marriage its core foundation. The development of human creation requires that man and woman come together in a special union which makes procreation possible and which distinguishes marriage from every other relationship between the sexes. In creating man as male and woman as female God was already instituting bride wealth in culturally binding the two together for the purposes of legalizing sexuality in the broad sense as integral to creating humanity.

Therefore, God instituted marriage as a specific expression and fulfilment of the sexual relationship which, in African terms, is only possible through bride wealth. Whoever becomes engaged to a woman without exchange of gifts is seen as committing an offence. So dowry for a family goes back to God's beginning with us and ours with God. Incidentally, it also carries with it the origin of the family and the continuing possibility of marriage, so that both marriage and family have their origin, basis, and goals in the divine purpose, word and action (Bromiley 181:4). In other words, the union of the two comes first, then bride wealth, followed by family. These three go hand in hand for a marriage to be a marriage and it is all in the plan of God. For this reason, humanity was created, man and woman, to be God's mutually responsible stewards without any monopoly of one over another. Men and women are different but the difference is what makes them stay together. God created them as two different persons who should bear one another's burdens without domination. The bride wealth is what makes both women and children feel as though they belong, while men equally feel they are part of that family.

In a nutshell, dowry is the key to success in an African marriage. It is a part of the culture that cannot be ignored. The gospel of Jesus Christ does not exclude culture. When God took the initiative to redeem humankind, Christ came among people (Bate 2000:38). So he became human; a person in a culture, with a cultural name, a local language, education and even conformed to the morals of his people (Neibuhr 1951:12). He did not become an African or Roman but a Jew, so that he would be able to participate in a particular culture performing deeds of mercy among his people (1951:3). So one major aspect of the gospel is incarnation, and a very important dimension of this is that the son of man revealed the father in a particular cultural tradition (Okure 1990:59). Without dowry there is no marriage, without marriage there is no community and without a community the great commission will not go on. Van Engen (1996:11) argues that in order for the Church to be able to communicate the gospel meaningfully and serve effectively as God's prophetic agent, calling for conversion and transformation of people, societies and cultures, it must know the social and historic contexts in which it lives and ministers. So when one gives dowry it is one way of obeying the great commission. Mugambi points out that transmitting the gospel from one culture to another in Africa has raised many challenges, which were due to cultural beliefs and the understanding of the people (1989:10).

Therefore, when the gospel comes to a culture, it must be like the Good Samaritan who came where the wounded, oppressed man was, not to crush him further but to nurture him because Christ's healing must meet people where they are. So the better the Church understands the context of a people's culture the better it will be able to serve them. Jesus, as we know, met people where they were and perfected his image in them (Hunter 1978:27). The purpose of Christ's coming was not to abolish our culture, so we need to let Christianity interact with culture for its blending.

In sum up, it is our contention that the challenge is to contextualise the Gospel of Christ to the culture of a given society. Dowry is an element of African culture which has a positive aspect that can be utilized for the sake of the gospel. Dowry is a way of inculturation and a tool to be used in marriage maintenance. It makes marriage relevant and applicable to the African culture. The message of Christ clearly supports what is good in culture and eliminates what does not agree with the Christian faith.

Since the role of Christ is to approve the best in the past and guide the process of civilization to its proper goal, he is part of culture in the sense that he himself is part of the social heritage that must be transmitted and conserved. In our case, dowry is one aspect that we need to maintain. If marriage is Christian then inculturating Christianity in Africa means making Christians conscious of their identity, their own history, their own weakness and lives, and the role of marriage. They must not only condemn unacceptable practices but come to see the importance of affirming their differences from others in order to liberate marriage from any foreign dependency. The main way is indeed to return to the painful history of marriage, to its failure and not sweep things under the carpet and hide them behind a huge smile saying 'I am a Christian'. So dowry allows a woman to be regarded as a human being in her own right and affirms her both as a member of a new family and of her own.

In African culture the wife is both an individual and part of a community once dowry is given. Dowry discourages polygamy, because unless one has enough to keep on giving one cannot afford multiple marriages. So Christian marriages should be organized in a way that will encourage dowry which is not exorbitant but that is primarily about property being endowed to the young couple by parents of both sides. Thus may we all adhere to the African way of marriage and there will be fewer stories of divorce.

In conclusion, giving and receiving of a dowry is a way of legalizing marriage and must be encouraged by those who believe 'you are because I am'. However no dialogue would be complete without a reflection on translation, which opened the Bible to all meaningful transactions on African soil.

A Cultural Transaction Through Translation

When the translation becomes the focus of the encounter between the African culture and the Bible, the emphasis is almost always on the role of the Bible in Africa. Recently Mbiti (2009:142) talked of the 'challenges of language, Culture, and Interpretation in Translating the Greek New Testament' in order to make the Bible available in local languages which then will enhance the dialogue between it and the African culture. I think no any other area is more fertile than translation in terms of dialogue.

Translation has resolved the misconception that missionaries brought God to Africa (hence the God of the white people), but it was God that brought them here. According to Mbiti (2009:147) by the end of 2008 the Bible had already been translated into 718 African languages, whereby the common indigenous word for God has been applied. This explains clearly the kind of dialogue that has been taking place in this field. Nevertheless, in some a controversy has arisen in the transaction, because missionaries did not feel comfortable with using the indigenous terminologies. For Mbiti the problem in this dialogue is caused by prejudice, where some people felt that the God they preached was not equal to the God of the heathens already acknowledged before the new era. Although I can understand their fears or hesitations in using indigenous names, this created a translation problem that will not be resolved soon. For example, the word 'spirit' in Kikuyu language is *Ngoma* and only needed to be qualified as to whether it was good or bad *ngoma njega kana njuru* (good or bad spirit); instead of this the translators borrowed a Swahili word *roho* for spirit which does not make sense in the dialogue. It is like two people talking and all of a sudden a foreign word is thrown into the conversation and they both rush for a dictionary to confirm its meaning.

However translation enabled the Bible to negotiate its own position as a yardstick by which to test, and sometimes to reject, what western missionaries taught and practised and in so doing provided the basis for developing new, indigenous forms of Christianity (Bediako 1977:246).

A Transaction between the African Culture and the Bible

CHAPTER NINE

Revelation

I have attempted to demonstrated in this book that African culture and Biblical culture can dialogue in order to produce common ground for the furtherance of the Gospel of Christ. In this book we have already established that the Bible has its own culture, which can easily be interpreted within a given culture. It explains the life of a people with humanness, which affirms humanity by recognizing the humanity of others in its variety of content and form. The core meaning of this statement is that humanness defines a person in terms of his or her relationship with others. The assumption is that this is a vital force, a universal force that is able to unite humanity and this gives the impetus for the potential inclusive and pluralist orientation of humanness.

As such it tends to bend towards accommodating cultures in which communality takes precedence over the individual. This is the value and the uniqueness of intercultural dialogue. The dictum is 'we can only be people through other people'; hence the African mantra 'I am because you are and because you are therefore I am'. In this understanding the transaction between African culture and the Biblical culture is open. The Biblical culture is pluralistic in nature, however its pluralistic nature can only work when it recognises that people have their own contexts, which must be respected. For without context the Bible is not, and without African context we are not. For this kind of understanding one needs to understand the historical overview of the intercultural transaction.

Church leadership today has to accept that we have come from a cultural background with its own leadership. Hence Christ is seen only as one who came to restore the true leadership, having come from God with a divine position. The African leadership has to be incorporated into Christ's body through the sacrament of both the age-grading and of baptism. This sacrament of Christ in the church serves as an alternative to the traditional practices, which Africans may have counted as their own sacraments. Christ is the present source of strength and wisdom in carrying out the role of leadership that once was popular within African culture. Therefore as much as the Gospel plays the role of restoration and purification of the African traditional culture, such purification is a two-way process in demanding the conversion of the leaders. The role of Christianity today in the midst of all this is for African Christians to be true to the gospel of Christ.

Therefore it is good to note that in the transaction between African culture and the Bible, Africans are more concerned with their own identity. This resulted from a loss of initiative and forward thinking within post-independent African nations. However, the time to blame colonialism or neo-colonialism is over; it is now time to blame ourselves. It is we who have damaged Africa – perhaps more than our former colonial masters. The situation of Jerusalem is a paradigm for Africa; where does Africa go from here? Reconstruction of our societies is essential; we must accept responsibility for revamping and reshaping Africa. Going back to our traditional practices sounds like an old song that no one wants to sing. There is a need to understand this revelation and ask, 'What is the vision for the future?' 'How do we proceed from here?', hence a call for a theology of social action, which produces a growing interest in the social life of the Bible. Such will then give birth to authentic Christian experience. So the transaction between African culture and the Bible ends up with a genuine transformation in the Church and in the Christians. This is only possible through a genuine inter-religious dialogue between peoples of different backgrounds.

African hermeneutics have emerged in order to fill the gap within African biblical interpretations, as we saw in the historical overview.

African hermeneutics flourish within the fundamental axes of liberation, love and justice, which characterise God's dealing with his people. The context of contrapuntal analysis is the harmony resulting from listening to the Biblical texts and our own oral texts as they interrogate each other. Africans must learn to make choices in their reading of the Bible. If they choose to read from the perspective of the oppressed, the grieved, and the marginalised, they have their own stories to reflect such perspectives within biblical texts. It is not only justifiable to do so, in order to understand in what way the stories of the Bible may contribute to our life and our faith in a hostile global environment, but is also a worthwhile study, because biblical stories range over a spectrum from simple, unilinear, tightly plotted sequences (such as a joke) to complex, multilinear sequences wherein any number of possible connections between events may be inferred (as in epic).

Hence, worship in Africa is not an individual phenomenon, but also a social and religious phenomenon, very similar to that of the Bible. It generates social and spiritual influences (mission) within the people. The character of the people is influenced by mission activity either from the Bible or African traditions. In Africa, worship does not necessarily distinguish between 'African religion' and 'Christianity'. However, it is the interpretations of images and symbols that were given different descriptions, and labelled either Christian or heathen, and the subsequest action are ostensibly done in a Christian manner. African people participated wholeheartedly in African religion as a means of mission.

But when translation took place it resolved a thousand and one problems, particularly the misconception that Christianity meant abandoning one's culture for another culture. It is clear from our discussion that by the end of 2008 the Bible had already been translated into 718 African languages, in which the common indigenous word for God was applied, making the transaction easier. Such an example explains clearly the kind of transaction that has been taking place in this field.

However this transaction has not been without controversy, because missionaries were not comfortable with some indigenous terminologies. Such a problem was caused by prejudice, because some people felt that the God they preached was not equal to the God of the other people. Although I can understand their fears or hesitations in using indigenous names, this created a transaction problem that will not be resolved soon. So, for any transaction to be meaningful, textuality and orality must be considered. Hence in this book we have done a reflection on a number of terms in order to show that common language can be found between the African culture and in the Bible. This dialogue is healthy and should be encouraged if African Christianity is going to have concrete foundations within the African societies.

Bibliography

Arndt, William E., and E. Wilbur Gingrich 1979. *A Greek-English Lexicon of the New Testament and Other Christian Literature.* 2nd ed. Chicago: The University of Chicago Press.

Arnold, Matthew. 1869. Culture and Anarchy.

Atieno Odhiambo & J. Lonsdale (eds.), *Mau Mau & Nationhood* (Oxford: James Currey Ltd): 79-120.

Bates, S.2000.*Theology of inculturation.* Cedara, Pietermaritzburg: St. Joseph   Theological institute. Unpublished.

Barr, L D 2003. The Story John Told: Reading Revelation for Its Plot in Barr(ed),
      Reading the Book of Revelation (2003), 11-23.

Barr (ed.). *Reading the Book of Revelation. 11 -23.* Draper, A J 2002. "Reading the Bible as Conversation: A Theory and

Beasley-Murray, 1978. *The Book of Revelation* (London: Oliphants).

_____1997. "Book of Revelation," in Martin &c David (eds.), *Dictionary of the Later New Testament and Its Developments* (Downers Grove, Illinois: IVP): 1025-38.

Bell, C. 1992. *Ritual Theory, Ritual Practice* (New York & Oxford: Oxford University Press).

Bewes, T. F. 1953. *Kikuyu Conflict: Mau Mau and the Christian Witness* (London: The Highway Press).

Bhabha, H. 1994. *The Location of Culture* (London: Routledge).

Boer, R. 1998. "Remembering Babylon: Postcolonial and Australian Biblica Studies,"in Sugirtharajah (ed), *The Postcolonial Bible* (Sheffield: Sheffield Academic Press, 1998), 24-48.

Bromiley G. 1980. *God and Marriage.* Grand Rapids, U.S.A: Erdmans Printing Press.

Brown, D. M. 1997. "Except a corn of wheat fall into the ground and die...The Bible and Christianity in Ngugi's Novels," *Bulletin for Contextual Theology in South Africa* 4/3: 30-35.

Brown, Raymond 1979. *The Community of the Beloved Disciple.* New York: Paulist Press.

_____ "Roles of Women in the Fourth Gospel." *Theological Studies* 36 (1975): 688-699.

Caird, G. B. 1984. *The Revelation of St. John the Divine* (2 ed). London: Black.

Cavicchi, E.1977. Problems of Change in Kikuyu Tribal Society. Bologna: Emi.

Comaroff, J. & Comaroff, J. 1991. *Of Revelation and Revolution: Christianity, Colonialism and Consciousness in South Africa* 1. Chicago: University of Chicago Press.

Decock, P. 1990. "Albert Nolan's Eschatology," *Grace & Truth* 10/2: 75-84.

_____1993. "The Reading of Sacred Texts in the Context of Early Christianity," *Neotestamentica* 27/2: 263-82.

_____ 2003. *Christians Theology and Social Reconstruction.* Nairobi: Acton.

Mbiti, J S 1971. *New Testament Eschatology in An African Background:A study of the Encounter* between *New Testament Theology and the African Traditional Concepts.* London: SPCK.

Chinkwita, M 1993. *The Usefulness of Dreams: An African Perspective.* London: Janus Publishing Company.

Culpepper, Alan R 1983. *Anatomy of the Fourth Gospel.* Philadelphia: Fortress Press.

Daube, David. "Jesus and the Samaritan Woman." Journal of Biblical Literature 69 (1950): 137-147.

Dickson, K1973. The Old Testament and African Theology, *The Ghana Bulletin of Theology* (1973), 4:4.

_____ 1984. *Theology in Africa* (London: Darton, Longman & Todd, Maryknoll: Orbis).

Draper, A. J. 1997 "The Bible in African Literature: A Contrapuntal Perspective," *Bulletin   of Contextual Theology in South Africa & Africa* 4/3: 1-3.

_____ 2002. Reading the Bible as Conversation: A Theory and Methodology For Contextual Interpretation of the Bible in Africa, in Grace & Truth, vol 19, 2 (2002), 13-25.

_____2004. "George Khambule and the Book of Revelation: Prophet of the Open Heaven," *Neotestamentica* 38: (2004) 250-74.

Dube, M. 1996. "Reading for Decolonization (John 4:1-42," *Semeia* 75 (1996) 37-59.

_____1998. "Go Therefore and Make Disciples of All Nations (Matt 28:19a): A Postcolonial Perspective on Biblical Criticism and Pedagogy," in F. F. Segovia &C M. A. Tolbert (eds), *Teaching the Bible. The Discourses and Politics of Biblical Pedagogy* (Maryknoll, New York: Orbis Books) 224-246.

_____1999. "Consuming a Colonial Bomb Translating Badimo in to 'Demons' in the Setswana Bible (Matthew 8:28-34, 15:2, 10:8), in JSNT 73, (1999) 33-59.

_____2001. "What I Have Written I Have Written' (John 19:22) in Getui & Maluke at el (eds.), Interpreting the New Testament In Africa (2001),145-164.

Ellis, Peter E 1984. *The Genius of John: A Composition-Critical Commentary on the Fourth Gospel.* Collegeville: The Liturgical Press.

Esler, P .1994 *The First Christians In Their Social Worlds.* London: Routledge.

Fabella, V. & Sugirtharajah, R. 2000. *Dictionary of Third Word Theologies.* Maryknoll, New York. Orbis Books.

Findley, Carther Vaughn and John Alexander Rothney (2006). *Twentieth-century World.* Sixth edition, (2006) 14.

Fiorenza, S. E. 1996. *The Power of Naming a Concilium Reader in Feminist Liberation Theology.* Maryknol, New York: Orbis Book.

Foley, M 1991. *Immanent Art: From Structure to Meaning in Traditional Oral Epic.* Bloomington: Indiana University Press.

_____1995. *The Singer of Tales in Performance.* Bloomington: Indiana University Press.

Gadamer, H.-G. 1989 *Truth and Method* (New York: Continuum; Michigan: Eerdmans).

Gottwald, N. K. 1983. *The Bible and Liberation.* Maryknoll: Orbis. Howard-Brook, W. & Gwyther, A. 1999 *Unveiling Empire: Reading Revelation Then and Now* (Maryknoll, New York: Orbis Books).

Geddert, Timothy J. 1989. *"Jesus and Women: A New Vision for Human-ity."* Unpublished paper, Mennonite Brethren Biblical Seminary, Fresno, CA.

Goodall, J 1986. *The Chimpanzees of Gombe: Patterns of Behavior.*

Goodday, J and Tambia, S.J (ed) 1973. *Bride Wealth and Dowry*. London: Cambridge University Press.

———. "Roles of Women in the Fourth Gospel." Theological Studies 36 (1975): 688-699.

——— 1984. *Theology in Africa*. London: Darton, Longman and Todd, Maryknoll: Orbis.

Guma, M 1997. Ithongo Dream Narratives: Healing Texts. Wholeness and Social Justice Among Nguni Healers of the Western Cape, in Guma & Milton (eds), *An African Challenge to the Church in the 21st Century* (1997), Cape Town: Salty Print. 12-29.

Hall, J 1983. *Jungian Dream Interpretation: A Handbook of Theory and Practice*. University of Toronto: Press Incorporated

Haenchen, Ernst. John, 1984. *Hermeneia. 2 vols*. Trans. Robert W. Funk. Philadelphia: Fortress Press.

Harper, Douglas (2001). Online Etymology Dictionary.

Hermanson, E 2001. Badimo a ba robaleng ka kagiso (Let the Ancestors Rest in Peace): Colonisation or Contextualization in the Translation of the Badimo in Setswana (Matthew 8:28-34; 15:22; 10:8). A Paper Read at the SNTS Post-Conference Hammanskraal, Campus, Pretoria, August 1999.

Hobley, C.W 1967. *Bantu Beliefs and Magic*. London: Frankcass.

Hunsberger, G.R and Van Gelder, C 1996. *Church Between Gospel and Culture*. Grand Rapids, Michigan: Williams B. Eerdmans Publishing Company.

Hunter, A.M 1978. *The Gospel: Then and Now*. London: S.C.M. Press.

Hurley, James B 1981. *Man and Woman in Biblical Perspective*. Grand Rapids: Zondervan.

———*Immanent Art: From Structure to Meaning in TraditionalOral Epic*. Bloomington: Indiana University Press.

———1995. *The Singer of Tales in Performance*. Bloomington: Indiana University Press.

John Berger, 1971. *Ways of Seeing*. Peter Smith Pub. Inc

Kabira, W. and Nzioki, E. 1993. *Celebrating Women's Resistance: A case study of Women's Groups Movement in Kenya*. Nairobi: African Women's Perspective

Keener, C. 2000. *The NIV Application Commentary: Revelation* (Grand Rapids, MI: Zondervan.

Kenyatta, J. 1938. *Facing Mount Kenya* (Nairobi: Heinemann).

Ketter, Peter 1952. *Christ and Womankind.* Trans. Isabel McHugh. West-minster: Newman Press.

Kibicho, S 1968. *The Interaction of the Traditional Kikuyu Concept of God with the Biblical Concept,* Cahiers des Religions Africaines. 2.4

_____ 1972. *The Kikuyu Concept of God: Its Continuity Into the Christian Era, and The Question it Raises for the Christian Idea of Revelation,* Ph.D Dissertation, Vanderbilt University.

_____ 2006. God and Revelation in an African Context. Nairobi: Acton Publishers

Kirwen, M.C. 1979. *African Widows: an empherical study of the problems adapting Western Christian teachings on marriage to the leviratic custom for the care of widows in four rural African societies.* Maryknol, New York: OrbisKinshasha: Saprientia Publishers.

Kopas, Jane. "Jesus and Women: John's Gospel." Theology Today 41 (1984): 201-215.

Kovacs, J. & Rowland, C. 2004. *Revelation.* Oxford: Blackwell Publishing.

Kraybill, J. 1996. *Imperial Cult and Commerce in John's Apocalypse* (Sheffield: Sheffield Academic Press).

Kroeber, A. L. and C. Kluckhohn, 1952. *Culture: A Critical Review of Concepts andDefinitions.*

Loba-Mkole. 2005. *Triple Heritage: Gospels in Intercultural Mediations.*

Lonsdale, J. 2003. "Authority, Gender & Violence: the war within Mau Mau's fight for land & freedom," in E. S. Atieno Odhiambo & J. Lonsdale (eds.), *Mau Mau & Nationhood* (Oxford: James Curry), 46-75.

Luz, V 1989. *Matthew 1-7: A Continental Commentary.* Mineapolis: Fortress.

Maluke at el (eds.). *Interpreting the New Testament In Africa,* 145-164. Foley, M 1991.

Minear, Paul S. "We don't know where . . ." Interpretation 30 (April 1976): 125-139.

Mpier, M 1992. "Dreams Among the Yansi", in: Jedrej & Shaw (1992), 100.

Mpier, M 1992. Dreams Among the Yansi, *Jedrej & Shaw* (1992), 100.

Mugambi, J.N.K. 1989. *The African Heritage and Contemporary Christianity*. Nairobi: Longman.

_____2003. *Christians Theology and Social Reconstruction*. Nairobi: Acton.

Muriuki, G1974. *A History of Kikuyu, 1500-1900*. U.S.A: Oxford: University Press.

Ngugi wa Thiong'o 1964. *Weep Not Child* (London: Heinemann).

____1965. *The River Between* (London: Heinemann).

____1978. 'An interview with Ngugi'. *The Weekly Review* 9 Jan: 10.

____1981. *Writers in Politics* (London: Heinemann).

____1982. *Decolonizing the Mind: the Politics of Language in African Literature* (London: Heinemann).

____2004. Murogi wa Kagogo (Wizard of the Crow) (London: Heinemann).

Ndung'u, N 2003. Towards the Recovery of African Identity, in Getui & Obeng 2003, 258-265.

Nolan, A 1997. 'The Paradigm Shift", in *Grace & Truth* 10:2, 97-103.

Nyamiti, C 1991. "African Christologies Today", in Schreitcr (ed.). *Faces of Jesus In Africa*. Maryknoll, New York: Orbis Books, 3-23.

_____1996. Trinity From an African Ancestral Perspective. ACS 12, 41-42.

Nthamburi, Rosemary 1987. "On the Possibility of a New Image for an African Woman". Voices From the Third World 10:1, 103-110.

Oduyoye, M 1990. *Who Will Roll the Stone Away?* Geneva: WCC Publication.

Okure, T 2001. "Invitation to African Women's Hermeneutical Concerns", in Gietui & Maluleke (eds.). *Interpreting the New Testament in Africa*. Nairobi: Acton Press, 42-63.

Peel, J 1968. *Aladura: A Religious Movement among the Yoruba*. London: Oxford University Press.

____1994. 'Violence Against Women: Challenge to Christian Theology. Journal of Inculturation Theology. 1:1,(1990), 38-52

____1995. *Daughters of Anowa: African Women and Patriarchy*. New York: Orbis Okure, Teresa 1990. 'Women in the Bible', in Fabella, Virginia, Oduyaye M, (eds).

With Passion and Compassion: Third World Women Doing Theology. New Orbis, (1990), 47-59.

_____ 2001. Invitation to African Women's Hermeutical Concerns in Interpreting the New Testament in Africa Eds. Getui *at el.* Nairobi: Acton Publishers, (2001): 42-58.

Payne, B 1981. *The Theology of the Old Testament.* Grand Rapids, Michigan: Zonderman.

Peel, J 1968. *Aladura: A Religious Movement among the Yoruba.* London: Oxford University Press.

Pugliese, C. 1994. *Publisher and Gikuyu nationalist. The Life and Writings of Gakaara wa Wanjau* (Nairobi: IFRA).

_____ 2003. "Complementary or Contending Nationhood & Songs 1945-52," in E.

Ramn, B. 1970. Protestant Biblical Interpretation: Text of Hermeneutics. Grand Rapids, Michigan.

Raymond Williams (1976) Keywords: A vocabulary of culture and Society. Rev. Ed. (New York: Oxford UP, 1983), 87-93 and 236-8. Williams, Raymond. *Keywords,* "Culture"

Richard, P. 1995. *Apocalypse: A People's Commentary.* Maryknoll: Orbis.

Richter, P. J. 1984. "Recent Sociological Approaches to the Study of the New Testament," in *Religion* vol. 14 (1984): 77-90.

Robinson, J.A.T. 1976. Redating the New Testament (Philadelphia: Westminster).

Rohrbaugh, R (ed.) 1996. *The Social Sciences and New Testament Interpretation* (Massachusetts: Hendrickson Publishers).

Rossing, B. 1999. *The Choice between Two cities: whore, bride, and the empire in the Apocalypse* (Harrisburg, Pennsylvania: Trinity Press International).

Rowland, C. 1982. *The Open Heaven: A study of Apocalyptic in Judaism and Early Christianity* (London: SPCK).

Ruiz, J. P. 2003. "Taking a Stand on the Sand of the Seashore: A Postcolonial Exploration of Revelation 13," in D. L. Barr (ed.) *Reading the Book of Revelation. A Resource for Students* (Atlanta: SBL): 119-135.

Said, E. 1978 *Orientalism* (New York: Patheon).

_____ 1993 *Culture and Imperialism* (New York: Knopf).

Sangree, W 1966. *Age, Prayer and Politics in Tiriki, Kenya.* London: Oxford University Press.

Schnackenburg, Rudolf, 1968. *The Gospel According to St. John*. 3 vols. Trans. Kevin Smyth. New York: Herder and Herder.

Schneiders, Sandra M 1982. "Women in the Fourth Gospel and the Role of Women in the Contemporary Church." Biblical Theological Bulletin 12 (1982): 35-45.

Schtissler Fiorenza, E.1996.*The power of naming: A Concilium reader in Feminist Liberation Theology.*

Seoka, J 1997. African Culture and Christian Spirituality: An Interpretation, in Guma & Milton (eds.), An African Challenge to the Church in the 21st Century (1997), 1-11.

Shao, J. 2001. "Alleviating Poverty in Africa," in D. Belshaw, C. Sugden & R. Calderisi (eds.), *Faith in Development: Partnership between the World Bank and the Churches of Africa* (Oxford: Regnum), 19-30.

Shorter, A (ed) 1975. *Church and Marriage in East Africa*. Eldoret: A.M.E.C.E.A.

Stagg, Evelyn and Frank,1978. *Women in the World of Jesus*. Philadelphia: Westminster Press.

Sugirtharajah, R. 1998. *The Bible and Postcolonialism* (Sheffield: Shield Academic Press).

_____1999. *Asian Biblical Hermeneutics and Postcolonialism* (Sheffield Academic Press).

Sundkler, B 1948. *Bantu Prophets in South Africa* (2nd ed. 1961). London: Oxford University Press.

_____1960. *The Christian Ministry in Africa*. London: Oxford University Press.

Swidler, Leonard, 1976. *Women in Judaism: The Status of Women in Formative Judaism*. Metuchen: The Scarecrow Press.

Tidball, D. 1983. *An Introduction to the Sociology of the New Testament* (London: Paternoster).

Turner, H 1967. *African Independent Church: History and Life and Faith of the Church of the Lord Aladura*, Vol. II. London. Oxford University Press.

Tylor, E.B. 1874. *Primitive culture: researches into the development of mythology, philosophy, religion, art, and custom.* UNESCO. 2002. Universal Declaration on Cultural Diversity.

Ukpong, J. S. 1995. "Rereading the Bible with African Eyes: Inculturation and Hermeneutics," in *Journal of Theology for Southern Africa*, vol. 91 (1995): 3-14.

_____2000. "Developments in Biblical Interpretation in Africa: Historical and Hermenutics Directions," in West G 8c Dube M. (eds.), *The Bible in Africa:*

_____ *2000. Transactions, Trajectories and Trends,* Leiden, Boston: Brill, 11-28.

_____2001. "Bible Reading with a community of ordinary Readers," in Getui &

Maluleke *et al* (eds.), *Interpreting the New Testament in Africa.* Nairobi: Acton Press, 188-196.

Vilakazi, B at el. 1986. *The Revitalization of African Society.* Johannesburg: Skotaville Publishers.

Waltke, H. and Guthrie 1978. *Biblical Criticism: Historical, Literary and Textual.* Grand Rapids, Michigan: Zonderman.

Waweru, H.M. 2005. A critical Analysis of the Vision of the New Jerusalem in Revelation 21:9-22:5 in Light of the Kikuyu Concept of Dreams and Visions. Unpublished PhD thesis: University of Kwazulu-Natal.

_____2005. "A critical Analysis of the Vision of the New Jerusalem in Revelation 21:9-22:5 in Light of the Kikuyu Concept of Dreams and Visions". Unpublished PhD thesis: University of Kwazulu-Natal.

_____2006. Reading the Bible Contrapuntally: A Theory and Methodology for a Contextual Bible Interpretation in Africa, in Swedish Missiological Themes: Svensk Missions Tidskrift. Vol. 94, No. 3 2006,333-348.

_____2007. Postcolonial and Contrapuntal Reading of Revelation 22:1-5, in Churchman Vol121. No.1 2007, 23-38.

West Gerald, 1999. *Contextual Bible Study.* Pietermaritzburg: Cluster Publications.

West, G 1995 *Biblical Hermeneutics of Liberation. Modes of Reading the Bible in the SouthAfrican Context* (Pietermaritzburg: Cluster Publications; Maryknoll, New York:Orbis).

_____1997. "Finding a place among the posts for post-colonial Criticism in Biblical Studies in South Africa," *Old Testament Essays* (1997): 10, 322-342.

West, G. & Dube M. 1996. "An Introduction: How We Have Come To read With," *Semeia* 73, 1996: 7-19.

White, L. 1949. *The Science of Culture: A study of man and civilization.* Wholeness and Social Justice Among Nguni Healers of the Western Cape", in: Guma & Milton (eds). *An African Challenge to the Church in the 21ˢᵗ Century,* 12-29.

Williams, J. J. 1930. *Hebrewisms of West Africa: from Nile to Niger with Jews.* London: George Alien & C Unwin.

Witherington, Ben, III 1984. *Women in the Ministry of Jesus.* Cambridge: Cambridge University Press.

Works Consulted

Ambler, C 1988. *Kenyan Communities in the Age of Imperialism: The Central Region in the late Nineeteenth Century.* London: Yale University Press.

Balogun, F O 1997. *Ngugi and African Postcolonial Narrative: the Novel as Oral Narrative in Multigenre performance.* Quebec: World Heritage Press.

Barker, M 1991. *The Gate of heaven: The History and Symbolism of the Temple of Jerusalem.* London: SPCK

Barthes, R 1967. *Writing Degree Zero.* London: Jonathan Cape.

_____1987. 'The Struggle with the Angel: Textual Analysis of Genesis 32:22-32'. *In the Bible,* ed. Harod Bloom. 83-94. New York. New Haven and Philadelphia: Chelsea House Publishers

Bauckham, R 1978. *Tudor Apocalypse: Sixteenth-Century apocalypticism, Millenarianism and the English Reformation.* Sulton Courtenary: Appleford.

_____1993. *The theology of the book of revelation.* Cambridge: Cambridge University Press.

Barnett & Karari, 1966. *Mau Mau from Within: Autobiography and Analyses of Kenya Peasant Revolt.* Modern Reader Paper backs. London: Monthly Review Press.

Beasley-Murray. 1978 *The book of Revelation.* London: Oliphants.

_____1997. Book of Revelation. (In Dictionary of the Later New Testament and Its Developments, 1997, 1025-1038. Martin & David Eds.) Downers Grove, Illinois: Inter-Varsity Press.

Beckwith, I T 1979 <1919> *The Apocalypse of John Studies in Introduction with a critical and exegetical Commentary.* Twin Books. Grand Rapids. Mich.. Baker Book House.

Bewes, T F 1953. *Kikuyu Conflict: Mau Mau and the Christian Witness.* London: The Highway Press.

Beya, M 1990. Doing Theology as African Women &. Voices from the Third World 13:1 (1990): 155-156.

Belshaw & Calderisi at el. Ed. 2001. *Faith in Development: Partnership between the World Bank and the churches of Africa.* Oxford: Regnum.

Bhabha, H 1994. *The Location of Culture.* London Routledge.

Boer, R 1998. Remembering Babylon: Postcolonial and Australian Biblical Studies. *The Postcolonial Bible.* Sigirtharajah (ed.), 24-48.

Boesak, A 1987. *Comfort and Protest.* Edinburgh: St. Andrews Press.
_____1984. *Black and Reformed: Apartheid, Liberation and Calvinist Tradition.* Johannesburg: Skotaville Press.

Brown, D M 1997. 'Except a corn of wheat fall into the ground and die...' the Bible and Christianity in Ngugi's Novels. *In Bulletin for Contextual Theology in South Africa.*vol.4 No.3 Sep. 1997, 30-35.

Cagnolo, C 1933. *The Agikuyu: Their Customs, Traditions and Folklore.* Nyeri: Mission Printing School.

Caird, G B 1984. *The Revelation of St. John the divine*, 2 ed. London: Black.

Chinkwita, M 1993. *The Usefulness of Dreams: An African perspective.* London: Janus Publishing Company.

Decock, P 1990. Albert Nolan's Eschatology in the Catholic Journal of Grace & Truth vol.10, no. 2 September 1990, 75-84.

Diop, Cheik A 1974. *The African Origin of Civilisation: Myth or Reality?* Westport, Connecticut: Lawrence Hill.

Douglas, M 1982. *Natural Symbols.* New York: Pantheon books.

Draper, A J 1988. 2002. Reading the Bible as Converstion: A Theory and Methodology for Contextual Interpretation of the Bible in Africa. *Grace & Truth a Journal of Catholic reflection for Southern Africa* vol. 19. No.2 (2002), 13-25.
_____2004. George Khambule and the Book of Revelation: Prophet of the Open Heaven. *Neo Testamentica* (2004), 250-274.

Dube, M 1996. "Reading for Decolonization (John 4:1-42)", *Semeia,* 1996, 75, 37-59.

_____1998. "Go Therefore and Make Disciples of All Nations" (Matt 28:19a): A Postcolonial Perspective on Biblical Criticism and Pedagogy. *Teaching the Bible.* Segovia & Tolbert (Eds), 224-246.

Ela, J 1994. Christianity and Liberation in Africa. *In Paths African Theology*, Ed. R.Gibellini Maryknoll: Orbis (1994), 146-147.

Elliot, J 1988. "The fear of the Leer: The Evil Eye from the Bible to Lil Abner" *Forum* 1988 (4), 42-71.

_____1993. What is Social-Scientific Criticism? Guides to Biblical Scholarship. *New Testament Series.* Minneapolis: Augsburg Fortress.

Empson, J 1989. *Sleep and Dream.* London: Richard Clay LTD.

Esler, P 1994. *The First Christians In Their Social Worlds.* London: Routledge.

Fabella, V & Sugirtharajah, R 2000. *Dictionarary of Third Word Theologies*: Maryknoll, New York. Orbis Books.

Faley, R 1999. *Apocalypse Then & Now: A Companion to the Book of Revelation.* New York: Paulist Press.

Farrar, A 1949. *A Rebirth of Images: the making of the Revelation of St. John's Apocalypse.* Westminister: Dacre Press.

_____1964. *The Revelation of St. John the divine.* London: Oxford University Press.

Fekkes, J 1994. *Isaiah and Prophetic Traditions in the Book of Revelation: Visionary Antecedents and their Development.* Sheffield: Sheffield Academic Press.

Felder, C.H. (Ed) 1991. *Stony the Road We trod:* Africa American Biblical Interpretation. Philadelphia: Fortress.

Ferguson, E 1988. "Irenaeus", New Dictionary of Theology, eds. Ferguson & Wright *at el.* (Downers Grove, Illinois: Intervarsity Press 1988), 340.

Foley, J. M 1991. *Immanent Art: from structure to meaning in traditional oral Epic.* Bloomington: Indiana University Press

_____1995. *The Singer of Tales in perfomance.* Bloomington: Indiana University Press.

Ford, J 1975. *Revelation, Introduction, Translation and Commentary.* Doubleday: NewYork Press.

_____1975. *Revelation Anchor.* Garden City: Doubleday.

Fornari, A 1989. *'Understanding Dream Psychology.* London: Hamlyn Press.

Friesen, J 1998. 'Revelation, Realia and Religion: Archaelogy in the Interpretation of the Apocalypse'. *Havard Theological Review* 88, 1998, 291-314.

Gadamer, H.-G 1989. *Truth and Method.* New York: Continuum.

Gager, J 1975. *Kingdom and Community: The Social World of Early Christianity.* EngleWood Cliffs: Prentice Hall.

Garrow, A 1997. *Revelation.* London: Routledge.

Geertz, C 1968. 'Ethos, World view and the Analysis of Sacred Symbols' in Dundes, A (Ed) 1968 Every man his way: Reading in Cultural Anthropology. Engle wood Cliffs, New Jersey: Prentice Hall (1968), 301-315.

Gehman, R 1985. *Ancestor Relations among Three African Societies in Biblical Perspective.* Amarbor University Michigan: Microfilms International.

Getui & Obeng (ed.) 1999, *Theology of Reconstruction: Exploration Essays.* Nairobi: Acton Press.

Geyser, R 1982. The Twelve Tribes in Revelation: Judean and Judeo Christian Apocalypticism. *New Testament. Stud. Vol.* (28), 388-399.

Giblin, C H 1991. *The book of Revelation: the open book of prophecy* Collegeville. Minnesota: Liturgical Press.

Glasson, T 1965. *The Revelation of John.* London: Oxford University Press.

Green, J 1979. *Christ in glory.* London: Skeffington.

Griffiths, M 1988. *'Forward' in David Burnett 1988 Unearthly Powers: AChristian perspective on primal and Folk Religion.* Eastbourne: MARC.

Guma, M P 1997. Ithongo dream Narratives, in An African Challenge to the Church in the 21stCentury. (Eds) Guma & Milton. Cape Town: Salty Print (1997),12-31.

Gundry, R 1987. 'The New Jerusalem: People as Place, not Place for people', *Nov. T* 29 (1987), 254-264.

Gustavo, G 1973. A Theology of Liberation. Maryknoll: New York: Orbis Books.

_____1975. "Liberation Praxis and Christian Faith", in Gibellini, R (Ed) Frontiers of Theology in Latin America, London: SCM 1975, 14-24.

Guthrie, D 1981. 'The Lamb in the Structure of the Book of Revelation', *Vox Evangelica* 12 (1981), 64-71.

_____1990. New Testament Introduction (4ᵗʰ Ed). Downers Grove: Intervarsity Press.

Hanson, P 1979. *The Dawn of Apocalyptic*. Philadelphia: Fortress Press.

_____1992. 'Apocalypse and Apocalypticism: The Genre'. The Anchor Bible Dictionary, ed. D.N. Freedman (New York, New York: Doubleday, 1992), 1. 280.

Hall, J 1983. *Jungian Dream Interpretation: A Handbook of Theory and Practice*.University of Toronto: Press Incorporated

Heinnisch, P 1952 *History of the Old Testament*. Collegeville: Liturgical Press.

Hemer, C 1986. *The letters to the seven churches of Asia in their local setting*. London: Sheffield Academic Press.

Hengel, M 1974. *Judaism and Hellenism*. London: S C M.

Hellholm, D (ed.) 1983. Apocalypticism in the Mediterranean World and the Near East: *Proceedings of the International Colloquium on Apocalypticism*. Uppsala, August 12-17, 1979. Tûbingen: Mohr, (1983).

_____1986. 'The Problem of Apocalypse Genre and the Apocalypse of John' *Semeia* 36, 1986, 13-64.

Helms, C 1991. *The Apocalypse in the Early Church: Christ, Eschaton and the Millenium*. Dphil. Thesis, Oxford University.

Hobley, C 1971. *Ethnology of AKamba and Other East African Tribes*. London: Frank & Co. LTD.

Homer, 1997. *The Odyssey*. Tr. Roberts Fagles, 1996. (The Softback Preview 1997).

Hopfe, M 1979. *Relations of the World*. Encino, California: Glencoe.

Horst, B & Gerhard, S 1993. *Exegetical Dictionary of the New Testament* .Michigan: Eerdmans

Howard & Gwyther, 1999. *Unveiling Empire: Reading Revelation Then and Now*. New York: Maryknoll.

Hoyt, T.Jr 1991. 'Interpreting Biblical scholarship for the Black church Tradition', in C.H. Felder (ed.) *Stony the Road we Trod: African American Biblical Interpretation*. Mineapolis: Augsburg-Fortress. (1991), 34-39.

Hughes, P 1990. *The Book of Revelation: A Commentary*. Leicester: Inter-Varsity Press; Grand Rapids: Eerdmans.

Humphrey, E 1995. *The Ladies and the Cities: Transformation and Apocalyptic Identity in Joseph and Aseneth, 4 Ezra, the Apocalypse and the Shepherd of Hermas. JSPS Suppl.17.* Sheffield: Sheffield Academic Press.

_____2003. A Tale of Two Cities and (At Least) Three Women: Transformation, Continuity, and Contrast in the Apocalypse, *in Reading the Book of Revelation: A Resource for Students,* (Ed) *Barr D L. Atlanta: Society of Biblical Literature.* (2003), 81-96.

Husser, J 1999. *Dreams and Dream Narratives in the Biblical World.* Sheffield: Sheffield Academic Press.

Idowu, E B 1973. *African Traditional Religion: A defination.* London: SCM Press.

Igenoza, A 1988. 'Medicine and Healing in African Christianity: A Biblical Critique'. *AfER Ecclesiash Review* 30 (1988), 12-25.

Isaac, E 1980. 'Genesis, Judaism and the Sons of Ham'. Slavery and Abolition: *Journal of Comparative Studies* 1:1 (1980), 4-5.

Isaac, E 1964. Relations between the Hebrew Bible and Africa. *Jewish Social Studies* 26.2

Jack, A 2001. Out of the Wilderness: Feminist Perspectives on the Book of Revelation. *Studies in the Book of Revelation.* Moyise, S (ed.), Edinburgh & New York: T & T Clark (2001), 149-162.

Jessie, O. L 1965. (Ed) *The Cambridge Bible Commentary: understanding the New Testament.* Cambridge: Cambridge University Press

Jeske, R L 1985. Spirit and community in the Johannine Apocalypse. *New Testament Studies* Vol.31.1985, 452-466.

Jung, C. G 1963. *Dreams,* (ed.) Hull. New Jersey: Princeton University Press.

Käsemann, E 1969. 'On the Topic of Primitive Christian apocalyptic', in R. W. Funk (ed.) *Apocalypticism* (JTC, 6; New York: Herder).

_____1969. The Beginnings of Christian Theology in Apocalypticism. *Journal for theology and Church* 6, 17-46.

Kalilombe, P 1980, AThe Salvifc Value of African Religions: A Contextualised Bible Reading for Africa. *In Christianisme et Identite Africaine: point de vue exegetique- Actes de ler Confres des biblistes Africains, Kinshasa,* 26-30 Décembre 1978, Eds A.Agang et al, 205-220. Kinshasa: Facultés Catholiques.

Kato, H 1975. *Theological Pitfall in Africa.* Nairobi: Evangel.

Keener, C 2000. *The NIV Application Commentary: Revelation.* Grand Rapids, Mich: Zondervan.

Kenyatta, J 1938. *Facing Mount Kenya.* Nairobi: Heinemann.

Kelsey, M 1978. *Dreams a Way to Listen to God.* New York: Pualist.

Kepler, T S 1957. *The book of revelation.* London: Oxford University Press.

Kershaw, G 1997. *Mau Mau from Below.* Nairobi: East African Educational Publishers.

Kibicho, S 1968. *The Interaction of the Traditional Kikuyu Concept of God with the Biblical Concept.* Cahiers des Religions Africaines. 2.4

Kiddle, M 1940. *The Revelation of St. John.* London: Hodder.

Killam, G D 1980. *An Introduction to the Writings of Ngugi.* London: Heinemann.

Knight, J 1999. *Revelation.* Sheffield: Sheffield Academic Pres.

Kittel, G 1964. *Theological Dictionary of the New Testament.* Vols. I & III. Grand Rapids,   Michican: WM. B. Eerdmans.

Koch, K 1972. *The Rediscovery of Apocalyptic.* London: SCM Press.

Koester, H 1982. *History, culture and religion of the Hellenistic age.*Philadelphia: Fortress Press.

Kraft, H 1975. *Die Offengbarung des Johannes,* HNT 169 (Tübingen: JCB Mohr (Paul Siebeck).

Kovacs, J & Rowland, C 2004. *Revelation.* Oxford: Blackwell Publishing.

Kraybill, J 1996. *Imperial Cult and Commerce in John's Apocalypse.* Sheffield: Sheffield Academic Press.

Kümmel, G 1975. *Introduction to the New Testament.* Nashville: Abingdon Press.

Kyle, 1998. *The Last Days Are Here Again.* Grand Rapids: Baker.

Ladd, G 1960. Revelation: In Baker's Dictionary of Theology.(ed.) Harrison & Bromiley. Grand Rapids, Mich.: Baker. 1960, pp 50-65.

_____1972. *A Commentary on the Revelation of John.* Grand Rapids. Mich..: William B. Eerdmans.

Lambert, H 1956. *Kikuyu Social and Political Institutions.* London: New York.

Lategan, B 1984. "Current Issues in the Hermeneutical Debate", in *Neotestamentica,* 18, 1984, 1-17.

Lawrence, D 1966. *Apocalypse.* New York: Viking.

Leakey. S 1952. *Mau Mau and the Kikuyu.* London: Methuen Press.

Lee, P. 2001. *The New Jerusalem in the Book of revelation.* Tübirgen: Morh Siebeck.

Le Marquand, G 1997. *'The Historical Jesus and African New Testament Scholarship'. In Whose Historical Jesus?* (Studies in Christianity and Judaism, no7), Eds William E.Arnal and Michael Desjardins. Waterloo: Wilfrid Laurier University Press.

Le Roux, J. 1993. *A Story of two Ways: Thirty Years of Old Testament Scholarship in South Africa.* Pretoria: Vita Verba Press.

Lieberman, S 1965. *Greek in Jewish Palestine.* 2nd Ed. New York: Philip Feldheim.

Limdsay, Hal with C Carlson 1970. *The Late Great Planet Earth.* Grand Rapids, Mich.: Zondervan.

Linton, G 1991. 'Reading the Apocalypse as an Apocalypse' In Society of Biblical Literature Seminar Papers. (Ed). Eugene H. Lowering Jr. 161-186. Atlanta, Ga. : Scholars Press.

Loomba, A 1998. Colonial/Postcolonialism. London: Routledge.

Lohmeyer, E 1953. Die Offenbarung Des Johannes, HNT, Ed. G. BornKamm (1953) (Tübingen JCB Mohr (Pul Siebeck) 1970.15, 141.

Long T 1996. Narrator, Audiences, and Message: A South African Reader-Response Study of Narrative Relationships in the Book of Revelation (Unpublished PHD Thesis University of Natal 1996).

Lonsdale, J 2003. Authority, Gender & Violence: the war within Mau Mau's fight for land & freedom in E S Atieno Odhiambo & J Lonsdale (eds), 46-75. Mua Mau & Nationhood. Oxford: James Curry.

MacFall, ernset A 1970. *Approaching the Neur through the Old Testament.* Pasadena. William Carey Library.

Maficao, T. 1989. *"Evidence fro African Influence on Religious Customs of the Patriarchs".* In American Academy of Relogions/Society of Biblical Literature 1989, Eds J.B.Wiggfins & D.J.Lull, 100. Atlanta: Scholars Press.

Magesa, L 1997. *From privatized to popular Biblical Hermeneutics in Africa*: Bible in African Christianity. Kinoti & Wahiggo (Ed). Nairobi: Acton.

Magie, D 1950. *Roman Rule in Asia Minor,* (2vols; Princeton : Princeton University Press.

Malina, J 1983. *The New Testament World Insights From Cultural Anthropology.* London: SCM Press

_____1994. 'The Book of Revelation and Religion: How did the book of Revelation persuade' *Scriptura* 51, 27-50.

_____1994a. 'Establishment Violence in the New Testament World' *Scriptura* 51, 51-78.

_____1994b. 'Religion in the Imagined New Testament World' *Scriptura* 51, 1-26.

_____1995. *On the genre and message of Revelation: star visions and sky Journeys.* Peadoby, Mass: Hendrickson.

Malina & Pilch, 2000. *Social-Science Commentary on the Book Of Revelation.* Minneapolis: Fortress Press.

Mare, G 1992. Brothers Born of Warrior Blood: Politics and Ethnicity in South Africa. Jonneburg: Ravan press.

Metzger, B M 1965. *The New Testament: Its background, growth, and content.* Nashville: Abingdon Press.

Mbiti, J S 1969. 'Eschatology', in K.A. Dickson & P. Ellingworth (Eds). Biblical Revelation and African Beliefs. London: Lutterworth Press, 159-184.

_____1970. *Concepts of God in Africa.* London: SPCK.

_____1971. *New Testament Eschatology in an African background: A study of the encounter between New Testament Theology and the African traditional concepts.* London: SPCK

_____1975. *Introduction to African Religion.* Nairobi: Heinemann.

_____1994. The Bible in African Culture. In Paths of African Theology. (Ed.) Gebellin. Maryknoll.NY. Orbis.

_____1997. Dreams as a Point of Theological Dialogue between Christianity and African Religion. *Missionalia* 25:4 (December 1997), 511-522.

_____2002. Aspects of the Hebrew Bible in African Independent Churches: Paper presented at the Old Testament Seminar, University of South Africa Pretoria.

McLean, A 1996. *The Seventh Week of Daniel 9:27 as a Literary Key for Understanding the Structure of the Apocalypse of John.* New York: Mellen Biblical Press.

Mealy, J W 1992. *After the thousand years.* England: Sheffield Academic Press.

Michaels, J R 1992. *Interpreting the Book of Revelation.* Grand Rapids: Baker.

Middleton& kershaw 1972. *The Kikuyu and Kamba of Kenya.* London: Lowe and Bryrone.

Moignan, C 2000. *Following the Lamb: A Reading of Revelation for the New Millennium.* Peterborough: Epworth Press.

Moore, B1974. ABlack Theology Revisited@ Bulletin for Contextual Theology 1 (1974) 7.

Morris, L 1965. *The cross in the New Testament.* London: Paternoster.

_____1969. *Revelation.* Leicester: Inter Varsity Press.

_____1972. *Apocalyptic.* London: Inter Varsity Press.

_____1992. *Tyndale New Testament Commentary Series: Revelation.* Grand Rapids. Mich. Eerdmans.

Morley, J 1992. *All desires known,* enlarged ed..London: S P C K.

Mosala, I 1989. *Biblical Hermeneutics and Black Theology in South Africa.* Eerdmans, Grand Rapids.

Mouce, R H 1998. *The Book of Revelation.* Grand Rapids Michigan: Eerdmans.

Moule, C 1981. *The birth of the New Testament* 3rd ed. London: Black Acton Publishers.

Moyise, S 1995. *The Old Testament in the Book of Revelation.* Shefield: Shefield Academic Press.

_____2001. *Studies in the Book of Revelation.* Edinburgh & New York: T&T Clark.

Mugia, K 1979. *Urathi wa Cege wa Kibiru* (the Prophecy of Cege wa Kibiru). Nairobi.

Mundle, W 1986. "apokalyptô" in New International Dictionary of the New Testament Theology, ed. C. Brown (Grand Rapids, Michigan: Zondervan, 1986), 309.

Murray-Brown J 1972. *Kenyatta.* Chatham: W&J Mackay Limmitted.

Muriuki, G 1974. *A History of the Kikuyu People 1500-1800.* Nairobi: Oxford University Press.

Mwaura, P 1996. Women's Healing roles in Traditional Gikuyu Society. Groaning In Faith: African Women in the Household of God. Kanyoro, Musimbi (ed.etl.), 253-269. Nairobi: Acton Publishers.

Mpier, M 1992. Dreams among the Yansi, in Jedrej & Shaw 1992, 100

Nasimiyu-Wasike, 1991. Christology and an African Woman's Experience. *In Faces of Jesus in Africa,* ed. Robert J. Schreiter, 73-80 Maryknoll: Orbis,

_____1992. 'APolygamy: A Feminist Critique' in the Will to Arise, eds. Mercy A. Oduyoye and Musimbi R.A. Kanyoro, 108-116. Maryknoll: Orbis.

Nessan, C 1995. When Faith Turns Fatal: David Koresh and Tragic Misreadings of Revelation. *Currents in Theology and Mission* 22 (June 1995).

Newsome, J D 1992. *Greeks, Romans, Jews, Currents of Culture and Belief in the New Testament World*. Philadephia: Trinity Press.

Ngugi wa Thiong'o 1964. *Weep Not Child*. London. Heinemann.

_____1965. *The River Between*. London: Heinemann.

_____1975. *A Grain of Wheat*. London: Heinemann.

_____1977. *Petals of Blood*. London: Heinemann.

_____1978. 'An interview with Ngugi'. *The Weekly Review* 9 Jan 1978, 10.

_____1981. *Writers in Politics*. London: Heinemann.

_____1982. *Decolonizing the Mind: the politics of Language in African Literature*. London: Heinemann.

_____1998. *Penpoints, Gunpoints, and Dreams: Towards a critical theory of the arts and the state in Africa*. Oxford: Claredon Press.

_____2004. *Murogi wa Kagogo* (*Wizard of the Crow*). London: Heinemann.

Niditch S 1980. The visionary: I deal Figures in Ancient Judaism. Nickelsburg& J Collins (eds.). Chico: Scholars Press. 1980, 153-180.

Niles, D 1961. *As Seeing the Invisible: A Study of the Book of Revelation*. London: SCM Press.

Nolan, A 1987. 'The eschatology of the Kairo's Document' Missionalia, 15 (1987), 61-69.

_____1990. The Paradigm shift in the Journal of Grace & Truth vol. 10, no.2 September 1990, 97-103.

Nthamburi, Z 1991. *The African Church at the cross roads: Strategy for indegenization*. Nairobi: Uzima Press.

Nthamburi & Waruta, 997. *Biblical Hermeneutics in African Instituted Churches*. Nairobi: Uzima press.

O'Donovan, W 1996. *Biblical Christianity in African Perspective*. Carlisle: Paternoster Press.

Ogude, J 1999. *Ngugi's Novels and African History: Narrating the Nation*. London: Pluto Press.

Okure, T 1985. Biblical Perspectives on Women: *Eve, the Mother of All Living (Genesis 3:20)*.Voices from the Third World. 8:3 (1985), 82-92.

Onwu, N 1985. @ The Current State of Biblical Studies in Africa. The Journal of Religious Thought 41:2. (1984-85)

_____1988. The Parable of the Unmerciful Servant (Matt! 8:21-35) In Gospel parables in African Context, Ed Justin S. Ukpong, 43-51. Port Harcourt: CIWA Publications.

Osborne, G R 2002. Revelation: baker exegetical Commentery on the New Testament (Grand Rapids, Michigan: Baker Book House 2002),4.

Osei-Bonsu, J 1990. 'The Contextualization of Christianity: Some New Testament Antecedents'. Irish Biblical Studies. 12:3 (1990), 129-148.

Osiek, C 1992. What are they saying about the social setting of the New Testament? New York: Paulist Press.

_____1999. *Shepherd of Hermas: A Commentary*. Minneapolis: Fortress Press.

Parrinder, E 1974. *African Traditional Religion*. London: Sheldon Press.

Paulien, J 1987. *Decoding Revelation's Trumpets: Literary Allusions and Interpretation of Revelation 8:7-12*. Barrien Springs: St. Andrews University Press.

Peel, J 1968. *Aladura: A Religious Movement among the Yoruba*. London: Oxford University Press.

Perterson, D 2003. Writing in Revolution: Independent Schooling & Mau Mau in Nyeri in E S Atieno Odhiambo & J Lonsdale (eds). Mau Mau & nationhood, 79-96. Oxford: James Curry.

Peterson, T. H and Japhet 1978. *The Mystic World of Whites in the Antelelum South*. Metuche, N.J. London: Scarecrow Press.

Pippin, T 1992. *Death and Desire: The Rhetoric of Gender in the Apocalypse of John*. Louisville: Westminister/John Knox.

Pobee, John S1979. *Toward an African Theology*. Nashville: Abingdon Press.

Preston, R H & Hanson, A T 1949. *The revelation of St. John the divine*. London: S C M.

Price, F 1984. *Rituals and Power: The Imperial Roman Cult in Asia Minor*. Cambridge: Cambridge University Press.

Prior, M 1997. *The Bible and Colonialism*. Sheffield Academic Press.

Pugliese, C 1994. *Publisher and Gikuyu nationalist: the life and writings of Gakaara wa Wanjau*. Nairobi: IFRA.

_____2003. Complementary or Contending Nationhoods & Songs 1945-52, in E S Atieno Odhiambo & J Lonsdale (eds). Mau Mau & Nationhood, 79-120. Oxford: James Currey Ltd.

Ranger, S 1983. The Invention of Tradition in Colonial Africa in The invention of Tradition (eds) Hobsbawm E and Rnager S. Cambridge: Cambridge University Press.1983, 211-262.

Rice, Gene 1972. 'The Curse of That Never Was' (Genesis 9:18-27), Journal of Religious Thought 29 (1972), 17,25.

Richard, P 1995. Apocalypse: A people's commentary. Maryknoll: Orbis.

Riss, M 1972. *The future of the world.* London: S C M.

Robinson J A T 1976. *Redating the New Testament.* Philadelphia: West Minister.

Roetzel, C 1987. *The world that shaped the New Testament.* London: S C M.

Rohrbaugh, R (ed.) 1996. *The Social Sciences and New Testament Interpretation.* Massachusetts: Hendrickson Publishers.

Rolof, J 1993. *The Revelation of John* (Trans/JE Alsup) Menneapolis: Fortress.

Rosberg& Nottingham 1966. *The Myth of "Mau Mau": Nationalism in Kenya.* Standford University: Hoover Institution Press.

Rossing, B 1999. *The Choice between Two cities: whore, bride, and the empire in the Apocalypse.* Harrisburg, Pennsylvania: Trinity Press International.

Rowland, C 1982. *The open Heave: A study of Apocalyptic in Judaism and Early* Christianity. London: S P C K.

_____1993. *Revelation.* London: Epworth Press.

Rowley, H 1950. *The Relevance of Apocalyptic-A study of Jewish and Christian Apocalypses, from Daniel to Revelation.* Second ed. London: Lutterworth Press.

Ruiz, J-P 1989. *Ezekiel in the Apocalypse: The Transformation of Prophetic Language in Revelation 16, 17-19, 10.* Frankfurt Main: Peter Lang.

_____1992. 'Betwixt and between on the Lord's Day: Liturgy and the Apocalypse'. In the *Society of Biblical literature Seminar papers.* ed. Eugene H Lowering Jr. 654-72 Atlanta. Ga.: scholars Press.

_____2003. Taking a Stand on the Sand of the Seashore: A Postcolonial Exploration of Revelation 13, in *Reading the Book of Revelation: A Resource for students.*(ed) Barr D L. Atlanta: SBL,119-135.

Russell, D S 1965. *Between the Testaments*. Philadelphia: Fortress Press.
_____1978. *Apocalyptic: Ancient and Modern*. London: SCM.
_____1980. *The method and message of Jewish Apocalyptic*. London: SCM.
Said, E 1978. *Orientalism*. New York: Patheon.
_____1993. *Culture and Imperialism*. New York: Knopf.
Sangree, W 1966. *Age, Prayer and Politics in Tiriki, Kenya*. London: Oxford University Press.
Saldarini, A J 1989. *Pharisees Scribes and Sadducees in Palestinian society*. Edinburgh: Clark.
_____1979. Apocalypses and Apocalyptic in Rabbinic Literature and Mysticism'. Semeia 14: 187-205.
Schmithals, W 1975. *The Apocalyptic movement: Introduction and Interpretation*. Nashville: Abingdon Press.
Schüssler-Fiorenza 1977. Composition and Structure of the Revelation of John in *CBQ* 39, 366, 344.
_____1985. *The book of the Revelation: Justice and Judgement*. London: S C M.
_____1989. 'The phenomenology of Early Christian apocalyptic: Some reflections on the method' in David Hellholm (Ed), *Apocalypticism in the Mediterranean world and the Near East. J C B. Mohr* (Paul Siebeck) Second edition. 1989, 229-314.
_____1990. The Crisis of Scriptura Authority: *Interpretation and Reception Interpretation* 44:353-68.
_____1991. *Revelation. Vision for the World:* Philadelphia: Fortress Press.
_____1999. *Ethics and the Bible*. Philadelphia: Fortress Press.
Scott, E F 1940. *The book of revelation*. London: S C M.
Scott, J 1990. *Domination and the arts of Resistance: Hidden Transcript*. New Haven: Yale University Press.
Scott, H E. A Harvest Thanksgiving Kikuyu News No. 24 December 1910, 3-5.
Segovia, F & Tolbert, M 1998. *Teaching the Bible: The Discourses and Politics of Biblical Pedagogy*. Maryknoll, NY, Orbis.
Shao, J 2001. Alleviating Poverty in Africa: in Faith in Development: Partnership between the World Bank and the Churches of Africa. Eds. Belshaw & Calderisi at el. Oxford: Regnum, (2001), 19-30.
Sinclair, S G 1992. *Revelation, a Book for the Rrest of Us*. Berkeley: Bibal.

Slater, T B 1998. *On the Social Setting of the Revelation to John*. Cambridge: Cambridge University Press.

_____1999. *Christ and Community, a Socio-Historical Study of the Christology of Revelation*. England: Sheffield Academic Press.

Smith C R 1990. The Portrayal of the Church as the New Israel in the Names and Orders of the Tribes in Revelation. *JSNT* 39, 111-118.

Smith, R.H 1995. Why John Wrote the Apocalypse Rev. 1:9. *Currents in Theology and Mission*. 22 (5), 356-361.

Sugirtharajah, R 1998. *The Bible and PostColonialism*. Sheffield: Shield Academic Press.

_____1999. *Asian Biblical Hermeneutics and Postcolonilism*. Sheffield Academic Press.

Sundkler, B 1948. *Bantu Prophets in South Africa* (2nd ed. 1961). London: Oxford University Press.

_____1960. *The Christian Ministry in Africa*. London: Oxford University Press.

Sutherland, S 1985. *'Mixing Memory and Desire'*, Book Review in TLS, 22 November1985.

Stone, E. M 1990. *Fourth Ezra*. Minneapolis: Fortress.

Swete, H B 1977 < 1911> *Commentary on Revelation* Kregel Reprint Library. Grand Rapids.Mich: Kregel Publications.

Sweet, J 1979. *Revelation*. London: SC M.

Tenney, M C 1985. *New Testament Survey*. London: Eerdmans Publishing Company.

Thompson, L 1990. *The Book of Revelation: Apocalypse and Empire*. New York: Oxford University Press.

_____2003. Spirit Possession: *Revelation in Religious Studies in Reading the Book of Revelation: A Resource for Students* ed. Barr (2003), 137-150.

Tidball, D 1983. *An introduction to the sociology of the New Testament*. London: Paternoster.

Tillich, P 1957. *Dynamics of Faith: World Perspective Series*. London: Allen & Unwin.

Tooker, E 1979. *Dreams, visions, speeches, healing formulas, rituals and ceremonies*

Turner, H 1967. *African Independent Church*: (*History and Life and Faith of the Church of the Lord Aladura*), Vol.II. London. Oxford University Press.

Ullman, M 1987. *Working With Dreams*. Los Angeles: Aquarian Press.

Ukpong, J.S 1987. *Sacrifice, African and Biblical:* A Copmparative study of Ibibio and Levitical Sacrifices. Rome: Urbaniana University Press.

_____1994a. 'Inculturation and Evagelization: Biblical Foundations for Inculturation' Vdyajyoti 58:5 (1994), 298-307.

_____1994b. 'Towards a Renewed Approach to Inculturation Theology'. *Journal of Inculturation Theology.* 1 (1994)3-15

_____1995a. Reading the Bible with African Eyes. *Journal of Theology for Southern Africa.* 91:3-14.

_____1995b. Development in Biblical Interpretation in Modern Africa. *Missionalia* 27 (3), 313-329.

Vermes, G 1987. *The Dead Sea Scrolls*. London. Penguin.

Wainwright, A W 1993. *Mysterious Apocalypse*. Nashville: Abingdon.

Walvoord, J 1974. *Armageddon, Oil and the Middle East crisis*. Grand Rapids.Mich.: Zondervan.

Wambutda, Daniel N. 'Savannah theology: a Reconsideration of the Biblical Concept of salvation in the Africa Context'. Bulletin of African Theology.3:6 (1991),137-153.

Wanjiku, K & Mutahi, K 1986. *Gikuyu Oral Literature*. Nairobi: English Press.

Wanjohi, G J 2001. *The Wisdom and Philosophy of African Proverbs: The Gikuyu World View*. Nairobi: Pauline Publications.

Waweru, H 2001. A Critical Analysis of the Millennial Reign of Christ in Revelation 20:1-10. (Unpublished, University of Natal 2001).

Webber, R 1999. *An Idealistic Reading of the Apocalypse*. London: International Scholars Publications.

Wehmeir, S 2003 (ed.) *Oxford Advanced Learner's Dictionary*. Oxford: Oxford University Press.

West, G 1995. *Biblical Hermeneutics of Liberation: Modes of Reading the Bible in the South African Context*. (2nd.ed.) Pietermaritzburg: Cluster Publications; Maryknoll: Orbis.

_____1997. "Finding a place among the posts for post- colonial Criticism in Biblical Studies in South Africa", *Old Testament Essays*, (1997) 10, 322-342.

West, G & Dube M 1996. 'An Introduction: How We Have Come To read With' *Semeia* 73, 1996, 7-19.

Wilcock, M 1975. *The message of revelation*. Leicester: Inter Varsity Press.

Williams, C 1976. *The Destruction of Black Civilisation: Great Issues of a Race from 4500 BC to 2000 AD*. Chicago: Third World Press.

Williams J.J.1930. *Hebrewisms of West Africa: fron Nile to Niger with Jews*. London: George Allen and Unwin. New York: Lincoln MacVeach/ the Dial Press.

Wilson, R 1980. *Prophecy and Society in Ancient Israel*. Philadelphia: Fortress.

Wilson, J C 1993. The problem of the Domitianic date of Revelation. *NTS* 39 (1993), 587-605.

Wilson, M 2004. The early Christians in Ephesus and the date of Revelation, Again. Neotestamenica 39.1 (2005), 163-193

Wink, W 1992. *Engaging the powers, discernment resistance in a world of Domitian*. Philadelphia: Fortress Press.

Bibles

The Greek New Testament and Dictionary 1983. United Bible Societies.
The Revised Standard Version 1993: The Bible Societies.
Ibuku RIA Ngai 1996. Nairobi: The Bible Societies of Kenya.

Index

Index of Personal Names

Index of Subjects

Auditing Priniples: A Stuents' Handbook by Musa O. Nyakora (2007) *The Concept of* Botho *and HIV/AIDS in Botswana* edited by Joseph B. R. Gaie and Sana K. MMolai (2007)

Captive of Fate: A Novel by Ketty Arucy (2007)

A Guide to Ethics by Joseph Njino (2008)

Pastoral Theology: Rediscovering African Models and Methods by Ndung'u John Brown Ikenye (2009)

The Royal Son: Balancing Barthian and African Christologies by Zablon Bundi Mutongu (2009)

AIDS, Sexuality, and Gender: Experiencing of Women in Kenyan Universities by Nyokabi Kamau (2009)

Modern Facilitation and Training Methodology: A Guide to Best Practice in Africa by Frederick Chelule (2009)

How to Write a Winning Thesis by Simon Kang'ethe et al (2009)

Absolute Power and Other Stories by Ambrose Rotich Keitany (2009)

Y'sdom in Africa: A Personal Journey by Stanley Kinyeki (2010)

Abortion and Morality Debate in Africa: A Philosophical Enquiry by George Kegode (2010)

The Holy Spirit as Liberator: A Study of Luke 4: 14-30 by Joseph Koech (2010)

Biblical Studies, Theology, Religion and Philosophy: An Introduction for African Universities, Gen. Ed. James N. Amanze (2010)

Modeling for Servant-Leaders in Africa: Lessons from St. Paul by Ndung'u John Brown Ikenye (2010)

HIV & AIDS, Communication and Secondary Education in Kenya By Ndeti Ndati (2011)

Disability, Society and Theology: Voices from Africa By Samuel Kabue et al (2011)

If You Have No Voice Just Sing!: Narratives of Women's Lives and Theological Education at St. Paul's University By Esther Mombo And Heleen Joziasse (2011)